TWO YEARS IN THE ANTARCTIC

TWO YEARS IN THE ANTARCTIC

by

E. W. KEVIN WALTON

E. W. Kevin Walton

THE KNELL PRESS
UPPER COLWALL
MALVERN

First published by the Lutterworth Press in 1955
Republished in 1982 by the Knell Press, Colwall.

This new edition is dedicated to my son-in-law
JIM BISHOP
Sometime British Antarctic Surveyor
Killed in the Karakoram 1980.

ACKNOWLEDGEMENTS

The photographs are published by courtesy
of the British Antarctic Survey, Cambridge.
The maps were drawn specially by Mr. V.
Nehring of the Royal Geographical Society.
I am grateful to the Lutterworth Press for
their permission to use the original printed
text.

This new edition is offset litho printed from the original printed text
and includes many new illustrations.

Kevin Walton.   ISBN   0-9508218-0-2

Printed and bound by Hillman Printers, Frome, Somerset.

Contents

                                                           PAGE

FOREWORD BY THE RIGHT REV. THE LORD BISHOP OF
  PORTSMOUTH

PREFACE

CHAPTER

  1 FROM THE RED SEA TO THE ANTARCTIC   13

  2 SETTING UP THE BASE   23

  3 LIFE IN THE HUT   29

  4 HUSKIES AND THEIR TRAINING   39

  5 THE LONG WINTER NIGHT   50

  6 EQUIPMENT IN USE   61

  7 UP TO THE PLATEAU AND A NEAR-TO-FATAL-ACCIDENT   78

  8 THE FIRST ANTARCTIC SUMMER   93

  9 ARRIVALS AND DEPARTURES   101

 10 THE AUTUMN RECONNAISSANCE, MARCH 1947   109

 11 AMERICAN NEIGHBOURS   128

 12 A CREVASSE RESCUE   143

 13 THE WEST COAST JOURNEY THAT RETURNED   151

 14 THE LOSS OF THE AIRCRAFT   161

 15 THE COMPLETION OF THE TWO MAIN JOURNEYS   168

 16 THE LAST SUMMER AT BASE   180

 17 GOOD-BYE TO MARGUERITE BAY   183

 18 RETROSPECT   188

INDEX   191

GRAHAM LAND

Miles
50   0   50   100

Route of the Southern Party — · — ·
   „   „   Hope Bay · · · · · · ·
   „   „   M.V. Trepassey ————
Proposed American West
      coast journey – – – –
   F. I. D. S. Bases

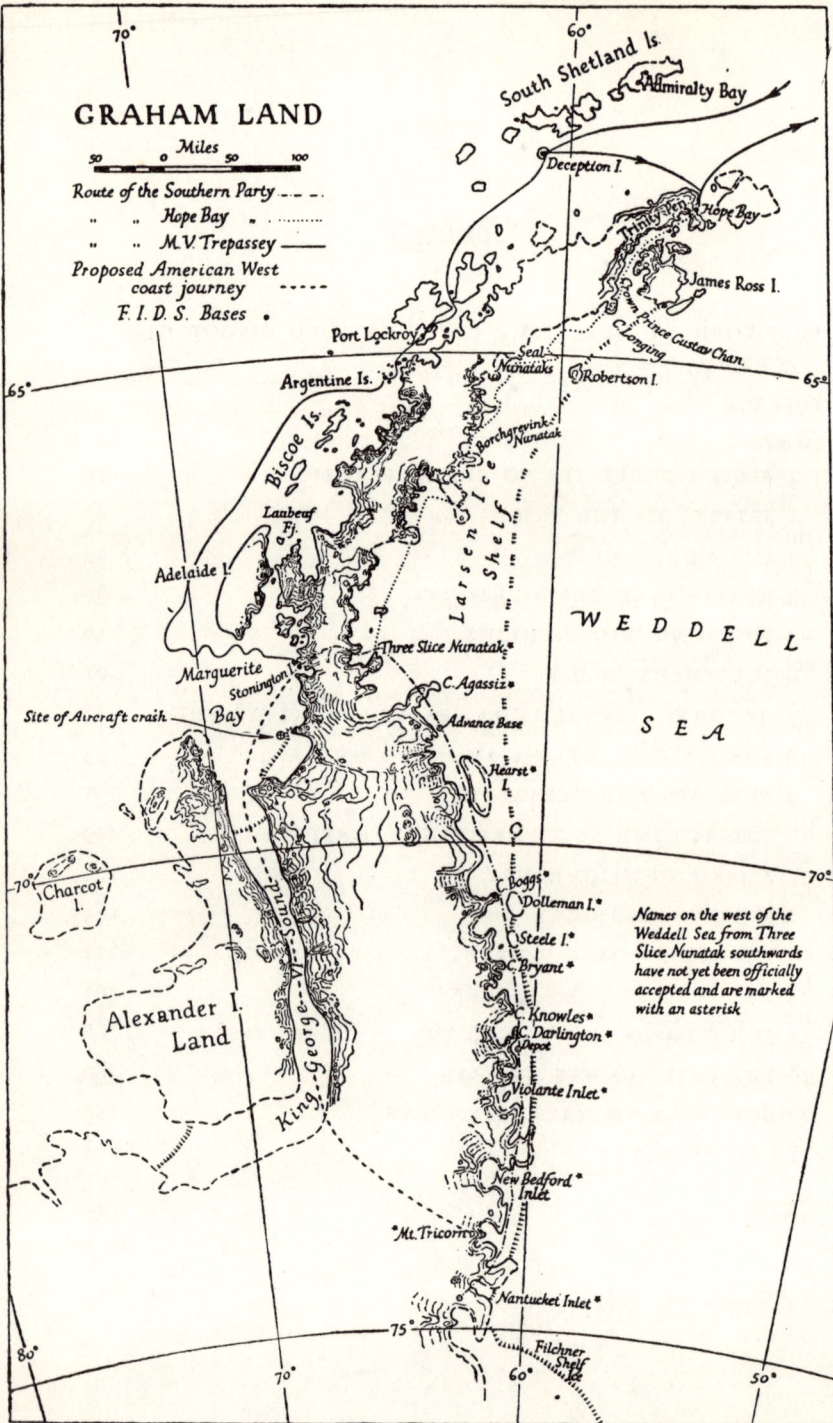

South Shetland Is.

Admiralty Bay

Deception I.

Hope Bay

Trinity

James Ross I.

Prince Gustav Chan.

C. Longing

Robertson I.

Port Lockroy

Seal Nunataks

Argentine Is.

Borchgrevink Nunatak

Biscoe Is.

Lanbeuf Fj.

Larsen Ice Shelf

Adelaide I.

WEDDELL

Three Slice Nunatak *

C. Agassiz *

Marguerite

Stonington I.

Bay

Advance Base

Site of Aircraft crash

Hearst I. *

SEA

Charcot I.

70°

C. Boggs *
Dolleman I. *

Steele I. *

C. Bryant *

Alexander I. Land

C. Knowles *
C. Darlington *
Depot

Violante Inlet *

King George Sound

New Bedford Inlet *

* Mt. Tricorn

Nantucket Inlet *

Names on the west of the
Weddell Sea from Three
Slice Nunatak southwards
have not yet been officially
accepted and are marked
with an asterisk

Filchner Shelf Ice

70°   60°   50°

Preface

WE RETURNED from two years in the Antarctic in May 1948, and if any one had suggested at the time that I should write a book about my experiences I should have ridiculed the idea. Our time in the Antarctic had, I felt, been very personal, and as such it never occurred to me that it would be of interest outside the family circle.

Yet now, six years later, just such a book is finished. Why the change?

Firstly, I found that the picture of Antarctica in everyone's mind was thirty years out of date and I felt we owed it to those great men of the polar past to put the matter right; secondly, to my astonishment I discovered that the smallest details of life in polar places *did* in fact interest many people; lastly, no other Englishman who has wintered south of the Circle since the war has seen fit to write.

This book is written essentially from my point of view. I make no apologies for this, but point out that it must not be regarded as the official story of the expedition; none has been written.

The reasonings and conclusions, though often mellowed by the passage of time, are based on the facts as they appeared in my diary, and I have made no attempt to alter them by reference to official diaries kept in the archives of the Colonial Office.

I do not vouch for accuracy, though I have made every effort to eliminate factual errors. I am deeply grateful to Mr. James Wordie, Dr. C. G. Bertram, and Dr. Brian Roberts, all of the Scott Polar Research Institute, and to Dr. V. E. Fuchs of the Colonial Office, for reading through the manuscript, giving invaluable encouragement and advice, and for their help in pointing out factual mistakes. This does not make the book official, and if errors still exist and views are controversial I alone am to blame.

Many apologies are offered to those members of the Falkland Islands Dependencies Survey whose names do not appear. For reasons of space I have had to stick carefully to descriptions of life at my base and by so doing I do not intentionally belittle their efforts.

Canon Gordon Hewitt proved a kind and skilful adviser in giving the book shape and helping to correct grammatical errors. To him and to those who typed from my appalling handwriting and halting dictation I offer my grateful thanks.

Many people have had the privilege to have been influenced by the ubiquitous Launcelot Fleming. It may have been while he coached an eight on the river at Cambridge, or perhaps in the forward messdeck of a wartime battleship while he was naval padre. Equally well it might have been in Arctic or Antarctic parts, while he was Padre Scientist, with a dog team of his own and a parish larger than Europe. In his present capacity as Bishop of Portsmouth he is one of the busiest men I know, yet he has found time to write the Foreword and to give his blessing to this book. The debt that I owe to him is not just one of putting pen to paper, for it goes far deeper than that. He has been and will continue to be an inspiration to many of us in the widest sense, and I for one can never be too grateful.

It savours of insolence for a young Naval Officer to thank his Commanding Officer, and I know that Surgeon-Commander E. W. Bingham may whimsically point this out. I know however that I can never express the debt that I owe him as leader for taking me south, for helping me when I was there, and above all for giving me the longing to return. All those who went to Antarctica with him in 1946 learnt the technique of polar travel soundly and well at his hands: in the years to come, if the history of British polar exploration in the years after the war comes to be written, I venture to predict that the full debt which we owe to him will be realised: he alone provided the active bridge between pre-war and post-war British polar explorers.

The last thank-yous must be personal ones, and therefore brief. To my parents, for without the background they provided for me I might never have wanted to go south, and to my wife, for without her inspiration I could never have written this book, and most certainly would not have been able to finish this Foreword with the words: "Completed while stationary in the Polar Pack-Ice somewhere west of Greenland and north of the Arctic Circle. August 1954."

E. W. KEVIN WALTON

Foreword

ON A COLD December day in 1940 a young Sub-Lieutenant (E) sought me out in H.M.S. *Queen Elizabeth*, when we were in dry-dock at Rosyth. He told me he wanted to go to the Antarctic when the war was over and had come to ask how to set about it. In such circumstances this might have seemed an unrealistic dream, but in point of fact the dream came true.

This young officer, Kevin Walton, had an eventful war. He won the D.S.C. when serving in the destroyer H.M.S. *Onslow* in the action off North Cape against the German pocket battleships *Lutzow* and *Hipper*. Later in North American convoys he was mentioned in despatches. As soon as the war was over Walton immediately volunteered to join the Naval Antarctic expedition "Operation Tabarin", which came to be known later as the Falkland Islands Dependencies Survey. This book is an account of his experiences with the Survey.

Many books have been published recently about polar expeditions, but there are two good reasons to justify this addition to their number.

In the first place *Two Years in the Antarctic* should commend itself on its own merits as a story well told. Mr. Kevin Walton has the happy knack of describing his experiences in such a way as to enable his readers in their imaginations to share in them. He gives a vivid and an authentic impression of what it really feels like to be a member of a polar expedition—to be wintering in a base hut or to be sledging with dogs (which is perhaps the most exhilarating part of such an expedition). He is honest enough to admit the disagreeable things and not to allow his enthusiasm to exaggerate the rest. He obviously enjoyed himself—good company, an exhilarating mode of life (at least for a time!), and absorbing work, in a land which can boast some of the world's most impressive natural scenery. There was plenty of excitement too, and some occasions for anxiety. The author was responsible for the hazardous rescue of John Tonkin from a crevasse which earned him the Albert Medal, and received the Queen's

Commendation when he extricated another companion from a similar situation in South Georgia in 1951.

The other reason why this should be a welcome addition to polar literature is that it is the only book to have been written about a very important British effort in Antarctic exploration by someone who has spent two years in the Antarctic since the war. The Falkland Islands Dependencies Survey has differed from other expeditions in that it has been planned as a long-term project to carry out an ambitious programme of scientific and geographical research. So that in addition to the personal light which the story throws on expedition life, it is a record of successful Antarctic exploration which yielded valuable results and laid the foundations of the work that was achieved in the years that followed. For their part in this work, the author and his colleagues were awarded the much prized Polar Medal. Especially notable were the 1,000- and 600-mile sledge journeys on the east coast of the Graham Land Peninsula. To carry out journeys of this magnitude across difficult country is no mean feat, particularly when one remembers the laborious stages of reconnaissance, route-finding and depot laying which were involved.

It is a tribute to Surgeon-Commander Bingham that the story which Walton tells is a happy one, for on the leader necessarily falls the chief responsibility of keeping such a party—most of whom have plenty of ideas of their own—working together as a team.

The chief reason why I have enjoyed this book so much is that the author carries you along with his own enthusiasm. There is no need to ask what makes people do these things. To Walton that would be a superfluous question. Anyone who reads this book will, I think, be bound to agree with him.

LAUNCELOT FLEMING

Bishopswood
Fareham
Hampshire

List of Illustrations

These all appear between pages 96 and 97.

1. "Drift". Taken in a high wind on a plateau journey.
2. M.V.Trepassey, a wooden trading ship built for the Labrador coast
3. Icebergs off the coast of Graham Land.
4. Unloading stores at Stonington Island.
5. Expedition motor boat as deck cargo.
6. Construction of Base hut. Day 6.
7. The same, four days later.
8. Early reconnaissance for the route to the plateau.
9. Mike Sadler rests on the plateau edge.
10. Aerial view of the Neny Fjord area looking north towards Adelaide Island.
11. The final haul up to the plateau.
12. Hoar frost over everything. The sledger's nightmare.
13. Sodabread slope, the bugbear of the haul to the plateau.
14. Evening camp scene taken through the tent door.
15. The rare luxury of seeing one's route when sledging on the plateau.
16. Tonkin and Mason setting up camp.
17. Sadler, Mason, Slessor and Joyce after 35 days in the field.
18. Returning to base with light sledges.
19. Bouncer and Sister enjoy a breather.
20. Smooth glacier surface destroyed by high wind.
21. A glacier camp that survived a 70 knot wind.
22. Wonderful sledging on the east coast.
23. Exercising teams round base.
24. Stonington Island from the air.
25 & 26. Aircraft hangar under construction.
27. Dave Jones services the aircraft engine.
28. Ice cold Katy warms up on the sea ice.
29. Bernard Stonehouse and..... 30. Tommy Thomson on their walk home after the loss of the aircraft.

List of Illustrations

31. Puppy training.
32. Aerial view of N.E. Glacier and the route to the plateau.
33. Base hut drifted over in early spring.
34. Base hut in early summer losing the snow cover.
35. 6 sledges, 8 men and 43 dogs in convoy up Bill's Gulch.
36. Auster Glacier from the air.
37. Penguin visitor swimming close inshore.
38. McLary's leap.
39. Evening scene inside the base hut.
40. J.Tonkin taking an evening bath.
41. Exercising a dog team on the sea ice round base.
42. Bouncer and Sister at base.
43. George, a midnight base visitor.
44. An unclimbed rock spike bagged on a mountaineering interlude.
45. An eleven dog team in Neny Fjord.
46. Base party at the end of the second year.
47. The Marguerite Bay Hope Bay sledging party on return to base.
48. Delivering the ship's pilot by dog team.
49. U.S.S. Edisto breaking a channel for the John Biscoe.
50. U.S.S. Edisto leads the John Biscoe out of Neny Fjord.

Line Illustrations in the Text

	page
The Stonington Island base hut at the end of the first year	31
American and British methods of harnessing dogs	41
The Stonington Island base hut at the end of the second year	131
Menu card of the Mid-winter's Day dinner	140
Map of Graham Land Peninsula	10
Map of Marguerite Bay showing the journeys undertaken during 1946-47	149

CHAPTER I

From the Red Sea to the Antarctic

THE hot airless cabin of a destroyer steaming northwards up the Red Sea is the strange starting point for the story of an Antarctic expedition, yet for me that is just where it all began.

I, as a Lieutenant (E), was the Engineer Officer of the destroyer *Relentless*, and the war was just finished. I had spent two years fighting the hot, rather sticky naval part of the war in the eastern waters of the Indian Ocean, and barely a month before at Singapore had witnessed the surrender of the Japanese forces to the Allies. For the flotilla of R-class destroyers active duty was over and we were on our way to cooler weather and home.

On October 23, 1945, I turned in late, but it was too hot to sleep easily for the wind was following us and there was no coolness in the ship. I was awakened before dawn by a seaman knocking at my door with a signal in his hand. He passed it to me with the remark, "With the Navigating Officer's good wishes, sir, and it should be cooler than this." It read: "If Walton is still a volunteer for two years in Antarctica he should be flown home forthwith."

Forty-eight hours later, loaded with a bunch of bananas unknown in wartime Britain, I walked into the family home unannounced and told my parents that I was off to Antarctica.

The next day I went up to London, and by the evening knew that I had ten days in which to collect my thoughts before I left for the far south: I was due to join the peacetime counterpart of the secret wartime operation "Tabarin". Apart from the fact that the commander of the expedition was Surgeon-Commander E. W. Bingham I knew very little about the job. He interviewed me in a small office near Charing Cross Station, where he was surrounded by a motley collection of items which belonged to polar regions: plywood ration boxes, pairs of snow-shoes, tins of pemmican,

13

and sea-boot stockings all helped to complete the picture. In the peaceful moments when the telephone was not ringing he signed me on.

On November 9, in a misty English dawn, I bade my parents good-bye; by noon I was in Lisbon, and the adventure had started.

In January three ships dropped anchor in the desolate harbour of Deception Island on the fringe of the Antarctic, and for the first time ever the whole party were able to gather together over a rum punch while Commander Bingham explained the background of the expedition of which we were all members.

South of Cape Horn, extending northwards from the Antarctic continent, is the Peninsula of Graham Land. It is roughly 1,000 miles from north to south, averages fifty miles wide, is heavily glaciated, and well endowed with high and rugged mountains. Together with off-shore groups of islands—the South Shetlands, South Orkneys, South Georgia—they form the most southerly part of the British Commonwealth under the overall title the Falkland Islands Dependencies, and we were all members of the Falkland Islands Dependencies Survey. The region was first explored in the early 1800's by adventurous seamen in search of seals, but it was not until 1902 that the first purely scientific party, under the Swedish Professor Nordensjöld, visited its inhospitable shores. His ship was lost, crushed in the pack-ice. In 1908 the French explorer Dr. Charcot, in his ship the *Pourquoi Pas*, spent a year exploring the length of the deeply indented and highly dangerous western coastline. From 1908 to 1928 there was considerable whaling activity but few discoveries were made public. In 1928 Sir Hubert Wilkins explored widely with a small single-engined aircraft flying from Deception Island, and in 1935 the American Lincoln Ellsworth flew down the length of the peninsula on his transantarctic flight. The first truly land-based expedition since Dr. Nordensjöld was in 1934, when the British Graham Land Expedition, led by John Rymill, spent over two years surveying and exploring by sea and sledge along the length of the west coast. This eminently successful expedition returned to the United Kingdom in 1937, and steps were put in hand to follow it up. The horrors of war overtook our nation, plans had to be shelved, and instead, in our absence, the Americans set up a base in Marguerite Bay some five miles from Rymill's winter hut of 1936. This base travelled widely and was evacuated by air in 1941, when exploration ceased. In 1944 it was decided to inaugurate a secret naval operation, "Tabarin", with the dual purpose of supplying written reports from the region of Antarctica and maintaining a look-out in case of enemy use or occupation. With the war drawing to its close this naval operation expanded, more bases were set up, and exploration in the widest sense was under way.

The first stage of this expansion had taken place the previous year when a landing had been made at Hope Bay at the northern tip of the peninsula, and an eleven-man base with dogs and travel equipment had been established.

This year, with Commander Bingham in overall command, the expansion was to continue. A small base was to be built in the South Orkneys, and a ten-man survey base was to be set up in Marguerite Bay. There he would pass on the art of polar travel and dog-handling: it was no enviable job, but he was well qualified. He had served with Watkins in Greenland, and sailed southwards with John Rymill's British Graham Land Expedition as doctor and dog expert, and had himself wintered in Marguerite Bay in 1936. He was a small, intensely energetic Irish doctor who had in his wide polar experience become a fanatic about huskies. This fanaticism he passed on to us as the years went by.

His task of collecting members for the expedition cannot have been easy. In the days before the war there was always a nucleus of explorers, and would-be explorers, from which to draw in the form of University scientists who banded together in exploration clubs. Now no such source existed, and he had found us by reference to our various wartime backgrounds as recorded in the archives of Whitehall.

For most of us Deception Island formed the gateway to Antarctica, and I don't suppose it could be bettered as a place where an expedition such as ours could sort and re-shuffle its stores.

It is an ancient volcano crater, several miles across, which has been flooded by the sea through a narrow entrance on the eastern side. High ridges of black volcanic rock screen the sun from the

sullen place, but as a harbour it more than makes up for its dour
drabness. For over a century it had provided a secure anchorage
for the sealers and whalers, where their ships could lie in safety
while the blubber was stripped from carcasses floating alongside.
At the turn of the century it became the site of a land-based
whaling station, and many of the factory buildings still stood.
Three ships now lay at anchor. The S.S. *Fitzroy*, which normally
plied between Montevideo and Port Stanley, and which had come
south with a load of expedition stores, lay alongside the R.R.S.
William Scoresby, a whaling research ship. Made fast alongside an
old oiling barge was the expedition's own ship, M.V. *Trepassey*.
She was a sturdy wooden vessel of some 200 tons, built in Newfoundland for coastal sailing and trading on the Labrador coast.
She was manned by a Newfoundland crew and had brought our
dogs as deck cargo from the far north.

Ashore was one of the original wartime bases: four men occupied one of the old whalers' barracks where not twenty years
before a hundred Norwegians had lived and worked. The derelict
factory itself seemed ghostly and eerie like a city of the dead. Vast
deserted cooking sheds lay open to the winds of heaven, and the
dreary clanging of corrugated iron gave life to an otherwise lifeless place. A rusty fence and a few crude crosses set in the shadow
of large empty fuel tanks formed the whalers' cemetery and told
strikingly of the rough toughness of the days that were gone. The
island itself stands well to the west of the mainland of Graham
Land, and it is high enough to provide a vantage point from
which to view the ice conditions to the north and south.

The movement of the pack-ice varies from year to year; sometimes drifting north from the Weddell Sea it blocks the passage
from Graham Land to the South Orkneys, and the west coast of
the peninsula has open water. Sometimes the position is reversed
and the west coast remains ice-bound, only clearing late in the
season if it clears at all. This year ice conditions seemed favour-
able, and Commander Bingham had to think ahead to decide
upon the order in which the bases could be visited and replen-
ished. He sent *Fitzroy* to Port Lockroy to replace the inhabitants,
and the *Trepassey* and the *Scoresby* were to re-provision Hope Bay
and then build the new base in the South Orkneys. These plans
meant that we had to re-sort all our cargo, a process that, due to

Bingham's foresight, proved very easy. Every base had its own letter which was clearly stencilled on the six sides of its many store crates, each case had a four-figure number which by a simple code could tell us much about its general contents. All that we had to do was to off-load the complete cargo from the deck of the old barge and reload the ship with the South Orkney, Base C, stores at the bottom, and the Hope Bay stores on top. *Trepassey* was ideal for this job, for in the Labrador trade she was expected to handle all her own cargo, and the light derricks and efficient petrol-driven winches could deal with all the queer-shaped cases which we carried. On January 15 we left Deception Island, and twelve hours later were anchored in Hope Bay. Here the sullen security of the Deception anchorage was gone, and Hope Bay seemed wild and vicious. The open bay was surrounded by rugged mountains and dying glaciers and could fill with heavy pack-ice at the whim of the wind and tide.

We landed a hundred tons of stores and ten dogs while the weather was calm, and thirty-one hours after arrival we were on the move. *Trepassey* and *William Scoresby* in company headed for the open sea. The next stop was to be the South Orkneys, five hundred miles to the north-east.

Four of us were to travel as passengers in the *William Scoresby*, for the *Trepassey* was already overcrowded. We slept on couches in the saloon, and on the morning of the 18th awoke quite literally with a bump as we hit our first lump of floating ice. The sound of it grinding and scraping its way down the ship's side drove us on deck with remarkable speed. We had reached the edge of a belt of pack-ice floating northwards from the Weddell Sea. At first we followed its edge northwards, but soon after noon Captain Shepherd, master of the *Trepassey*, decided to turn his ship eastwards again to force his way through. There is something very exhilarating in steaming through pack-ice if the sun is out and the weather is quiet. The whiteness of the ice contrasts strikingly with the blueness of the sea where it is visible between the floes. The bright sun on the rough ice produces a deep-shadowed whiteness that gives the eyes no rest.

After the long ocean passages, when the ship was the centre and extent of our world, the vast icebergs which we passed provided a yardstick against which we could measure ourselves. This was the real Antarctic, and it was truly humbling to feel so insignificant in the vastness of the Universe.

We backed and bumped our way through the evening and night, and at daybreak were in open water again, rolling heavily and longing for the shelter of the South Orkneys which lay ahead. We steamed round to the eastern side of Laurie Island, and, after examining twenty miles of coastline from the ship through binoculars, Commander Bingham went ashore and selected a site for the new hut. Nine days later eighty tons of cargo were ashore and the hut was nearly completed: we had been roughly treated by the weather, the landing place was bad, especially when the wind was from the east. There were no landing places where we could beach the boats if the sea became rough; whenever the weather looked menacing we had to hurry back to the ship and hoist the boats on board. If we were lucky and it was still calm, hoisting the landing scow was an easy process; with the ship rolling its heart out in biting sleet and a rising storm it could behave like a devil, however. On February 3 the hut was completed, the base wireless had spoken for the first time, and we could leave. We were entertained for a good-bye party by "Mac" Choyce (so named because his initials were M. A. C.), who was the base leader, and afterwards returned to the ship to wait until the fog should lift. The weather cleared with the early dawn, and we watched the shore party of four wave good-bye to us from the hut door.

Their isolation was more complete than they realised, for their wireless broke down in the first week. It says much for Mac's wise leadership that a year later, after twelve months' isolation, all volunteered to stay a further year with the Survey. We set course for Deception Island; the belts of pack-ice that had delayed us three weeks earlier had dispersed. We passed a mile-long iceberg on the 6th and steamed close to Elephant Island to examine the coastline where Shackleton's ill-fated *Endurance* Expedition had finally beached their boats. They had lost their ship, crushed by the ice nearly a thousand miles to the south, and had drifted northwards on the pack-ice watching their security melt away from under them.

From that desolate coastline Shackleton, with five others, had

sailed an open boat to South Georgia, civilization, and safety—
six hundred miles across the stormiest ocean in the world.

On February 8 we were back on Deception Island again. The
next part of the plan was to establish the new Marguerite Bay
base. From past experience Commander Bingham knew that it
would be unwise to start southwards until the middle of February,
for the pack-ice moving north along the coast of Graham Land
would still be heavy, and we could not afford to be caught.

There were ten days to wait at Deception and we intended to
make good use of it. After three days the ship was reloaded with
the Base E stores and topped up with fuel from the oil barge.
We could consider ourselves ready for sea, and enjoyed the luxury
of a few days' leisure.

I spent one very happy afternoon wandering round the tumble-
down whaling station with the Commander. For him it must have
evoked memories of his visit there in *Penola* in 1935. In those days
the buildings were still standing, the hospital had been clean and
well equipped, and the process of decay had scarcely started.

One evening, just as we sorted through the last few cases on
the deck of the oil barge, I spotted one of my family packing-
cases. It was my Christmas hamper that had been lost in the cargo.
I opened it on deck in the light and warmth of the evening sun.
Opening a Christmas parcel such as this, that had been packed
with all the loving care of those at home, made me realise that
the wrench in family life such as our expedition demanded was
far harder for those I had left behind than it was for me. For the
wanderer life is ever interesting and colourful; for those at home
it can be so colourless and humdrum, and for them the separation
is greater as a result.

On February 15 we collected the dogs that had been roaming
loose on the island for the last month and put them on board. At
the best of times *Trepassey* was crowded, for she was designed to
carry a crew of nine and now carried thirteen. Add to this forty-
five dogs and a cargo which left thirty tons on deck. Squeeze on
forty drums of extra diesel fuel and the description "deeply laden"
begins to have meaning. On top of this dump the landing scow
sitting athwartships with bow and stem projecting over the ship's
side, put the motor-boat inside it, and the picture of the expedition
ship is almost complete.

For sleeping space we really were cramped. Four of us slept in the forward saloon, which was only six feet square. Three more slept in the galley on the benches and table, and the remainder fitted in where we could in wireless or engine room. We saw no sign of pack-ice between Deception and the mainland, and motored in flat calm into the entrance of Neumayer Channel. Here were coastal mountains carved on the grandest scale, and the humbling delight of steaming through pack-ice could count for nothing by comparison with the beauty of this fjord. The afternoon sun had not yet started to shelter behind the mountains, it was warm and comfortable watching the world go by from the ship's crow's-nest or upper bridge. Seals abounded everywhere and lay in groups of two or three idly watching us as we passed. We could watch penguins in their thousands playing "last man in" at the water's edge, using their neighbours as bait for their enemies, the leopard seal. The game is almost human. Groups of twenty or thirty would stand back from the water's edge and then without warning would make a united run towards the sea in the pretence of jumping in. All would stop at the last possible moment, all save one or two unfortunates who would slip and overbalance into the sea below. The remainder would crowd to the edge and, like spectators at a tennis match, follow the movements of the swimmers and judge for themselves if leopard seals were on the prowl.

Perhaps as we passed an empty ice-floe a swimming penguin would decide to have a look at us more closely and would pop several feet into the air, like a cork on a champagne bottle, landing feet down on the floating grandstand. More would join him, and they would watch us and gossip with each other as we motored on.

In this channel the mountains rise from sea-level to 8,000 feet with scarcely a break, sometimes as steep black cliffs from sea to summit, and sometimes as smooth guileless-looking snow-slopes that end suddenly in treacherous ice-cliffs. *Trepassey* seemed but a toy ship in the grandeur of this scenery. The sun dipped lower and left us, and the stillness seemed to intensify the cold. The sea, clear and blue and quiet as a millpond, mirrored the high mountains until the ripple from the ship's bows disturbed the surface and made them vanish. The channel narrowed to a few hundred yards, turned sharply to the east, and Port Lockroy was in front of us.

The original F.I.D.S. base was here, but ours was a purely social visit, for the *Fitzroy* had called earlier to replenish the stores and change the personnel. We stayed the night and then turned southwards down the Peltier Channel. If anything it was even more spectacular than the Neumayer Channel of the previous afternoon, and the impression of austere beauty was enlivened by the frequent ice avalanches which rumbled down the upper slopes as the sun touched the tops. Inside the channel it was sunny and still, but as soon as we lost the shelter of the coast the weather and sea worsened and we were glad to reach the shelter of the Argentine Islands thirty miles to the south. It was here that Rymill had spent his first winter in 1935, so Commander Bingham knew it well. We anchored close inshore and rowed up a narrow channel to the hut which he had occupied in 1935; it stood as dry and as sound as the day in which it had been built. Some humorist had written "To let for 1936–37 season" across the entrance. It must have been odd for the Commander to revisit his old house, and to see again the scenes of his previous labours. There were still the stone shelters there he had built for his dogs, and the gay "Welcome to Brighton" poster was pinned above his bunk.

The next morning was spent topping-up the ship's tanks with fresh water, and by lunch time we were ready to leave. In the hut we left a cache of stores for the possible use of shipwrecked whalers, fixed a Union Jack and a notice-board to record our visit on the hut wall, and by early afternoon we were gone: our next stop was to be Marguerite Bay.

With the motor-boat in the lead Captain Shepherd felt his way out of the dangerous waters, and by evening we had turned southwards in open ice-free water to work our way past Adelaide Island into the ill-charted waters of Marguerite Bay. Twenty-four hours later, at dusk on February 21, we could recognize the high mountains that guarded the entrance to Neny Fjord, our ultimate destination. It would be unwise to close the coast in darkness, so we hove to and rolled and wallowed all night waiting for the dawn. At first light, in a rapidly rising wind, Captain Shepherd uneasily nosed the ship into the entrance of the fjord and dropped anchor in the shelter of an ice-cliff, close beside the island where the Americans had built their base in 1940.

Even in this anchorage the wind seemed to blow the sea flat, such was its force, and the flying spray lay like a white blanket over the surface of the water. Drift snow was being whipped off the glacier above and thrown like desert sand on the ship beneath. That biting vicious wind that came without warning taught us an early lesson. From that time onwards we never trusted Antarctic weather, and the "fumigator", as we nicknamed this local wind, was ever watched for and guarded against. There were ten of us to go ashore here, to build our hut and to spend the next two years together. I looked round at the world outside and then at the nine men who were to be my companions and found myself longing for the ship to stop rolling and the years' work to begin. Commander Bingham, or "the Commander", was leader. Robbie Slessor, a naval doctor and specialist in midwifery, was second in command; it was he who had bought our huskies in Labrador and nursed them through the tropics. "Reg" Freeman, an R.E. officer with the most infectious smile of anyone I know, was one surveyor, and "Duggie" Mason, sometime Oxford scholar and R.E. captain, was the other. "Willie" Salter, bearded and bald, was to run the meteorology. John Joyce, a wartime Army captain, came as geologist. "Ken" Butler, a signals officer, was to work the wireless. The remaining three of us signed on as "dog's-bodies", or handymen. Mike Sadler was a major with the Long Range Desert Group and had a reputation for accurate navigation, ingenuity, and independence. John Tonkin was from the Special Air Service and he had a reputation a trifle more stable but equally distinguished. I was the last, a lieutenant (E) from the Royal Navy, with a love of mountains and five years of driving turbine warships in wartime to fit me for this life of wind and snow. February 23, 1946, was the date, ten years to the day since the rugged little ship *Penola*, with Commander Bingham on board, had entered those same waters, and Rymill's expedition had set up its winter base on the Debenham Islands only a few miles away.

It was nine years since he had left the same base, leaving much of his heart behind. Once, in the blustering wind, I watched him on the ship's bridge looking for peaks and places that he knew. I left him silent with his thoughts and memories.

CHAPTER 2

Setting up the Base

THE next morning all was quiet. The mountains were
mirrored in the still, blue water, penguins and seals had time
to stand and stare, and we were tempted to forget the bitter
blowing of the day before.

The history of the exploration of Marguerite Bay is rather
complex, and as such needs explanation. The area was first
charted by the Frenchman Dr. Charcot in his ship *Pourquoi Pas*
in the first decade of the century. He spent the summer of
1908–9 exploring Marguerite Bay, wintered his ship at Peterman
Island, north of the Argentine Islands, and returned to Marguerite Bay the following spring; as a result, many of the names
in the region are of his choosing and are French.

Except for short visits from passing whale-catchers the area
remained unvisited until, in 1936, John Rymill had sailed in with
the *Penola* and established his base on the Debenham Islands, a
few miles north of Neny Fjord.

The American Antarctic Service base, established in 1940, was
on Stonington Island, some five miles south of Rymill's old hut.
This was the island beside which we lay anchored, and was the
place where we intended to put up our own hut.

With Antarctica so unexplored it seemed stupid to have three
huts in so close an area, but we, as government servants, were not
there to argue the point. Our job was to carry on where Rymill
had begun and the American party had left off.

We all landed on the morning of the 24th to examine for ourselves the state of the American huts, while the Commander
wandered all over the island to decide on a site for our own.

The American huts and their surroundings were not good to
behold. All around lay the rotting debris of a year's kitchen refuse,
and further afield, still chained to their tethers, lay the carcasses

23

of their dogs, shot when they evacuated the base. The hut itself was a vast barn-like structure showing clear traces of hurried evacuation: plates were unwashed on the table, meals stood stale and uneaten, and washing-up water lay frozen in its bowl— exactly as it had been left six years before. Alongside the main sleeping quarters was the workshop; the door had been left open and a five-foot layer of clear ice covered the floor, encasing the debris that was there. The corner of a sewing-machine looked out from the ice alongside a caribou sleeping-bag; on both rested a broken sledge. It was hard to believe that the base could have been left in such a shambles, and one got the impression that there had been thoughtless visitors exploring the huts since the Americans had left.

The immediate decision was to dry out and to occupy the main American living hut, so that once the wood was ashore we could continue our own hut-construction without waiting for wind, weather, or boatloads of cargo.

After the cramped conditions on board *Trepassey* our temporary quarters seemed luxury indeed. Now, each of us had a bunk of our own, even though the blankets did smell rather musty and the remains of sticky sweets stuck the mattresses to the boards beneath. As the hut warmed up, so the ice that had formed between the roof-boards thawed out, and the silence of the night was always broken by the noise of continuous dripping.

I became cook and took on the job of cleaning out the American kitchen and coaxing the temperamental stove into doing some work. The others were involved in clearing up outside, removing the dead dogs and preparing to bring our own animals ashore.

Judging by the way the American huts had drifted up and become engulfed by ice, it was quite obvious that the Commander would have to think carefully before he decided where our own huts should be built.

Bingham knew from experience that the siting of a polar hut is of vital importance. The main thing is to hit a happy medium between being completely covered in drift snow and being so exposed to wind that the snow coverage would be impossible. A drift-covered hut is certainly warm, yet it multiplies the risk of fire and asphyxiation; it entails continuous work to keep its

24

exits always open, and with the windows snow-covered it is as dark as a tomb. Yet equally well it must not be on top of a hill or else the first breath of the first "fumigator" would make it airborne. Careful study of the remains of old snow-drifts and local ice formation were made, and finally Bingham selected a site sixty yards from the shore facing the open sea, and about two hundred yards from the American huts.

Within a week all the stores were ashore. This went rather more efficiently than at other bases, for we had built a temporary floating jetty and could handle the cargo fast. In any case, after all our cargo-handling at the other bases we were now incredibly fit and were able to work eighteen hours a day, sleeping only between the boatloads. We certainly became very tired; John Tonkin, I remember, fell asleep over his soup and only woke when his cigarette had burnt its way through all his clothes to his thigh. We all knew the cargo by that time and could recognize the cases that looked light and yet were brutes to handle.

Robbie Slessor was a tower of strength, ever cheerful and ever able to exert the little extra effort where others had failed. John Tonkin always made me think of myself as a small boy when I would only handle the more interesting pieces of a picture-puzzle, with the unfortunate result, in his case, that the "interesting" loads always formed far more than his share of the cargo. Our attitude to coal sacks changed too. In Port Stanley we had regarded them as difficult and heavy items of cargo. By now we were used to them and were able to handle their hundred and fifty pounds as if they were mere half-hundredweight sacks of corn.

The hut itself grew rapidly, resting as it did on the heavy timbers collected on Deception Island, and these in turn were securely bolted down to concrete and brick foundations.

The framework of the building had been first erected in England and every part numbered according to a master-plan. All we had to do was to collect a portion of the master-plan, select all the numbered parts which it indicated and then, as we assembled this jig-saw around the prefabricated windows and doors, the hut structure grew. On the outside of the framework we laid aluminium foil, which would stop most of the heat-loss by radiation; we covered this with tarred paper and then secured the whole with five-eighths of an inch thick, tongued and grooved boarding. The inside we finished off in much the same way, but with much thinner wood. A single-thickness cedar floor, one inch thick, was now all that was left to do.

This prefabricated-framework method of hut-building is not quick in comparison with the simpler method of bolting six-foot-square sections end to end, but it has the great advantage of occupying a very small cargo space. Motionless air sealed in between wooden walls is still the best insulator against heat or cold, but a cargo of large hut-sections filled with English air is a terrible waste of good shipping space. Our hut was assembled with care and thoroughness, and only later when the winds of winter started to blow did we discover its weaknesses in the badly fitting windows and doors.

Apart from the actual building of the hut, the collection of stores from the beach-head had to go on. It was a wearying job, for the fifty-yard track was very rough, and our backs were aching by the end of the week when the last case had been carried up.

Meanwhile the internal fittings of the hut took shape. I assembled the modern slow-combustion Esse stove, which was to serve us so well, and fitted it into the minute kitchen. The wireless room filled up with equipment, and piles of blankets—and even sheets—appeared on the bunks. Some fifteen days after our arrival at Stonington Island we were ready to move into our new home, and *Trepassey* felt she could leave with a clear conscience.

While all these hut preparations were going on the *Trepassey* crew were not idle. For the first time since we had known the ship her holds were empty, and she needed ballast. The extra fuel carried on deck was run into her tanks, and the drums which had carried it were filled with water and were bedded down in the hold, along with sixty tons of good Antarctic.

Even this simple operation was not without excitement, and involved us in quite unnecessary risks. I had to tow the scow across the harbour with the motor-boat, and watched the *Trepassey's* crew make it fast to the lower side of a steep, unstable slope of rock debris. To fill the scow it was merely necessary to loosen the lower stones, stand back, and in a matter of seconds the scow would be fully laden. The Newfoundlanders seemed quite oblivious to the fact that such a stone slide could rapidly reach the proportions of a major landslip, and the chances of the scow and its crew surviving with this mishap would be very small. No such accident occurred, but it was more by luck than good seamanship.

By March 14 they were ready for sea, and that same night our own base wireless spoke to Port Stanley for the first time; at last we could be considered utterly independent of the ship.

We laid on a good-bye party that night to thank the ship's crew for their assistance, with gin and rum and a sing-song to send them on their way. With Newfoundlanders a little drink goes a long way, and we watched the boats pursue a perilous zigzag course back to the ship that night.

There was a frantic rush to finish the mail the following morning, and, with this completed, we were too busy really to notice when our last tangible link with the outside world finally left us. Towards the evening the *Trepassey*, looking absurdly small against the vast panorama of the fjord, had hooted her last good-byes on the siren and was gone.

That night we toasted wives and sweethearts with high hopes for the morrow—and for the seven hundred other to-morrows that were still to come.

Bingham had warned us that he would drive us hard until the base could be considered secure for the winter, and, though the hut was built and secure, there was, in fact, a month's hard work still ahead of us. The stores were clear of the sea and covered with tarpaulins but still needed endless sorting, compacting, and re-stowing before the snows came; we still had two more huts to build, one for the year's food and one to house the petrol-driven generator necessary for the wireless. There were only seven seals left for dog-food, and there would be no more after mid-April until the spring came.

Just before *Trepassey* had left, Bingham declared a free day with no duties, to give us time to write letters, but a holiday of this sort went against his ever-busy nature and at lunch time, grinning broadly, he suggested a whole series of voluntary jobs in case time should hang heavy on our hands. We completed both our letters and the voluntary jobs, and worked harder on that Bank Holiday than we had ever worked before. To the end of our stay in Antarctica, whenever some long, arduous, and disagreeable job came up, John Tonkin would, in his own inimitable way, ask for another such "public holiday" in which to get it done.

The month's estimate proved about right, for by the middle of April our daily routine slackened and we could relax and look around. All our stores were now sorted into weather-tight dumps and our equipment was well dispersed from the main hut so that the fire disaster, which we always dreaded, could not prove fatal to our livelihood. By dint of dropping everything that we were doing whenever a seal was sighted, we had a safety margin of dog-food. The dirty coal-heaving work was over, and we could discard the clothes that we had worn threadbare in the last six weeks and start to use all the excellent equipment which we had brought with us. In the two months since early February we had handled about twelve hundred tons of equipment either out of or into the ship, and had mislaid but two cases. We had worked extremely hard, and enjoyed it.

We were in excellent health and looking forward to the supposed rest of the long winter night.

CHAPTER 3

Life in the Hut

THE hut itself was not very complicated in design and I have included a rough diagram in this chapter. In actual fact it was formed by two similar huts placed in the shape of the letter L, with all our living quarters in the upright section and our workshops in the horizontal part of the L.

The front door opened into a long porch extending the whole width of the hut and here Robbie Slessor kept all the "ready use" foodstuffs where they were handy to the kitchen. A week's supply of coal was kept here in a box, and a brush for sweeping snow off one's clothes completed the furnishings. From the porch the door opened into the kitchen portion of the main living room. To the right of this door was the small kitchen some 6 feet by 8 feet, the greater part of which was occupied by the Esse stove and the snow-melting tank that formed our main water supply. The kitchen itself was very compactly fitted out with rows of shelves designed to house all the bottles and jars so necessary to a chef. These shelves and those in the porch gave the impression of a well equipped grocery shop and Robbie took endless care to keep them filled. In theory every time a tin of food left our outside food store it was noted in his food stock book. A special occasion might arise when the cook would beg him to release some luxury item such as ham or asparagus. Robbie would consult his book and after long Scottish deliberation pronounce that we had "a few tins in hand". To the left of the door Ken Butler had his wireless room; it was a soundproof rabbit hutch 6 feet by 4 feet, with a window overlooking the kitchen; the corner of this room and the water tank alongside the stove almost blocked the passage into the living room. The tank held ninety gallons when full and was painted black so that it would absorb all the waste heat from the warm hut: as long as we kept it topped up with snow or ice the warmth of the hut melted it into water for us. In midwinter, without any effort on our part, other than keeping it full of lumps of iceberg, we could draw off up to forty gallons a day.

The living room itself was about 23 feet long and 17 feet wide with bunks fitted all around the side. Ken Butler slept close beside his wireless room and the rest of the bunks were selected by ballot. Our bunk spaces were to represent the sole privacy that we had for those two years. It was a room of our own, 6 feet 6 inches long, 2 feet 6 inches wide, and extended from floor to ceiling. Willie Salter slept next to Ken and surrounded himself with countless self-recording weather instruments which ticked their clockwork life away above his head and by which we could always tell what clothes were demanded by the weather outside. I came next in the line and, knowing my untidy habits, I built countless shelves and stowages in the vain hope of keeping my bunk free to lie upon. Reg Freeman was in the bunk by the farthest window, the opening of which he of course controlled; he was lucky, for he is tidy by nature and owning a window of course reduces storage space. In the far corner, with a certain amount of privacy, Robbie Slessor hid himself and fitted a chest of drawers on roller wheels into the space under his bunk. Mike Sadler slept across the window with no more additions to his comfort than a few six-inch nails on which to hang his clothes. Bingham occupied the corner bunk and decorated it with a calendar dated 1935 which had been above his similarly sited bunk at the Argentine Islands. Duggie Mason was across the room from me, existed on a bare minimum, and seemed to keep everything of value underneath his mattress.

The door into the workshop came next and beyond it J. J., as Joyce was now called, had his bunk. His feet were warmed by the chimney of the kitchen stove and he could warm his hands at the living room fire as he lay in his bed. John Tonkin was even better off from the point of view of warmth, for he was warmed from both sides of his bunk.

Down the centre of the room was a long table which was the focal point of the hut; we did most of our work upon it and used it for all our meals. The door to the workshop opened into a small lobby which housed our library, and the Commander had a small office leading off it to the left. From the porch a second

The Stonington Island Base hut at the end of the first year

'DOC' SLESSOR | MIKE SADLER
'REG' FREEMAN
E.W.K.W.
WILLIE SALTER
KEN BUTLER
WIRELESS ROOM
SHELF SPACE

LIVING ROOM

Stove

CDR. BINGHAM
DUGGIE MASON
JOHN TONKIN
J. JOYCE
KITCHEN
Water Tank
Eng. Cooker
Shelves
PORCH

OFFICE
Library
Stove
GREEN HOUSE
WORKSHOP
DOG HOUSE

N

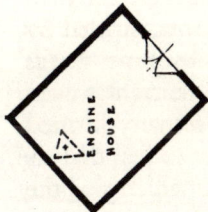

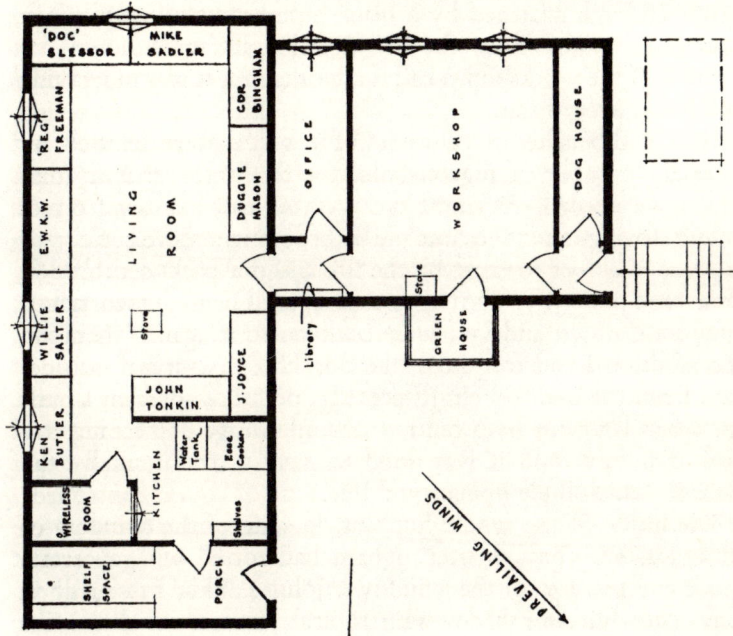

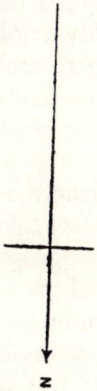

PREVAILING WINDS

ENGINE HOUSE

TREPASSEY HOUSE
MARGUERITE BAY
As it was at the end of 1946

0   5   10   15   20
feet

door opened into the workshop proper, which was about 13 feet square and was warmed by a black anthracite stove which also heated the water pipes for the double glass greenhouse that opened off the workshop. I call it a workshop; it was in fact used for almost everything.

We fitted benches on two sides of it with shelves for tools and a certain number of pigeon-holes for the small separate items which we needed. At night the washtub came down from its ceiling stowage and it became the bathroom where we could wash in peace, our toes roasting by the fire and our backs scrubbed by some kind passer-by. The back porch opened from the workshop; three steps down and you were back on rock again. There was one addition I had forgotten, the dog house, with a door of its own from the back porch. It seemed a pointless addition at first, but when later our lives centred around sweaty dog harness and cooked puppy food it was good to have a special smell-proof place in which these items could live.

The inside of the whole hut was, in spite of the comparative bleakness, very gay. Mrs. Bingham had sorted out gay scarlet check curtains for all the windows. John Tonkin had made up some cheerful lampshades with topical pictures on them. The hut-warming stove was bright enamel and always looked clean. We had a scarlet tablecloth and, on occasions, even had flowering hyacinths as decoration.

We had very good lighting from the wireless generator at 220 volts and Ken rigged up a secondary 24-volt battery circuit which was maintained by a wind-driven propeller dynamo.

By this time every member of the base had his own definite responsibilities and the more communal ones were shared. Everyone, for instance, did his share of cooking, by rota, so that for each of us one week's cooking was followed by nine weeks' break. I myself will always maintain that this is the right way to run the cooking in a small base such as ours. To many it was a thoroughly unpopular move; some scientists like to feel that the chores of the house should be done by the untrained dog's-body of handymen, but Bingham's feeling, with which I know I agreed, was that even the job of handyman in a polar base was as exacting and as skilful as that of the most scientific of scientists. What good was a field scientist if he couldn't train and handle a dog team and wasn't prepared to try? A scientist who wouldn't wash up was as useless to an expedition as a washer-upper who has no scientific appreciation.

These, however, are thoughts of the moment, and readers must ask just how the day filled up.

To preserve the smoothness of life some definite routine had to be adopted; ours went something like this.

The day would start with the cook slipping silently out of his bunk some time after 7.30. He might place in the oven the yeasty bread rolls which had been rising through the night in the warmth above the stove, and certainly would start boiling the huge pot of porridge on the hot-plate. He would invariably brew a cup of tea for himself and for anyone else who was awake early, and then would noisily lay the table at about ten to eight and hope that the noise would remind the others that it was nearly breakfast time. We adopted many methods of waking folk up in the morning. As often as not John would imitate sergeant-majors with a loud "Wakey wakey" shout; he was the only one who got away with it, because of his extreme good-nature. Most of us merely went round the bunks and shook everybody until they showed signs of life. Duggie Mason would wait until the last possible moment, yet was rarely late for a meal. One moment he would be lying asleep in bed, and the next time one looked round he would be fully dressed sitting at the table.

By eight o'clock the shout would be "Porridge up", and if there was a late riser, well, his porridge would just get cold. There would always be a second dish, bacon or beans, scrambled penguin eggs or sardines on toast, and the whole would be supplemented with coffee and bread rolls. The meal would break up when Willie left to take his weather recordings and went through the pantomime, peculiar only to him, of putting on his outdoor clothes; at about 8.40 Ken would go off to start the generator and gather by wireless the weather reports from the other bases.

Some volunteer would then get up and collect the washing-up water, set it on the table, and within ten minutes the room would have been cleared and the day's work could start.

Bingham always liked to keep careful check on what each one of us was doing and the dispersal each morning rather reminded me of the first lieutenant in a destroyer detailing off the seamen; we took it in very good part, however, and it was probably extremely good for us.

Two or three would probably take the kitchen waste down to the sea-ice, where it would pile up through the winter and drift away when the ice broke up in the summer sun; at the same time we would probably bring in two or three boxes of clear blue ice chipped off a local iceberg. This would be tipped into the water tanks that rested beside the Esse stove. Reg would go down the burrow that led to the snow-covered coal dump and emerge with the week's ration of coal. There would invariably be work for an hour or two carrying stores over to the American huts for dry stowage, and then a party would be detailed off to dig for several hours to help clear their ice-filled workshop; Duggie Mason and I were usually landed this job. Ken Butler was always busy, for his daily wireless schedules came every four hours and there was no relief person to operate his set. He was always fighting a losing battle with the electrical equipment; there is a terrible tendency in Antarctica to do a job temporarily, only to find the temporary repair still in use twelve months later. If the weather was fine Bingham would invariably decide on some puppy training, and two or three of us would be detailed to help him harness up the dogs.

Quite early on, we started to assemble the sledges and only then found that certain vital parts had been shipped to Hope Bay in error; the job of making the new parts fell to me. We had no timber suitable, and it took three weeks chipping away blue ice from around the American huts before we unearthed some planks of pitch-pine which Bingham felt would be able to do the job. In two days the sledge parts were complete. I enjoyed this job immensely for I prided myself on my woodwork, and even though pitch-pine is quite the wrong sort of wood the parts survived the first season's sledging.

Willie Salter managed, and we never could understand how, to make weather, Met for short, an absolutely full-time job. Oddly enough his successor in the following year was able to do a full-time zoological programme and run the weather in his spare time. Soon after breakfast, if the end of the month had just passed, Willie would be huddled over the end of the table working out the averages on a calculating machine, and we always suspected that he followed this up by checking the accuracy of the machine by mental arithmetic. His *sotto voce* whispering of figures would go on for days.

Sometime during the morning there was bound to be the cry of seal, and one or two of us would leave whatever jobs we were doing to kill it and bring it ashore. We couldn't afford to let any escape, for our dog food was still rather scarce and the seals would soon leave us for the eleven weeks of winter. As often as not the seals would be sitting on ice-pans in "Back Bay", which lay in front of the American hut, and we would have to punt and paddle ourselves on floating ice in order to reach them. Invariably they would slip into the water as we approached and would peep up through the ice-floes and wonder what all the fuss was about. The actual job of killing seals was not pleasant. Our only aim was to give minimum discomfort to the seal for the shortest possible time. At the end of our stay the whole rather bloody process of killing and cleaning them would take something under a minute; it gave no pleasure to any one of us.

By noon we would filter back to the hut for lunch. With ten cooks we fed extremely well, for competition among ourselves guaranteed variety. The rations from home were extremely generous and, to my sorrow, we rarely had to resort to eating seal or penguin. Dehydrated foods were available, vegetables in particular, and were excellent. Lunch always consisted of two courses and would invariably be a time for wholesale arguments of strictly unanswerable flavour. Arguing, or discussing, was a pastime in which it was always considered cheating to look up the answer in an encyclopaedia.

But soon lunch would end, as did all meals, with the arrival of the washing-up water and the clearing of the table. The afternoon until tea-time passed in much the same way and at the same speed as the morning, except that maybe we would take an hour off to learn to handle the 40-foot dog whip on the snow patch in front of the house. This is a long, heavy affair, copied, oddly enough, from a Labrador whip by a firm of London suitcase manufacturers. It was short-stocked and a gradually tapering lash of composite raw-hide and horse-hide strips.

The idea was to cast the whip out ahead in a straight line, using either hand, with considerable power and accuracy. In those early days while we were still learners this rarely occurred, for usually the lash would turn back sharply and finish up with a flip across the back of the knee or head, in a way that was powerful enough to raise a red weal.

Later on in the afternoon just before tea two or three of us would feed the dogs; each animal was given three or four pounds of raw, probably rather stale seal meat. If it were cold enough we could cut the seal with a cross-cut saw but if warmer we dealt with the oily and rather smelly lump with knives and axes. It didn't take long to distribute it, for we could load the barrels of meat on to a sledge and then tow it around distributing it as we went. As soon as the dogs saw us approach the meat dump, bedlam would be let loose, and they would leap to the full extent of their chains, howling their heads off. It was only when the last piece of meat was thrown to the last dog that life became peaceful again.

At 4.30 it was tea-time and woe betide any cook who couldn't put both cake and hot scones on the table. Tea would last an hour, and afterwards the hut living room would fill up with folk busy on the more sedentary sort of jobs. There were always items of equipment to be made, such as dog harnesses or covers for the sleeping bags, tarred rope to be spliced into dog traces, or clothing to be repaired. We had a sewing-machine but, unfortunately, no needles tough enough for the work we were doing until I found three in the sewing kit that my practical mother had made for me. They were precious as gold, and as a result I guarded the machine carefully and tended to monopolize it.

Supper was at 7.30, and by 8.30 the wireless schedules were over and only the battery lights were left on. Ken would be making up his wireless log and John would be reading with one foot on the stove and his leg on the bunk, quite oblivious of the noise around. Mike Sadler would probably be doing something photographic, for he was a meticulous worker with his Leica. There might be a theodolite on the table with Reg Freeman covering every metal knob with a chamois leather skin. It was a homely scene inside, noisy with the back-chat that made each one of us interested in the other's job, and to an outsider, it would have appeared incredibly warm and friendly.

Outside the hut it might be doing anything: it might be cold

and clear with bright stars—and down south they are very bright
—or it might be blowing a ninety-mile-an-hour "fumigator".
If it were quiet and windless you would hear the dogs still scratch-
ing around after bits of seal meat, and exciting the rest to join in
a friendly chorus. If it were windy the wind charger propeller
on the hut roof would be tearing its heart out and Mike Sadler
would probably be putting a strip of cellophane tape around the
windows to keep the drift snow out, or John would be demon-
strating the draught that came through the boards beside his head
by letting it blow out a burning match.

It would be somebody's bath night; it always was, for we
worked in exact rota, so he would put a couple of buckets of
water on the stove, stoke up the workshop fire, and put the old-
fashioned bath in front of it. The bather would collect his dirty
clothes, sort out the clean ones for the next day, find someone to
scrub his back, and retire for the few minutes of warm bath that
were his, once every ten days. As he dried himself the dirty clothes
would be put in the bath with a handful of soap flakes and, rather
after the style of a crusher of grapes, he would tread the dirt out
of them and leave the rinsing till the morning. By 10 o'clock at
night the battery lights would be turned off and we would resort
to candles, and it wouldn't be long before each of us would retire
to bed to read for an hour before going to sleep.

I've heard many folk criticize the fact that we washed, wore
pyjamas, rinsed our clothes, and used sheets. It was intentional.
We felt, and the feeling grew the longer we stayed in Antarctica,
that there would always be a sharp difference between conditions
of life at base and out travelling. We had no rules on the subject
but always shaved when we were home, kept our hair cut, and
did our best to wash for meals. Looking back, I know we were
right.

Another matter which sorted itself out in part the first year,
and was solved in full later, was that of our liquor ration. We
didn't have very much, and a little went a long way. Every Friday
night, the night when the cook changed, the week's bottle would
be produced and we would have our weekly party. The cook
would make his big effort; we might even "change for dinner";
jobs would be forgotten and we would be sociable, and probably
argumentative, one with each other. Arguments were entertain-

ment and rarely got out of hand. I am not sure who it was that first produced the remark "Has anyone read any good books recently?" which said in so many words "Stop this argument. It is becoming too heated". It was probably John, for no one else could say the magic words so innocently. If that phrase bore no result he would smile sweetly and produce his ultimatum, "Let's change the subject, let's talk about *women*."

I've missed out much about hut life, of the daily bread bake when the dough so easily caught cold if the door was left open, of the click of nails contracting from the wood of the roof in the silence of a very cold night, of the little irritating things which we knew we did and which we knew we must cease from doing if life was to remain bearable.

Hut life is the body of an expedition of which travellings are the limbs. If the body has no strength, the limbs have no value. We always longed to get away from the base and, oddly enough, always longed to get back.

CHAPTER 4

Huskies and their Training

U P TO NOW I have avoided talking about huskies except as animals to be fed and live cargo that required shipping.

All of us who went southwards in 1945 liked dogs after the manner of any normal Englishman; they were good companions, as long as they were well disciplined and did what they were told and so on; and we rather laughed to see Bingham's fanaticism about huskies as a breed.

We have, I know, all come back from Antarctica with a love and affection for huskies deeper and more personal than the most sentimental among us believed possible.

They were more than haulage animals that required care; they were companions that always gave a welcome whenever we were disgruntled or out of sorts. They helped us over the bad moments in life and, in spite of the general picture I have painted of base, there were such moments, when our human friends seemed irksome and petty.

Often I have been involved in some fiery discussion and watched tempers rise, and then noticed folk quietly slipping from the room, to return ten minutes later, more tolerant, and forgetful of the mind that was in them. They had slipped out to discuss the situation with the puppies or to find out what old Admiral thought about it all. You can't hold on to a bad temper when ten frenziedly friendly little balls of fun are competing for the doubtful honour of licking your hands or your sealskin boots, or when old Admiral, even in the worst of weathers, was prepared to shake the snow out of his fur and welcome you, after the style of Eeyore in *Winnie-the-Pooh*.

I myself don't think an expedition of our size could have run so happily without this leavening influence of dogs.

Robbie Slessor and Tom O'Sullivan had been sent by Bingham in September to collect the dogs in Labrador and to ship them south in the *Trepassey* to Montevideo. They left St. John's, Newfoundland, in a small trading schooner to call in at all the Labrador settlements and to select the dogs as they went. Unfortunately the reasons for the ship's visit were all too well known and all the best dogs were sent up to the backwoods, leaving only the unwanted misfits, the rag-tag and bobtail of the community, to be available for purchase. They were not expensive however, thirty shillings for each dog, and four pounds for the bitches; they were bought one or two at a time and shipped to St. Johns'.

There is a prayer for the dogs which says,

> "Look kindly, O Lord, on these Thy creatures for we are dependent on them and they, with us, are utterly dependent on Thee."

In the Labrador summer dogs live a hard life, being left to roam loose on the islands off shore, fending for themselves, catching fish in the creeks and becoming wild and thin and mosquito-bitten; small wonder that when Robbie collected them in the autumn it was a cowering, smelly, untrustworthy crowd that finally reached Newfoundland. In St. John's they had the free run of an old warehouse, and plenty of good whale meat was available for food. Robbie washed them and combed out the summer's grime, and finally shipped them south in kennels on the foredeck of the *Trepassey*, stopping but once at Trinidad on the way to Montevideo. He had been lucky enough to find an old scrap marine boiler in Newfoundland which was put in the ship's hold and filled with the extra water necessary to keep the dogs in good health through the tropics. It was a credit to the efforts of the two of them and a tribute to the detailed instructions given them by Bingham that the only dog who died on passage passed out from a meal of old rope ends. When they finally reached the Falkland Islands, in addition to the forty-nine old dogs, there was a flourishing nursery of six puppies. Three weeks later, by the time they reached Deception Island, they were thin, but very fit. We killed some seals on the foreshore and let the dogs run loose for a month, eating as much as they could, and free to take plenty of exercise. In the month that they roamed loose ashore they sorted themselves into rough groups, and when we were ready to ship them south for Marguerite Bay they were chesty and heavy and ready for work.

Once at Stonington Island, we arranged tethers for them, using chains recently discarded from the Horse Guards and obtained from Army stores by the Commander. From that time until the evacuation of the base in 1949, except for the joyous moments when they were at work, they lived tethered in the open, through wind or snow. Buying dogs, as we had to, in this haphazard manner, is not the way of getting the best teams quickly. It would certainly mean that one had seven dogs in a team, all "broken to harness", but this is quite a different matter from seven dogs working as a team. Bingham loved those dogs; he alone knew what their capabilities were and as we look back, big as the other debts were, the biggest that the expedition owes to him is on that score.

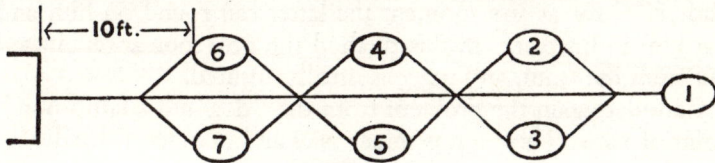

Figure 1

There seem to be two opposed schools of thought about driving dogs in Antarctica. The Americans, with experience in North Canada, tend to use a complicated and beautifully made harness made with hard leather-covered collars and webbing, and to hitch their dogs in the formation shown diagrammatically in figure 1, with the sledge itself perhaps ten feet behind the rear dog.

The British, on the other hand, mostly I suppose as a result of Greenland experience, have adopted rather a freer style. The lamp-wick harnesses are very much simpler and easier to make, and the system of harnessing the dogs together and to the sledge

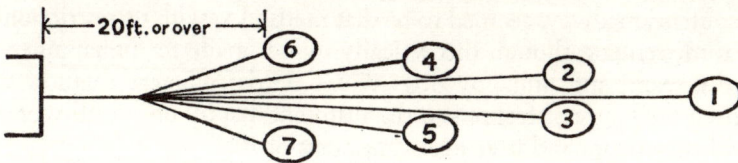

Figure 2

41

is in diagram something like figure 2, with the front of the sledge never closer than 20 feet to the rear dog of the team.

Mathematically, I suppose if one considers dogs as so much mechanical power, the first system is the only logical one but it has its limitations. Each dog quite obviously is securely fastened in the team; it is fastened, that is to say, in relation to the other dogs. As long as the leader will lead, the second pair have the option of being pulled along by their necks or else leaning into their harness and working. As long as the first three dogs pull, the rest have no option but to follow. It doesn't take long for number 5 dog, who is maybe a bit of a coward at heart, to discover that he can grumble all day at the dog in front and that the dog in front, perhaps a thoroughly aggressive type, cannot shut him up. If later on a fight does develop between these two it will be embittered by the day's back-chat. Now in the second method number 5 knows too well that he mustn't argue the toss with number 3, for at any moment the latter can round on him and put him in his place. In this method the boss soon sorts himself out from the team, and peace is usually ensured.

Consider again the problem from the "dog and a lamp-post" point of view. The team is under way and number 3 decides he must have a temporary halt; he does so, and in stopping receives a sharp jerk from his neck trace. Being a big dog his reaction quite probably will be that some other dog is the cause and has a grudge against him, so he will stop dead and duffy up number 5, who was entirely innocent. Quickly the team will join in, for, to a husky, there is nothing better than a good fight, except perhaps another one. With the second method, number 3 can draw clear and cause no trouble.

Bingham, and we soon learned to do the same, could never think of dogs as anything but personalities, and his experience was that dogs performed much better if they had the maximum chance to develop their personalities one against the other. His contention always seemed to be that method 1, with its restriction of movement, though theoretically sound, made for unhappiness in a team, and unhappy dogs won't work; whereas method 2 bred the happiest feelings in the team and happy dogs will work till they drop, and love every moment of it.

That is the human angle, as you might say; but how does it

line up with the purely practical problem of sledging in Antarctica? Quite clearly method 2 is valueless in any place where there are trees. If the team divides to go round a tree everything must come to a stop; but where there are enormous crevasses, potholes in the snow several hundred feet deep, the result is the opposite. If the leader falls into the hole, the dogs that follow will leap to one side and one dog only is swinging in space demanding rescue. If method 1 is used the difficulty among trees does not exist, but the crevasse problem can be fatal to a whole team, for if the leader falls he drags in all the rest.

This has been a long dissertation on dogs and I haven't started to describe our dogs and how we trained them. They were a motley-coloured crowd, black, black and white, brown, wolf-coloured and white, and plain white. The males weighed on the average about ninety pounds while the bitches ran at about seventy. Labrador dogs are notably tough sturdy animals, with the ability to work hard, if necessary, on remarkably short rations. Bingham preferred them to the West Greenland variety who themselves were better than the smaller almost weedy East Greenland type.

In our training we made use of several dog habits. First, a dog will invariably run after something, whether it be seal, human being, or another dog; secondly, the husky basically loves to pull; thirdly, though the odds are that he has never felt it, he loathes the sight of a whip, except maybe as chewing-gum.

We watched the dogs ashore in Deception and noticed very carefully which dogs ran together, and then at Stonington Island each group was tethered in a clump apart where they could get used to one another. From that group one dog would be selected who, perhaps because of better eyesight, was quicker than the rest at noticing things and making for them. Then one momentous day he would be slipped into a harness and fastened to the front of a sledge with a fine easily chaseable object out in front. He would be allowed to chase it, drawing the sledge as he went, and it wouldn't be long, as long as the relationship of firm friendliness was established between driver and dog, before the dog would realise that certain words meant pull and certain others meant stop.

Two more dogs would be paired in behind him; it might well

be that one was his worst enemy or, at best, the boss of the group to whom he was attached. The would-be leader would learn that the only way to keep clear of his enemy was to pull, and the boss would pull in the hope that one day he would catch the leader out in front.

Gradually the team would enlarge, and extra pairs would be fitted on behind the front three until a fine power unit would emerge, probably without sense of direction and certainly without brakes.

That, of course, was the theory of the training and the practice would probably take this form. The sledge would be firmly anchored, pointing towards the wide open sea-ice in front of base. The traces would be laid out in the snow and probably with one or two folk from the hut the dogs would be brought over in pairs, their harnesses put on, and the hauling traces attached. With luck there would be relative quiet, sufficient at least for some of the dogs to be left unattended and to give time for one of the assistants to walk out across the ice as an incentive to the leader. The anchor would be slipped, and the driver would jump on to the sledge and away it would go, each dog chasing the one in front and the lead dog determined to keep his distance and reach the black speck on the sea-ice first. Just to liven things up the last dog but one would probably decide that this was the exact moment to visit a bitch he was fond of under the nearby tarpaulin, so he would double out sideways, smartly tripping up a spectator with his trace as he did so. The lively team would finish up, in fact, with six dogs facing forwards pulling their hearts out and dragging, willy nilly, one spectator caught by the ankle, a dog facing backwards and a driver with nothing but his voice and the 40-foot whip with which to assert his authority.

After many attempts the pantomime of the start would disappear; the boss of the team, Bouncer in my case, would assert his authority and wander round the other dogs whenever they were lying down with the sort of expression which said, "If you move a muscle I'll knock your block off."

Lesson 2 was about to begin—the lesson that taught them a sense of direction. The mad rush would continue, the black spot would be reached, the purpose of the rush was lost, or was it? Rover—he was my leader—would turn his head to the right and spy the base hut or someone on the island taking weather observations and would decide to go that way when—zing— and the lash of the long whip would bar his path.

Around to the left there would be some other interesting attraction, so he would try that way, and once again—zing— and the tail of the whip would bring him up short. The whip itself was rarely used for punishment, sometime in a dog's life he had felt it, and after that—well it was a memory and he avoided it.

Slowly but surely, with the whip used to emphasize our authority, they would learn that "Irra" meant left wheel and "Auk" meant right, and the team was ready to go places.

With luck the whip could be left coiled on the sledge, and they would turn happily left or right by voice alone. Gradually they would be as easily steered as a car, prepared to plug along all day heading for nothingness, able to steer for mile upon mile upon a compass bearing or to zigzag like a dodgem car in and out of intricate crevasse patterns.

There was one more important lesson still to come and almost the most important, this was the lesson of working as a team.

With a heavy load on the sledge well and truly stuck in the snow only a united jerk will start it again. A syncopated series of jerks by seven dogs, each leaping forward against the tightness of its trace, achieves nothing; but a single solid jerk of all seven dogs moving as one will move a mountain. Each driver adopted his own method, but in general it was merely necessary to pull all the dogs back with the main trace a distance of a couple of feet, give a cautionary "Now, dogs," and at "huit", the dogs would leap forward as one and the whole load would be jerked on its way.

I have probably made the whole process sound quick and easy; it wasn't. My own team, "the Orange dogs", took eighteen months before I considered them up to scratch. Eighteen months of blood, sweat, and tears, but in retrospect I loved every minute of it. Rarely have I been so exasperated, rarely have I cursed so much as at the dogs when they showed the self-willed spirit of unbroken stallions. Those dogs are tough; if a walloping was required it had to be a real one that left me tired and exhausted, and the odds were, that as I sat taking my breath, the offender would lick my ear. If it was a kick up the backside for laziness that was required it would be the soft-booted foot that would be bruised. If it was encouragement and petting that was required they were as sloppy and soft as children's cuddly toys.

The actual dog training trips were a never-ending delight; they gave me a chance to get away from the restrictions of base and to see myself in proper perspective to base life. I know that I have spent many hours of dog travel, ostensibly looking for seals, yet actually worrying out details of travel drill or trying to cure myself of my irritating habit of telling others how my practical, somewhat impetuous mind thinks they should do some particular job.

Sometimes we would go out to collect seals, sometimes, if visibility were low, I would plot out a six-sided course on a piece of paper and then, using the compass on the sledge and some form of distance meter trailing along behind, I would try and trace it out on the sea-ice in front of base on a larger scale. Sometimes I would put on a couple of boxes of iceberg chippings and make the dogs take the load for a six-mile run while I ran beside the sledge to keep warm, and we would then deliver it to the hut as a contribution to the water tank.

All the training journeys were pleasure, yet all really necessary. At school I remember we had a rowing motto which read "Mileage makes champions", and it is the same with the dog teams. If you don't take them out and exercise them often they will never become a team.

I am often asked why he took so much trouble with our teams. Why for instance did we insist on their being self-leading? Why didn't we walk ahead? Or surely we could have spent much of the time on more productive pursuits. One thing Bingham taught us for our travels was never to tolerate a man walking in front as a continuous incentive to the dogs. Some nations allow it, but to him it was a waste. If the surface were hard the person would have to run, and a run of thirty miles a day is not my idea of efficient, tireless travel. Anyhow, with a man ahead, it is so much harder to maintain accurate direction than with a well-driven self-leading team being kept by voice on an accurate compass course. When travelling with heavy loads it is essential for the dogs to do the work, hence the necessity of training as a team. If training is bad it will be a weary person who turns into the tent at the end of the day, and at the end of a week's travelling he will be quite worn out; it will have been his personal efforts and not those of the dogs that have kept up the pace. The team, in short, needs more training.

Lastly a man walking ahead all the time spells danger. If the area ahead is crevassed he must be on a rope, and the rope dragging in the snow will worry the dogs. If he isn't roped it is an unjustifiable risk. Better a dog down a crevasse than a man; better still, neither.

As far as was possible with our limited number of dogs, each of us had teams of our own, and the owner was responsible for the team's training and equipment. He was responsible for making all the harness and keeping the traces in good order, for checking up the tethering of the dogs of his team, and if he was to maintain their confidence, for visiting them once or twice every day especially on those days on which exercising was not possible. He would deal with their minor sores or ailments, and would call the doctor in if necessary.

Many folk did not like the dog-house by the back door and the strange sour doggy smell that pervaded it.

It was moderately tidy, with a row of wall hooks, each belonging to a dog driver in the expedition. On the peg would be hung the owner's whip, and the traces belonging to his own team; with them would be a set of used dog harnesses, and a brand-new spare set ready for some future journey. The bundles of harnesses were gay to look at, as each was marked with its own combination of bright-coloured tabs.

Above all there was the strange dog smell. A queer mixture of sweaty harnesses and seal oil, crushed puppy meal, tarred rope, and new leather collars.

Even now, after several years, when I get out my old sealskin boots or my oil-soaked dog whip, they retain in part the smell of the dog-house and my thoughts go back to the rows of harnesses and the many happy miles that we worked and trained together.

The proof of the pudding is in the eating—and I can look back on all this in retrospect. In the 1946 season the longest journey was 300 miles. In 1947 with teams in better shape it was 1,200 miles with air support. In 1949 and 1950 the journeys were 1,000 and 1,200 respectively, without air support, and with the trained teams driven by folk who in most cases had never handled dogs before.

I have said enough about fully grown dogs and how we trained them, but cannot pass on without a mention of puppies. Among the bitches our birth-rate was not as high as we might have expected, and when happy events were imminent we all behaved like expectant fathers. A few weeks before she was due, the bitch would be brought nearer to the house, with the sire of her choice for company, and in a kennel by the back door would get all the tit-bits that were going from the kitchen, at the same time she would receive special attention from us all. Nearer the time, depending on the weather and the general layout of the snow drifts, we would try and coax her into a more secluded spot. It wasn't easy, as the creatures, like their human counterparts, liked to show a will of their own. Often we would get our way by securing her to a new, thoroughly hygienic, kennel with a light piece of string and would hide, somewhere else, an old box with a blanket in the bottom. It wouldn't be long before she would break the string and, with luck, in a few hours would have discovered the old blanket and settled in exactly as we had intended her to do. To maintain the quality of the stock only a proportion of the puppies born would be kept, and, from the very start, we would handle them daily, partly to get the bitch used to the idea, and partly to ensure that we never had fully grown puppies that were frightened of us. Weaning would probably start in about three weeks and would be complete by five or six; the puppies would then be shut into a large pen, with the mother free to hop in and out over the wire-netting side to keep up the daily hygiene. Six or seven weeks would see them as tough sturdy little brutes well able to fend for themselves. For the mother the work was ended and for us it had just begun. Hot meals three times a day was the rule; the menu was dog meal and seal blood, grated liver and blubber, or sometimes a large seal liver which they could tear to shreds in puppy-like ferocity just for the fun of licking each other clean afterwards.

As often as not they would escape from the puppy pen and would wander far. Many were the nights when our peace would be broken by the puppies who had decided that the hut roof would be an excellent playground. After twelve weeks we let them loose and for the next two months the puppies lived a glorious life. We did not attempt to keep them in the confines of a wire cage and allowed them to wander freely all over the island. In this way they were able to get plenty of exercise and build up good hefty bodies for future use.

The older dogs always treated them with kindly tolerance and affection, even though the puppies often took unheard of liberties in stealing some peculiarly luscious lumps of old blubber, or digging up some treasured bone. It seemed as if the older ones nodded their heads in wisdom and remarked to each other, "Let them be, they are only young once."

The puppies as a result grew up fearless and playful and bubbling over with good spirits. If the back door were left open they might wander into the hut and rampage in a pile of wood shavings under the bench in the workshop or play tug of war with someone's socks drying in front of the fire.

They slept where they wished, under the hut or in an old box, and as often as not when the bowl of hot breakfast mash appeared at the back door a bunch of dirty black pups would emerge from the hole in the snow that led down to Reg Freeman's coal mine.

All young animals inspire a sense of joy and affection and I believe young huskies beat the lot.

All good things come to an end and so at the age of four or five months they would be given a collar; their playing days were past and they would be tethered close beside their parents. For the first twenty-four hours after the change they would howl their heads off and sound terribly unhappy; but it wouldn't be long before they settled down to become as contented as the rest of the dogs around base.

CHAPTER 5

The Long Winter Night

IN MID-MAY the sun left us and we were not to see it again until the third week in July. For most of that time it was not daylight until 10 a.m., and even then it was a pale insipid sort of light that gave no shadow or contrast. By three in the afternoon it was dark again and in those short five hours all the outside jobs had to be finished. This in fact was the long winter night. It made very little difference to our general routine except of course that the outdoor jobs were concentrated into a much shorter time. Dog training, fetching coal and ice, or emptying kitchen rubbish went on exactly as before.

In many ways the early part of the winter was thoroughly disappointing, because the weather remained far too warm and little snow came to stay.

The sea in front of the base had shown no signs of freezing up and even the sheltered "Back Bay" between us and the mainland was only half frozen, with a layer of soft snow covering the treacherous ice. With no sea-ice our training runs with the dog teams were thoroughly restricted, and usually involved a steep haul up to the glacier behind the base. We were lucky in being able to get out of Stonington Island at all for at Bingham's old base in the Debenham Islands there was no such outlet, and there was no room for them to give their dogs the much needed exercise.

This restriction in movement that was imposed upon us did give us a real chance to set our own house in order for there were many small details which might otherwise have been neglected.

We were able to put up shelves and set out the expedition library. There were two sets of books, one a typical ship's library of novels and light reading, and the other an astonishingly complete set of scientific books which ranged from a complete encyclopaedia to all the polar literature and expedition reports which might possibly concern us: there was even the old faithful, *Whitaker's Almanack* which in the years to come solved so many arguments.

Few discussions on the polar technique did not call at some time upon this wealth of experience so carefully recorded by our predecessors.

As I look at it a large part of the success of an expedition must depend upon the speed with which individual members learn their job and a good library hastens this process enormously. I don't know who assembled our scientific library, for it was probably the best that had ever sailed south with a polar expedition; in any case our indebtedness was incalculable.

We fitted wire-netting protection to the greenhouse so that later on when the hut became half submerged in snow the windows could not be attacked by the uproarious puppies.

We were rather slow in becoming used to the ways of the Esse cooker. It demanded so little attention that as often as not it would be forgotten altogether. At the end of the day the cook would forget to shake out the ashes and top up the coal hopper and the first that we would know about it was the sound of a roaring primus cooking the morning breakfast.

Rarely did we let all the hut stoves go out at the same time, and the sound of the primus would mingle with the sulphurous smell of red-hot cinders that were being carried through the hut on a shovel from the workshop fire to the dead kitchen stove.

One long and tedious job which, as I have said, occupied Duggie Mason and myself, was the digging out of the American workshop and drying the whole place out for possible use. To excavate five foot of clear blue ice covering an area of twenty foot square is a quick job in the normal way, but mix it with a conglomeration of wood-working tools, sacks of nails, bags of soot, and a miniature billiard table that must not be damaged, and the job was quite different. Add to these items the body of an old husky and a barrel of paint or a small tin of anti-freeze compound, and the job had its messy side as well.

It was nearly a month before the workshop was clear to floor level and we were able to light the fire and dry the whole hut out.

The work did have its lighter side, however, for there was always the sense of "Lucky dip".

A power-driven circular saw emerged and the sewing-machine was found still to be in good order; odd souvenirs that had come from the Debenham Island hut lay alongside unopened packets of chewing gum and reels of sewing twine. The two diesel generators in the corner of the workshop block were examined and, apart from frost-cracked cylinder blocks, were deemed repairable. J. Joyce and I spent many evenings working by the light of a hurricane lamp drilling holes and fitting the copper patch which I thought would probably do the job.

Outside, awaiting removal and not yet covered by the new season's snow, was the incredible mass of old tins and evil kitchen refuse, dumped not five yards from the hut's main entrance. It never ceased to amaze us why the Americans, with all the advantages that numbers and mechanical aids must have given them, had left their supplies and fuel dumped so haphazardly all over the island. The kitchen refuse heap was utterly unforgivable.

We finished cleaning and drying the American huts by mid-June and about this time, after a week of zero temperature, the sea froze and at last we had space in which to move. All the seals had left us for the winter but now we were able to collect the various carcasses that had been left on the outlying islands by the crew of the *Trepassey* and to exercise ourselves and our dogs as we did so.

All the really dirty jobs were over and the Commander issued us with our personal sets of clothing. Some of the items belonged essentially to life at base, and the more specialized items were only for use when travelling.

I don't think any of us realised at the time how extremely good our equipment was, judged by any standards. The fact that we were still virtually at war and that we were only one of many bases has since made me realise how much work Bingham had achieved in England. Every item of clothing had been checked by him in the United Kingdom before it was packed.

In our daily life we used very ordinary clothes, for the temperature was seldom below zero and we were never far from the warmth of the hut. Thick wool underclothes, flannel trousers, endless socks, woollen shirt, and an old sweater formed the lower layer, and these would be covered, when outside the hut, by a heavy white duffel coat pulled over the head. If we expected to remain outside long we would put on a thin windproof outer covering, made in two parts, exactly similar to the clothes used by the seamen in the Navy for the wartime Russian convoys.

As soon as the permanent snow had covered all the rocks our sealskin boots were produced. These are knee-length boots made by the women of Labrador from specially prepared sealskin. Except for the actual killing, the women do all the work. The skin is first scraped and allowed to tan in a barrel of urine until all the hairs drop out. After that it is chewed until soft and only then is considered ready for use.

Rumour has it that in Arctic Labrador the suitor examines the teeth of his prospective bride rather on the lines of a horse dealer in England inspecting a possible purchase! A well-dentured bride can "chew" a complete skin in about two or three days.

Using caribou sinew for thread and a special type of watertight seam, the boots are then stitched together, and finished in a manner that any civilized seamstress would be proud to copy.

When we received them they were hard and parchment-like, but in use they rapidly became soft and pliable as chamois leather, water-tight as rubber sea-boots, and pervaded with a smell, offensive at first yet remarkably pleasant in retrospect. Worn with three or four pairs of socks these soft-soled boots are warm in temperatures down to 0° F., and their enemies are sharp rocks, broken bottles, and jagged tin cans.

All our specialized travel and clothing items had been obtained after endless difficulties at home and represented much time and labour. It was small wonder that Bingham reacted sharply when he saw moose-hide moccasins, for instance, which should only be used when travelling in sub-zero weather, used without thought in the salt slush of the tide-crack or as house slippers in the warmth of the kitchen. It certainly was not intentional on our part to misuse equipment; at the end of the year's travels, when we had learnt to appreciate its value, we were rarely offenders in this respect.

Often in May or June it blew for days on end. Outside chores tended to accumulate and only necessary outings such as feeding the dogs, reading thermometers, or the daily walk over the hill to the American-built privy, which we had cleared and put into use, were ever embarked upon.

On any one of these windy days, Robbie Slessor, if he were going out to feed the dogs, would ask somebody to tie up the cuffs of his anorak tight around his wrists and button up his hood so that it covered all but his eyes and nose. He would go into the back porch, shutting the workshop door behind him, open the back door and, as the swirling drift swept into the porch, he would slip out into the noisy murk and be gone. After an hour he would be back in the shelter of the porch, sweeping the loose snow off his clothes, thawing the ice out of his whiskers, shaking out the snow which, in spite of his precautions had blown up into his wrists. The hour had been well spent. With two others he had rolled a seal carcass out from under a snow drift and probably found it so hard that an axe would bounce off it as if it was stone. In any case using an axe was very dangerous, for as soon as the axe head left the shelter of his body the wind would play with it like a child's kite and accuracy of aim was quite impossible. Using a big cross-cut saw was moderately successful, and after forty-five minutes' hard work fifty lumps of seal, rock-hard and almost smell-less, were ready for distribution around the mounds of snow that were in fact sleeping dogs.

At each mound, as the sledge load of meat went on its round, a paw would come out and draw in the day's ration. The dog would be loath to uncurl himself from the protection of the hole in which he was buried. He would stick out a muzzle and pass a red tongue across his own nose by way of thank-you, and it would not be long before his bushy tail would seal up the hole through which he had dragged his meat, and it was time to feed the next dog, just visible ten yards away in the driving drift. The fact that the dogs didn't even get up really meant that it was blowing; for, for them, the delight of anticipating the meal, leaping up and down, howling their heads off at the full extent of their chain, was nearly as great as the meal itself.

Willie Salter's process of dressing had to be repeated four times a day, for he had to flounder, whatever the weather, up to the meteorological station fifty yards away from the hut. Even in that distance it was easily possible to lose one's way, so he rigged a safety line along which he could slide his hand, and we in the hut did not have to worry if he was late in returning.

Inside the hut it would be warm. The heating stove would be drawing like a blast furnace as the wind swept across the top of the chimney. Mike or Reg would be busy sealing up the window frames with cellophane tape or caulking the crack with twists of cotton wool. Leaky window frames and doors always annoyed me. It isn't difficult to design a draught-free window, or to make windows fit accurately in their frames. The Swiss achieve it so simply in their mountain huts. Our mass-produced articles were totally inadequate. Inside it certainly would be warm but also very noisy. The wind charger on the hut roof always sounded as if it were about to take off, shaking and shuddering like some chained beast. Every now and then some particularly vicious blast would rock the hut and somebody would glance up at the wind-speed recorder out of curiosity. Gusts of over a hundred miles an hour were not unknown. We had implicit trust in the security of the hut and we blessed the fact that the roof was well anchored with heavy steel cables to the rock beneath. While the "fumigator" blew it certainly wasn't unpleasant in the hut, yet it was an incredible relief when it all stopped.

At the end of a week's blow the whole contouring of the countryside had changed. Downwind from the hut, in its lee, so to speak, a long snow drift had formed, perhaps a hundred yards in extent. No longer was the way out of the back door a drop of three steps, for it had become a five-yard dig through the snow. Every loose object that had been left outside before the wind started had blown away, or become the nucleus of a second-ary drift of its own. The dirt of the week before had gone, all was covered with a new layer of hard wind-blown snow.

The Commander had certainly sited the hut well, for however hard it blew and drifted, the upwind side remained uncovered. Throughout the winter and spring the light from the world out-side could reach the windows and keep the inside of the hut clear and bright.

There were other days, not quite so frequent, of clearness, coldness, and stillness that are hard to describe.

Instead of the rush and roar of the wind there was an exhilarating coldness that froze the moisture in the nostrils and numbed the back of the throat. The wire supports for the wireless masts were coated in glistening hoar frost that fell off at the quietest touch: the propellers of the wind chargers lay stagnant and still. Above the chimneys the moisture in the smoke condensed and lay as a thin cloud immediately over the hut. The mountains of the mainland seemed near and welcoming and the silence was only broken by the rattle of a dog's chain or the muffled noise of the petrol generator's exhaust discharging under the snow. Then, to break the spell three or four rampaging puppies would chase each other out from the wood-pile, their white frost-covered noses making them look like funny old men as they rushed up eager and excited to be the first to lick one's sealy hand or dash off with the hammer that had just been put down.

Midwinter's day in the first year was enormous fun and formed the only real day's rest that I can remember in the first eight months. Robbie Slessor delved into his special hoard of luxury stores and produced items which we had known nothing about. Mincemeat and corn-on-the-cob appeared, with tins of Christmas pudding and chicken soup. I was officially cook of the week, but that did not stop everybody else in the hut from enjoying the luxury of preparation. The day was officially a public holiday and on this occasion there were no voluntary jobs to be completed.

Ken Butler and John Tonkin between them baked an enormous twelve-pound Christmas cake and the rest of us gave advice when the question of icing it came up. John had four attempts to produce an ersatz marzipan from things like almond essence and biscuit crumbs and he only finally solved the problem when he found a tin of almonds in the lucky dip over at the American huts. Ken, I remember, burnt his finger as he tried to push the water icing through a home-made decorating tube. I advocated "a touch of colour" and added too much Reckitt's blue and the cake took on a speckled effect. In spite of it all, the cake was an enormous success.

For the evening meal we changed into our best clothes, laid a tablecloth, and become thoroughly civilized. The chicken soup was followed by new potatoes, sweet corn, and a hot veal and ham pie that Duggie Mason had cooked. Christmas pudding, burning well, decorated with real holly sent by my young sister in the Christmas hamper, was followed with fresh mince pies and enlivened with strong rum sauce. Hot rum punch followed the coffee and a singsong started. The evening ended when the un-melodious songs were picked up and echoed in opposition by the dogs in the snow outside. For us in Antarctica the new year had started, the bottom of the hill was past.

The five weeks that followed while we waited for the return of the sun passed with incredible speed—five weeks of frantic preparation for the travels of the spring.

Most of the travel equipment that we had brought was quite ready for use, but several items had been left by Bingham for completion in Antarctica. The sledges, for instance, were still in pieces and had to be assembled, and it was a job in which every-one assisted. The design of these had not changed much since 1936 and, except for war-time modifications, they were copies of the ones Commander Bingham had used ten years earlier. Runners were of steamed hickory turned up at either end; the inverted U-shaped bridge pieces that joined the runners together were of split ash, flexibly jointed and strengthened with a metal bracket. The platform that took the main load was of split ash again in twelve-foot strips. There was always an air of crafts-manship about when we assembled these sledges, and we had pride in our work. Every joint had to be lashed with raw-hide or light-weight fishing line and every securing screw put in with care and precision. We treated the runners with a mixture of hot Stockholm tar and wax, and spliced on the ropes that were to take the main hauling load.

We set up all the tents and examined them for defects. Sleeping bags were aired above the workshop stove and fitted with canvas covers made for them on the heavy duty sewing-machine. All the ration boxes had to be checked and fitted with small wooden chocks that would prevent them sliding sideways off the sledge. The thirty 2-gallon cans that were to be used in the field had to be filled with filtered paraffin and tested for leaks. All the primuses had to be assembled and tried out and the medical kits for travelling completed. All these were bad-weather jobs, and as I read my diary again I find that on all the fine days we were busy training the dogs. The sea-ice was not firm enough for travel until well after midwinter and only then were we able to give the dogs the longer journeys which they so badly required.

Each day we would explore further and further afield and attach names to the various icebergs that formed for us that year the geographical features of the sea-ice. By the end of July the dogs were sufficiently fit to travel six or eight miles at full gallop and could be considered almost ready for real work.

We went over one day to Bingham's old base at the Debenham Islands. It was only a matter of five miles to the north, round the tip of a glacier that shoved its snout into the sea and then the group of islands with the hut on them could be seen. We felt that we knew a good deal about the B.G.L.E. Several of us had met and worked under other members of that expedition besides Bingham and had learnt much of how they had lived and worked.

This hut was made from timber rescued from the derelict Deception Island whaling station and it had been brought down in sections in *Penola*, pre-built much as ours had been. It was typically B.G.L.E., clean and ready for habitation, neatly stored, and still full of useful equipment; a coil of old sealskin dog traces that had come from Greenland when Watkins was still alive, a caribou-skin sleeping bag that had hardly been used, and the ski split by Stephenson and mended by him in the field with pieces of ration box; all had stories to tell.

The bunk of Hampton, the pilot, was still fitted with an ingenious tin contraption designed to divert drips away from his pillow and Bingham, in the corner bunk, had decorated the wall with a set of cigarette cards illustrating English flowers. The hangar was neatly fitted with useful remains: unopened drums of paraffin and aviation petrol were stacked in the centre with a pile of well-used sledges against the far wall; in the rafters of the roof was a dismantled and well-greased Greenland sledge which in its day had been dragged through a tent by Bingham's unruly team at the northern base; in the corner of the hangar was the old stove and bench where Launcelot Fleming as expedition padre and senior scientist had held his Sunday evening services. He was vicar of Antarctica for two years and I have often heard him say that each week, in the largest parish in the world, he could take an evening service with all his parishioners present and join with them in discussing the merits of his sermon ten minutes later as they sat down to an evening meal.

It always struck me as a most beautifully sited base. As often as not it was free from the main run of the "ill-tempered fumigator" and was but fifteen yards from the sea, with secure moorings available for the ship not fifty yards away. The hut retained the family atmosphere that comes from being sited on one of a group of small islands. It was obviously warm and snug and seemed to offer a welcome whenever we rounded the glacier tongue after leaving Stonington Island and drove towards it.

It must have been sentimentally strange to the Commander to visit his old base again. In the Argentine Islands the hut was clear of stores yet asking for inhabitants. The hut here was peopled by the ghosts of living men and memories of a job well done.

We brought back two Greenland sledges from the rafters, and they became our heavy-duty sledges from that time on. The seal-skin line replaced the worn out raw-hide tip of John's whip and I used a pair of skis that had been Bertram's for many miles. We brought back many old dog harnesses still marked with their owner's names and we discovered why Bingham had used such prosaic names as Mutt, Jeff, or Bouncer for our own dogs. They were the names of the B.G.L.E. dogs, that had come to life again.

As I have said already we had completely cleaned and dried the American huts. Many of our own stores had been sledged over the hills for safe keeping and much of the debris outside had been moved away to the sea-ice. The place at least looked cared for.

The patch on the smaller of the two diesel generators had been successful and Joyce and I persuaded it to run happily on load, but in general we neither needed nor wanted to use the large chilly building. Joyce, our geologist, had brought with him a simple rock-slicing plant which required electricity to run it. I remember well arguing in the evenings about the value of this equipment. In our limited knowledge of field work we all felt that a polar geologist neither requires nor expects to make microscopic rock sections in the field; as a result none of us was ever very serious about helping him to start the diesel generator and get his rock-slicing machine to work. We would often pull his leg about helping us train our rowdy, unruly dogs which in the future would provide him with transport, and he in turn would point out how simple it was to handle a whip and get the best out of a dog team. He was never prepared to give his theories a trial, however!

A week before the sun returned we awoke one morning to find the world around lit by a strange translucent light: high above the plateau was a single, enormous cloud lit from afar by the returning sun. It seemed as if it were made of mother-of-pearl with the delicate rainbows forming round its edge, gradually spreading to cover the whole area. The bright whiteness was our sun for that day and we had an inkling of what life would be like when the real sun returned. We had become used to the twilight of winter and had almost forgotten the glory of sunshine.

On July 21, high above the base on the mountain peaks the light of the sun appeared, day by day we watched it creep down the hills, and on the 26th it was with us at Stonington Island.

Few folk, unless they themselves have experienced it, can appreciate just what the return of the sun means. I have heard it likened to the emerging from a long tunnel into the bright beauty of an English spring: but no tunnel can be long enough for that to approach a true description. For us it was a day of great rejoicing, the confinement of base life was gone, the time for travel had really begun.

CHAPTER 6

Equipment in Use

TO UNDERSTAND fully what life was really like when we travelled with dogs in Antarctica it is essential to know the details of the equipment we used and the general way in which it had been thought out.

Not many people know that in England, at Cambridge, there is a building known as the Scott Polar Research Institute. It is a memorial to that great polar leader, Captain R. F. Scott, R.N., and has as its purpose the sorting and recording of all possible knowledge on polar matters; by so doing it helps us as a nation to carry on that spirit of polar adventure which is our heritage.

In the field of polar equipment this means that there is available to any would-be explorer a gigantic pool of information which covers the history of every little detail of polar life, from the moment when an idea for equipment germinated in someone's mind up to the stage when it could be judged in the light of actual experience.

The institute aims at the strictest impartiality. There is no insistence that one article of equipment, or another particular procedure for travel, is the only one. If one nation differs widely from Britain in its methods, the Institute's job is to record those methods and attempt to assess the efficiency of the results that have been achieved.

In Britain, therefore, as I see it, the attitude of those who have travelled and lived in polar regions, to those folk who want to learn how, is something like this: "Here is the equipment that we used on our recent expedition, this is the exact method in which we used it, it works efficiently and well, and is rugged enough to bring you back. When you have learnt to use it, then, and only then, start to improve it; above all record your improvements for future reference and don't change the details too fast."

This seemed roughly the course that Bingham followed. For us, all our items were modelled on their counterparts in the B.G.L.E., and these themselves were evolved from items used by Watkins in Greenland. Every item of travel equipment was proven and good, and until we had passed our "apprenticeship", new items were not to be tried.

This may sound like staunch conservatism, but to the polar traveller who intends to explore and to return with his results, it is sound common sense.

If for instance a new-fangled tent, or one of a type that has already failed in Antarctic conditions, blows away a hundred miles from home, the immediate problem is to return to base intact. There is no sense in sitting down in the field and arguing that its loss was a theoretical impossibility. The tent that must be used is one of the type that has stood through a hundred gales or the wildness of a polar winter and survived with colours flying.

In civilization, if some new type of house of revolutionary design falls down in service it doesn't really matter, for the world is full of welcoming neighbours. In Antarctica, when travelling far away from home, one's neighbours are usually many thousand miles away and life without a "house", to put it mildly, would be pretty exacting.

In shape they resembled a rectangular pyramid with seven-foot bamboo poles at each corner meeting together at the top in a canvas pouch. Suspended from the poles and some six inches inside them was a white inner tent which turned inwards eighteen inches at the bottom to form the edge of the inside floor. The dark outer tent dropped over the outside of the framework and its lower edge turned outwards to form a flap about eighteen inches wide on which we could shovel snow for anchorage. In the centre of one of the triangular sides there was a circular hole through both tents which formed the entrance. It was closed by a sleeve three feet long tied up for all the world like an old sack with a piece of tape or lamp wick. When once the tent had been erected for the first time the four poles were left permanently laced to the two covers and it was only necessary to lift the corners, push the bottom of the poles together, and the tent was folded and ready for transport.

Because of its pyramid form, re-erection was easy; the four poles needed only to be separated, and jumped into the ground, some snow shovelled on to the flap, and the tent would stand with no pegs to hold it, secure against the strongest winds and heaviest of snow falls.

The living space inside was about six feet wide by seven feet long and the height to the peak about five feet six inches. Right at the top there was a tube, some two inches in diameter, which passed through both tents and acted as a ventilator.

The material was non-rubberized, very tightly woven cotton windproof, a product of wartime research, which was quite unsurpassed for its durability and utter windproofness. Up to the present it has survived the rigours of seven Antarctic winters with various expeditions, and has never shown signs of failure. Unfortunately, by some obscure industrial monopoly, this proven Antarctic cloth is almost unobtainable for general use by mountaineers or campers.

The ground sheet that we used was made from the rubberized fabric used in the Services for self-inflating rescue dinghies and it fitted the floor of the inner white tent exactly.

We had sleeping bags that originated with the American Army, where they were known as Arctic mummy bags, and this name indicated their Egyptian mummy-like shape. There were two bags one inside the other, each filled with goose down, and the design was so thought out that no seam on the outer bag coincided with one on the inner. The entrance was not through one end, as is usual in British bags, but through the front by a long slit which extended from the head to the thighs, and so placed that both bags could be closed by a single strong zip. The mummy bag itself was always carried inside a strong canvas cover which I had made in the winter, and this served the double purpose of keeping it clean and providing a tough, non-tearing cover to the quilted bag itself.

Reindeer skins formed our mattress. This was not because snow is not in itself a soft and pleasant bed, but because it is essential to prevent the chill of the snow from reaching the body. Many types of skins will provide excellent protection in this respect for a short time, but will slowly ice up and become frozen solid with continuous condensation. Only the thick skins of certain animals will remain free from ice and warm for months on end, the caribou and the polar bear for instance.

The sledges that we used were of two distinct types. Around base where we could expect a good deal of travel on hard frozen blue ice we used a broad sledge with narrow runners that were shod with steel. It was based on the type used by the Eskimos in East Greenland and represented the results of several adaptations by previous British expeditions.

The heavy side timbers were fitted with strip steel loops which passed through the deck planks, and the whole was held together by hard wood wedges driven into the loops. In spite of its strength and weight it remained remarkably flexible. These were the sledges that we brought back from the Debenham Islands.

The other sledge, the broad runner Nansen type, was to be used continuously on our travels inland. It was a light wooden skeleton built up upon hickory runners twelve feet long and four inches wide. These were kept apart by bridges of split ash formed by a horizontal cross piece and two uprights, and the whole framework was carefully jointed and dowelled together and lashed up with strips of rawhide. In front a piece of ash of round section was bent into a semi-circle and formed a bumper against damage in the field. At the rear there were handlebars three feet six inches high and, mounted on a bracket between the uprights in an easily visible position, was a P.10 type aircraft compass, as used for navigation when flying.

The sledge was fitted with a foot-operated brake which lay between the runners and could be worked from the rear; the bicycle-type sledge wheel mounted to run in the exact track of one of the runners was our means of measuring distance.

The whole sledge was light and flexible yet oddly enough incredibly strong.

It had points of close resemblance to the sledges used by Shackleton or Scott, yet to the discerning eye, all sorts of details had been changed. Every change represented time and thought on somebody's part, a journey completed, or some repair that had become incorporated in the design. It was another case of tried evolution and as such typical of all our equipment.

The ice spear was always one of Bingham's favourite items of equipment. It had a six-foot shaft made of hickory, and at its lower end was fitted a steel head, shaped like a joiner's mortise chisel. They are used much in Labrador as a prodder for feeling out a track across rotting sea-ice: in Graham Land we used them all the time when crossing glaciers, feeling for crevasses to ensure that the surface ahead was firm and safe for travel.

In the matter of personal clothing when sledging, the thing that amazed me was the incredible simplicity. For travellers who hoped to live happily in temperatures that ranged from freezing to 30° or 40° F. below zero, we took and wore remarkably little.

On our upper half, if the weather were blustery and cold, we would wear a long-sleeved woollen vest and long woollen shirt. A silk scarf, invariably made from an old section of parachute, would be lightly twisted around the neck and a light-weight Shetland sweater was pulled on above the shirt. On our lower half, just as at base, we would wear long woolly pants and battle-dress trousers. I always wore three pairs of socks, each layer being a different bright colour, and over these slipped one or two pairs of slippers made from close-woven duffel blanket material.

Over all these clothes would be drawn a baggy and shapeless two-piece windproof outer. It was made from the same material as that we used so successfully for the tents.

Compared with the material available to previous expeditions, we were equipped with windproof outer clothing that really *was* windproof, and was light in weight, tough in wear, and hard to tear. If by chance they did become cut through by careless handling there was little tendency for them to rip down, as a sail rips in a stiff breeze.

When wet the fibres of this material become swollen, and the fabric itself becomes stiff and waterproof. Worn in a single thickness it provided all the protection that was needed.

When I say baggy and shapeless I really mean it, for much of the insulating value of light windproofs depends upon the volume and stillness of air that they trap inside them. Refinements of design were noticeably absent, for every button and buttonhole, drawcord or zip represented something which would catch the drift snow or provide an inlet for the cold winds. The lower half, made on the lines of pyjama trousers, had a waist of about fifty inches around, and drew tight with a lampwick drawcord. The anorak, or upper half, would look as if it had bats' wings if the baggy arms were stretched out sideways, and the hood edged with wolverine fur was balloon-like and shapeless.

Almost anything was used to keep our heads warm. I myself always preferred a wool gaberdine Army ski cap which had a peak that was large enough to keep the anorak hood out of my eyes; this wasn't warm enough in the coldest weather so I made a peaked cap of my own, lined with some odd scraps of beaver fur that my mother had sent down.

Our gloves were many and various. We all had white horsehide mitts of the semi-gauntlet type fitted with a draw-up strap at the wrist. They were large enough to take at least one woollen lining made from the same woven duffel material that we used for the slippers. They were excellently warm in the coldest weather as long as they were kept clean and dry, but obviously they had limitations when it came to using cameras or survey instruments. When we wanted to use our fingers we had thin white woollen fingered gloves and we rang the changes with white silk R.A.F. pilots' gloves or chamois leather ones made up at base in the long winter nights.

For footgear we stuck to types of boots which had soft soles, and required a minimum of maintenance in the field. The sealskin boots that we used, when worn with several pairs of socks and duffel slippers, were light, warm, and comfortable from above freezing down to zero degrees Centigrade, but below that temperature their watertight properties made them condense up and freeze on the inside. In really cold weather we would always use smoke-tanned caribou-skin moccasins made by the Red Indian folk in North Canada. Neither type of boot gave much support for the ankle and this criticism was often levelled at them, but for those who didn't mind padding about all day in footgear that were a cross between bedroom slippers and boxing gloves they were excellent and gave good service with negligible maintenance for many months in the field.

Because of their softness they are not easy to attach firmly to ski or snowshoes and as a result only a limited amount of control

over these items can be maintained. It is a case of weighing up
the advantages of hard ski boots, which fit the skis excellently
yet are heavy in use and much more troublesome in maintenance,
against the light-weight boots which provide poor ski control
yet demand no attention and are warm and blisterproof. Bingham preferred soft boots, so it was all that we carried. For the
explorer who wants to travel far for months on end behind his
dogs, and who is prepared to sacrifice a certain amount of control
over his skis so that he can live more comfortably under conditions which may vary from above freezing to −40° F. in a matter
of hours, they are items which are thoroughly proved, and as
such will certainly "bring him back".

Bingham loved snowshoes. I suppose this was because in
Labrador they are used so much in the forests of the hinterland,
but none of us ever achieved a satisfactory method of fixing them
to our feet. We used them around base when the snow was soft
and we wanted to potter around from hut to hut, but we never
liked them for travelling and I finally discarded them altogether.
In the end we found it was always easier to use skis, for earlier
expeditions had evolved a thoroughly adequate method of using
them with soft footgear in all temperatures. The binding took
the form of a canvas and leather boot whose stiff sole was
fastened direct to the ski. It was only necessary to insert one's
moccasined foot into the ski "boot", tie up the ankle straps
made of lampwick, and all was ready.

In man-rations we were particularly well off, for Bingham had
copied largely the scientifically calculated ration produced for the
B.G.L.E. and found by them to be so successful. The whole
problem of providing a reasonable man-ration for Antarctic
sledging is remarkably complex and the history of its evolution
could form a complete book in itself.

In our case the rations had to fulfil the following rigid require-
ments: they had to be light and packed to withstand a passage
through the tropics or a year's submergence in soft, slushy snow;
they had to be robust enough to withstand considerable rough
handling in transit; they had to be complete in themselves, except
for fuel, and capable of sustaining life in the field without loss of
health, indefinitely; they must be easily cooked or, better still,
completely pre-cooked and easily preared by heating in the

confines of the tent, for cooking by boiling wastes fuel; they must be easily digested and unlikely to upset the regularity of life; they must be packed in reasonable sized units to help with man-handling; they must be digestible in the uncooked state in case of emergency.

Our ration fulfilled all these points excepting perhaps the vexed question of weight.

In the form in which we took them each light plywood ration box represented exactly twenty days' worth of food for one man and provided him with 4,400 calories a day of a reasonably well-balanced diet. Each box contained exactly the same items, sealed in tins and packed in exactly the same positions relative to one another. The complete box contained thirty-three pounds of food and with all its packing it weighed about fifty pounds.

The contents were made up as follows:

7 lb. of Bovril Pemmican, a hard, brown meat product made from the best lean beef, dried, ground, and mixed with fat. It looks and tastes rather like the powdery dregs at the bottom of a cup of Bovril.

7 lb. of best butter.

2 lb. of full-cream dried milk. This was the same product that was used at the end of the war for special baby foods.

3 lb. of quick-cooking Quaker oats.

4 lb. of lump sugar.

3 lb. of chocolate in wrapped 2-ounce bars.

20 packets of biscuits made with a very high fat content and yet remarkably solid in spite of it.

½ lb. of cocoa powder.

2 lb. of pea flour for thickening soups, and a bottle of "babies" orange-juice to provide the extra vitamins.

Worked out on a day-to-day basis this provided about twenty-six ounces of food and it required a maximum of one-third of a pint of fuel for melting the snow and cooking the complete meal.

Described in terms that the practical housewife would understand this is quite remarkable. It was a ration that needed no larder, would keep indefinitely, and the whole day's cooking could be done in a bare half-hour at the enormous expense of two pennyworth of paraffin. All the items except pemmican were

obtainable from the village shop, and even with pemmican at
7s. 6d. per pound the cost per day works out at less than 5s.

In bulk it certainly was not a filling ration; and nobody can
deny that it is rather monotonous. To hungry travellers who are
prepared to think in terms of weight carried against miles
travelled or who prefer to "get the cooking finished and have
the evening to ourselves" this ration was proved, and it would, if
used sensibly, be sure to bring them back.

For the dogs the question of food was even simpler. Each dog
received one pound of pemmican daily, packed in hard blocks
about four inches square and one and a half inches thick and
wrapped up in paper. Basically it was the same as man's
pemmican but had a far higher fat content and a small proportion
of chopped maize was added to act as roughage. It was always
carried forty-eight blocks at a time in light plywood boxes with
tin linings and when deposited in the field the inside tin always
remained sealed.

All these items were simple, and only as we learnt to camp and
travel did we fully realise the value of this simplicity which could,
with careful use, provide us with such a comfortable life in the
bleakest of surroundings. The efficiency could only be maintained
by careful adherence to details of use in the field, and that is why
meticulous camp routine was so essential and to us all so very
interesting.

It would be of little value to describe our various journeys
if I did not first try to give the picture of a day's routine from
the moment when the tent goes up in the evening, at the end
of the day's travel, until it went up again twenty-four hours later.

Before midwinter's day Bingham, Robbie Slessor, John Tonkin, and I left for a short reconnaissance on the glacier behind
base. I will not describe our camp routine on that trip, for in spite
of several rehearsals on the snow patch outside the hut we were
slow and cumbersome; in any case during the next two years
camping routine underwent many changes and improvements.
Instead I will quote the text of a letter that I wrote in the spring
of 1947 for private circulation among my friends:

For me the day always starts in the evening when the leader
of the party decides to make camp. It has probably been blowing

all day with a bit of a cross-wind and the loads are still pretty heavy. We've had to help the dogs a good deal and our anoraks are hanging loose outside the trousers to keep us from sweating. The party is four men with three sledges travelling like ships in line ahead. The front sledge, with John Tonkin driving it, carries a complete campload for him and Doc Butson who is with him. Duggie Mason comes next with a load that consists mostly of dog rations, and I am "tail-end Charlie" with another campload for Mason and myself. Each sledge has its own ice axe and alpine rope on the top of the load, where it can easily be reached should an emergency arise.

John looks at his watch, turns into the wind, and stops, for he had told us at dinner-time that we would camp at exactly six o'clock and in the poor conditions we all have been counting the minutes. We close up on him and turn the dogs into the wind too so that our sledges finish up side by side, yet five yards apart.

Straight away we tether our dogs in groups of three, staking them down with light hickory stakes driven deep into the snow. We have tried other methods of tying the dogs up at night but have found that this is the quickest, and by selecting dogs that are friendly to each other for each group, it makes for peace in the camp. The other method that we tried and discarded was to use a long wire pegged at each end and fitted with chains spaced at intervals down its length. But we found it slower and much less certain. As soon as all our dogs are tethered and as quickly as possible we deal out the dog food, still wrapped in its paper; "dog feed" time always imposes the greatest strain on our tethering arrangements. The dogs are hungry and excited and the mere rustle of paper or the opening of a pemmican box sets them all off. After a meal they soon settle down and their twistings and turnings as they select their patch of snow for the night soon consolidate the snow around the picket and then, acting on the lamp-post principle, they quickly cement it into position.

As soon as the dogs have been fed, the sledges are unlashed and in the strong wind it is necessary for all four of us to take a hand with each tent. It is laid out on the snow with its peak pointing upwind, the poles spread wide apart, and the upwind corners of the snow flap held down with spare ration boxes. With a quick flip the peak of the tent is lifted, allowing the wind to catch it, and as it bellies out the downwind poles are opened out and stamped in. Some snow around the flap and a few more ration boxes, and all is quite secure and it is safe to put up the other tent.

Once this is up each tent's occupants fend for themselves. Duggie, the inside man for the day, prepares to go into the tent, brushing every bit of snow off his clothes before he enters. Snow inside a tent that is soon to be warm means melting, and water means a damp sleeping bag which in turn means a cold, sleepless night. Inside he spreads out the groundsheet, brushes off his feet as he draws them in, and shouts that he is ready. We always carried the sleeping bags and reindeer skins inside a large cotton bag made like a large pillow-case. To save brushing the drift snow off it was only necessary to push the open end of the bag into the tent entrance and the inside man could draw the bedding inwards, leaving the bag to be shaken free from snow outside the tent.

Each bed is rolled out along the sides of the tent with the reindeer skin underneath, fur side uppermost, as mattress. Between the beds there is a space about two feet wide which serves as a kitchen. The box full of pots and pans is brushed clean and passed in next and placed between the feet at the far end of the tent. The ration box that is in use forms a doorstep just inside the entrance between our heads, and the spare box, which contains the wireless set and medical kit, is left outside as an outer doorstep. The two empty cooking pots are pushed outside for me to fill up with snow. There are still a few more things to be passed inside: the two kitbags of personal clothes, the survey board on which the daily march is to be plotted, and the wireless aerial that is threaded in through the ventilation tube at the peak of the tent.

It is time for Duggie to undress and make the place warm. He removes his windproofs which are large enough to slip off very easily, and hangs them and his gloves and duffel slippers in the peak of the tent to dry off. He changes his socks into some spares that he had dried off during the previous night, and then slides down into his sleeping bag.

Outside I lay all the unused ration boxes around the tent flap and turn the unloaded sledge upside down to scrape the runners and brush off the snow.

The whip, which is popular for chewing gum to any wandering dog, is coiled up and placed inside the tent door on the left-hand side between the inner and outer tent and the current two-gallon tin of paraffin joins it. The dog traces have been collected and coiled up and all the loose bits and pieces such as ice axe and skis or snowshoes are stowed neatly outside the door. I have dug up a supply of hard snow with a high water content and placed it on the right of the door, between the tents, where it represents our supply of drinking water. The maximum and minimum thermometer is clipped on to the ice axe just outside the door and I am now able, after a last look round to see that nothing is left loose, to bid good night to the dogs, brush the snow off my clothes, and enter the warmth of the tent.

Inside, in strong contrast to the wildness outside, all is cheerful and warm. I slip off my windproofs and boots, hang up my clothes in the roof of the tent, and slide down into my sleeping bag to watch Duggie, as cook, preparing supper. If we have been efficient as a pair there is no need for either of us to leave those sleeping bags until it is time to break camp the next morning. The cook can reach the rations and the hard lumps of snow that are the water supply are just behind his head. If the primus runs low in paraffin the spare can is quite close and if the dogs are restless they are sited where they can be seen from the tent door. The noise of the primus drowns the sound of snow driving against the tent in the rising wind.

It is only twenty minutes since we stopped and already we are warm and comfortable. I roll around in my bag and decide that the snow under the reindeer skin has too many queer lumps in it, so, using my hip as a battering ram, I wallop my bed into a more comfortable shape and form a large pit for my hip and backside.

Duggie is busy melting the snow and then reaches for the tins of half-used rations. He chips the cold pemmican out of the seven-pound tin, and sprinkles it into the hot water. Two large dollops of butter follow, each the size of an egg, three or four dessert-spoonfuls of pea flour are stirred in, and some salt is added.

Supper always consists of pemmican made thick like blanc-mange or thin like soup according to taste. While it is coming to the boil he distributes the portion of the day's ration which we

are allowed to use as we think fit. Into my food bag he slips a
packet of biscuits, twenty lumps of sugar, a slab of chocolate, a
dollop of butter and a knob of pemmican which will be kept for
lunch the next day. After this the pemmican hoosh only requires
a couple of minutes to boil and is ready for consumption.

We invariably had a make-believe weekly menu to help us
remember the days of the week. Duggie would remind me that it
was Sunday as he passed me my pint mug of pemmican, referring
to it as cold meat, salad, and baked potatoes. I would slide partly
out of bed, break a biscuit or two into the soupy brew and get
on with supper. Meanwhile Duggie is melting more snow and is
brewing up the evening's cocoa in the other pot. He would make
it thick and sweet, using lots of milk and sugar, so that by the time
the pemmican was finished the cocoa was standing ready. In spite
of the very limited size of our supper I always felt full to capacity
at the end of the evening meal. On one or two occasions, when
we had surplus rations, we tried to eat more than our fair share
of pemmican but always found it rather a struggle.

We would not think of turning out the primus after supper,
for all the clothes in the peak of the tent would still be drying in
readiness for the next day. It is always a case of giving the primus
another pump, and using the extra warmth for some useful purpose. After lighting a candle Duggie would reach for the survey
board and plot in the day's course; I might well dig into my kit-
bag and produce a sock that had become thin round the heel and
required patching; later on I would connect the minute American
R.B.Z. wireless receiver to the aerial and tune in to London and
the B.B.C., using the excuse that we wanted a time-signal to
waste precious battery hours listening to the nine o'clock news. It
somehow emphasizes the remoteness of life to hear the measured
tones of the B.B.C. news-reader telling of events in the world
outside which we, in our remoteness, had tended to forget.

Often I would use the last flickerings of a primus to write a few
more lines to folk at home, and would invariably add some more
to my diary. After an hour or more we would wind up the
chronometer watches, set the alarm clock, shout good night to
the other tent, and let the primus go out. Lulled by the noise of
the wind on the tent we would wonder what the next day would
bring.

Duggie and I always found that we slept deeply, and had the most vivid and topical dreams in the moment before waking. They were dreams of a richness and clarity that we had never known before. (One morning I woke in worried horror and announced to Duggie that I had been married the night before and had recognized the church, the congregation, and my father as he took the service, but the bride's identity was quite unknown. Two years later when the dream became a reality the whole ceremony seemed like a repeat performance.)

In the night the wind died down and as we wake at 5.0 a.m. to the sound of the alarm and peep out of our sleeping bags, the whole of the inside of the tent is shimmering white with lace-like crystals of hoar frost. A rapid move or a vigorous uprising and the whole lot would shower down, so Duggie's hand slides out of his bag, feels for the matches, and lights the primus that he had primed the night before. His hand slides back and through a small opening in his sleeping bag he watches the warmth of the primus turn the hoar frost crystals to water vapour which leaves through the ventilator in the peak of the tent.

Porridge is ready in twenty minutes, for he used some water he had stored away in a thermos the night before to save the tedious process of melting down snow from scratch. It is a thick porridge, enriched by a dollop of butter, a spoonful or two of powdered milk, and some lumps of sugar dissolved in the water before cooking started. A mug of cocoa follows and forty minutes from waking it is time to get dressed and prepare to leave the tent.

It has been a pretty restful night, for we achieved eight hours of very deep sleep and were beautifully warm and cosy in spite of the cold world outside. The dogs hear the sound of our chatter and I can hear the bell on the collar of Rover, my lead dog, being shaken as he uncurls to greet the morning. In our tent we would always set the alarm a little early, so that we could enjoy the luxury of twenty minutes' dozing after our mug of cocoa and allow the porridge to digest and our thoughts to run their own course.

Duggie is still cook, so I get dressed first and slip on the clothes that I had so meticulously dried the night before, and probably stow the spare socks and duffel slippers in the mouth of my sleeping bag where they would be available in the evening.

Barely an hour after waking, I stick my head out of the tent door, say good morning to the dogs and start the day's work. I shout to Duggie what the weather is like and how much the tent has drifted up during the night. Outside everything is covered by a foot of snow but the snow shovel is where I had left it and it doesn't take long to dig everything else free.

Alarm clocks may sound rather luxurious, but they are not so. Look at it from the point of view of the first man out when the morning is bitterly cold and the wind is strong. Nothing is more irritating than creeping out of the tent dead on time, into the coldness outside, to find that the other tent failed to wake up, has not yet finished breakfast, and that there will be half an hour's delay. The day's travel will have got off to a bad start.

Outside I will be busy reversing the camping routine of the night before. I clean down the sledge runners and ice them with water passed out from inside the tent, and then turn the sledge over and start to load it with the boxes that have been holding the tent down.

By the time that Duggie has packed up all his bits and pieces inside, it is only necessary to lift the tent off the pile of bedrolls and rations that he has put in the centre of the groundsheet, load the whole lot on top of the sledge, and lash it up.

There is still a bit of digging to do around the second sledge, but with two to do the work it won't take long and when that is done it only remains to untether the dogs, clip them on their traces, and stand by for the word go. We ourselves are still beautifully warm, for we have been working hard, and with luck the other tent will have worked at the same speed and we will all be ready to proceed at exactly the same moment. As long as we act wisely we will stay warm all day. If life becomes strenuous we must pull the anorak out of our trousers and let the air circulate inside to prevent us sweating, but as soon as we stop we must close our windproofs again and keep the warm air in.

On this occasion it is a fine windless day and life is astonishingly pleasant. John, with the lead sledge, is taking the brunt of the work, for his dogs are breaking a new trail in six inches of powder snow and it is taking all his powers of concentration to keep them on course.

I, as "tail-end Charlie", have a very easy time, for the track that

I use has been well consolidated by the teams ahead. My dogs are hauling easily and as Duggie finds me continuously on his tail he drops off a fifty-pound ration box which I retrieve and take over, and the two teams run at a more even pace as a result.

Exactly two hours from the time of starting John halts for ten minutes to give the dogs a break and to allow them a few mouthfuls of snow and a well-earned roll. There is a certain trades-unionism about dogs, for they have fixed ideas about what constitutes work or rest. Lamp-post drill must always be carried out in working hours, and as soon as they are roused from their rest with the cautionary "Now, dogs", they all decide to demonstrate quite clearly why they must have "just two minutes more".

The ten minutes is well used by Duggie, for he takes a quick round with a prismatic compass and makes a sketch of the local mountains which I have already photographed.

We restart, and repeat the performance at hourly intervals for the rest of the day. The midday halt is obviously a little longer.

We collect our thermoses of hot orange juice from the snow-proof bags hanging from the handlebars, lay out our skis side by side on the sunny side of the sledge, we sit on them, and prepare to enjoy the only fully social meal of the day. John produces some joke that he had heard the night before in the Itma programme or sees what offers he can raise for half a bar of chocolate in exchange for other items of current rations. Each of us extracts his lunch from his own personal ration-bag and prepares the meal. The knob of butter is so cold that it cracks like a boiled sweet, and the chocolate is hard and brittle. We dilute the orange juice with snow, stir it with our fingers and drink it back. Within twenty minutes of stopping we are again on our way. After four more hours it is time to make camp and we are back where this letter started."

That was a typical good day and it would be useless to pretend that there were not an enormous number of bad days, but even these followed the same sort of pattern. There was always the great personal care to adjust our clothing to avoid perspiration, and the brief halts to "off sweaters" were never questioned. There was always the mutual watching of each other's sledges to prevent straggling or bunching up. There were always halts regularly timed so that the prospect of them could keep us in good heart, and there was always the knowledge at the back of our minds that no matter how cold, blowy, and miserable was the weather, we had the peace and warmth of a well-tried tent in which we could record our travels, plot out the day's survey, and complete the record of the day's scientific progress.

Even away from base the life of a polar traveller should in fact be remarkably comfortable, for he knows that only in this way can he achieve the soundest scientific results.

Conditions of wind and weather are still the same as they always were, cold is cold the world over and modern snow is the same as the snow which baffled Captain Scott's party forty years ago.

The tendency of post-war polar writers, who are very often the people who have never actually travelled but write by quoting the diaries of others, is to equip modern polar travellers with untold powers of endurance and physical toughness. They dwell on the conditions of wind and cold and forget to point out that methods have improved and tents are now warm and homely, whatever the weather outside.

Physical toughness was certainly necessary in the past but it is ungracious and forgetful of the polar heritage that is ours to pretend that it is so still. A member of a modern expedition is still capable of surviving hardships, if they arrive, but now he uses his head and the recorded experiences of his predecessors to keep those hardships at a sensible, respectable distance.

CHAPTER 7

Up to the Plateau and a Near-to-Fatal Accident

THE return of the sun at the end of July meant of course that the travelling season had begun, and the longer hours of daylight enabled us to take stock of the country around and to work out plans for the coming year. On the map it is quite clear that our base lay on the western and relatively well-explored side of the peninsula of Graham Land.[1] The Colonial Office at home decreed that all the efforts of Base D and Base E were to be directed towards the survey of the east coast.

For us this was not so simple as it looked, for a 6,000-foot plateau formed the backbone of the peninsula and this would have to be crossed, with all our loads, before we could start the survey proper. We first had to find a route from the base itself to the plateau, and then haul something like two tons of stores to the top; we had to reconnoitre a route across the high snows and find a glacier that would lead us safely to the ice shelf of the east coast.

We knew that the Americans in 1940 had used the glacier behind the base as an airfield and the chimneys of the small hut they had built by the landing strip protruded through the snow a mile above Stonington Island. From there they had worked out a route up the full length of this north-east glacier and had established a weather station at 4,800 feet on the very edge of the plateau; then, after crossing the plateau, they found a route down a glacier to the east coast and gave it the fine, mid-Western name of Bills Gulch.

Unfortunately the general details of their travels were so vague that the whole route had to be re-discovered and put on the map.

In early May we had managed to do a three-day reconnaissance

[1] See maps on pages 10 and 149.

journey up North-East Glacier, and were able to establish the general direction which we were to take, and in early August we made a real start on the job of hauling up the heavy loads. It was not until mid-October that we were able to report to those at home that we had three tons of stores depoted at 5,000 feet and we were ready to start our main journeys.

This chapter is the story of how we established the plateau depot, and some of the many incidents that occurred in the process.

In spite of the belts of heavy crevassing that had to be avoided, the first ten miles of North-East Glacier were relatively simple. A small reconnaissance party, usually consisting of Bingham, Mike Sadler, and myself would go on ahead, roped together, probing the general route to see how large were the crevasses, and how safe were the bridges that crossed them. The rest of the party would follow with the loaded sledges, carefully plotting their way with sledge wheel and compass as they came and leaving small flags stuck in the snow as signposts for future journeys. We soon realised that the glacier was by no means the smooth, safe highway that it appeared from base; wherever a smaller glacier entered from the side, vast areas of treacherous crevassing would develop which would have been difficult to cross even with a strong mountaineering party, so we would have to make an enormous detour. Sometimes without apparent reason, an enormous pit hundreds of feet deep would have to be skirted, or belts of narrow crevasses, regularly spaced, like so many parallel ditches, would have to be crossed at right angles instead of diagonally to allow the sledges and skis to act as mobile bridges.

Our aim was to find a route, however zigzag it might be, which avoided all these difficulties and to put it on the map in such a way that we could navigate our way up and down it in the same way as a ship sails up a dredged channel.

In the way that I have described it, glacier travel is not very difficult as long as there is sun and there are strong shadows, for every small rise and fall is easily apparent and suitable precautions can be taken.

In early spring these days are all too few and instead it is overcast and shadowless; there is no sense of height or distance and all is white and glaring. Ridges or hummocks, crevasses or potholes are all lost in the incredible whiteness. It is as easy to fall down a crevasse without ever knowing it has been there as it is to walk into a fifty-foot high snowbank.

Bingham had a story of his own experiences in Greenland where he and his companion Flight Lieutenant, now Air Vice-Marshal, N. H. D'Aeth were in a tent two hundred miles from base on the inland plateau; they were manning a weather station, waiting wearily to be relieved by a sledge party from the coast. As he emerged one morning he saw, far in the distance, the relief party arriving. D'Aeth came out to see it and agreed with him and they started to discuss who it might be. Binoculars were brought out and trained upon it and all that could be read in large letters was the word "Cadbury". The "sledge" was in fact a chocolate paper a few yards downwind. The story, when we first heard it, seemed quite fantastic, yet when once we had experienced sunless glacier travel ourselves we knew it to be true. Bingham would never let us cross glaciers when perception was bad, unless we were navigating accurately on a known route. It was only later in the second year when an American party started to cut corners off our charted track on North-East Glacier, and finally dropped one of their number deep into a crevasse, that we realised the full wisdom of this glacier navigation.

We had camped only twice on the main glacier and it always amazed me how carefully Bingham would site our camps. He knew from 1936 the incredible strength of the "fumigator" as it swept down the trough of the glacier valley.

By observing snow conditions we could judge the shelter that some slight undulation in the glacier would give to the tents, even then we would dig the whole square of the tent about a foot into the hard snow and use the debris to form a windbreak around the upwind side.

At the end of the first week we established a large depot about eleven miles from base and something above 2,000 feet from sea-level. From here the glacier steepened and seemed to rise to about 5,000 feet in a matter of two or three miles.

The depot site was well sheltered at the side of a horseshoe-shaped combe overlooked by high ice cliffs. All night we could hear the run and tumble of ice debris falling off, and every now and again a really large avalanche would start and enormous blocks of ice would rumble their way across the valley floor to stop a few hundred yards short of the tents.

From this camp we were able to do two good reconnaissances to assess the general problems of this last haul to the plateau. One day stands out as a nightmare and is one that I hope never to repeat. Bingham, Mike Sadler, and I, roped together, were examining a route on the north side of the valley and in so doing we needed to cross a very rugged icefall that barred further progress. The Commander was essentially a sledger, a polar traveller who hated mountaineering, yet this was a mountaineering problem. Instead of spiked crampons on our feet we wore smooth-soled moccasins; the bollards and ridges between the enormous crevasses were shiny glare ice, without any belays, and if any of us had slipped our chances of being stopped by the other two were negligible. But I was not man enough to argue the point and say that this misuse of an Alpine rope was more dangerous than no rope at all.

The result of the nightmare, however, was satisfactory, for we found a long smooth snow slope, free from all danger of avalanche from above, or crevassing from below, which led a thousand feet from our lower camp site to a horseshoe-shaped amphitheatre which seemed about a thousand feet from the plateau itself. It was steep, however, and averaged one in two and a half for the first half mile; it was a possible route, and a safe route at that.

We were still not getting the best out of our dogs and decided that the soundest way of getting our loaded sledges up the bank was to use a long rope passed round a pulley block, anchored in the snow at the top. It would then be relatively simple to walk to the top, harness ourselves to the short end of the rope, and as we walked down so the loaded sledge could be hauled up.

The weather worsened and blew a full gale and three days later we returned to base to collect the necessary rope and a further load of stores for the depot.

It didn't work out quite as planned and Bingham felt that before we started hauling the loads up this steep bank it would be worth investigating a glacier twenty miles further north which Stephenson had noted in 1937 as a "possible route to the plateau".

On August 24, four of us, Bingham, John Tonkin, Mason, and myself left base for a week's reconnaissance in the area to the east of Square Bay. We were comparatively lightly loaded and the surface was excellent.

In spite of this the dogs were very loath to leave base and on the lower glacier frequently turned round to watch all the goings-on around the hut, a bare half mile away. My dogs were performing even worse than John's and about a mile up the glacier Mason and I found the Commander with his sledge upturned, and no trace whatsoever of John. As he had walked just ahead of his dogs, coaxing them into reluctant life, he had fallen out of sight down a narrow crevasse and was wedged some forty feet down—and this in an area which we had traversed many times before and had pronounced as quite crevasse-free!

He was alive and shouting volubly, and was able to tell us that he was jammed by his chest with his feet hanging free and was finding it hard to breathe. We lowered ropes to him with loops on their ends so that he could pass them under his arms and take the weight off his chest. At least we knew he could drop no further.

I'm not sure why or how, but five minutes later I found myself being lowered into the crevasse to see what could be done. I was in no mood to do more than notice the austere beauty of the place. The hard blue walls were covered with large spine-like ice crystals and I could follow John's downward path by the line of their broken stumps. Thirty feet down, with three zigzags between me and the top, I stuck when the crevasse narrowed to less than eight inches. Lower down in the dim light I could see the top of John's head, and could just make out that he was stuck spreadeagled between the two ice walls. I asked to be pulled up twenty feet, moved a few feet to the right where the crevasse seemed an inch or two wider, and tried again. This time I managed to get my feet level with John's shoulders, but once again I stuck. I was pulled to the surface, where I made a small chipping tool from the bottom spike of an ice axe, for there was no room to use anything larger, and went down again.

All went well this time and I was able to chip my way down to John's level. There wasn't much room; his head faced away from me and the crevasse was too narrow for him to turn it round. By a combined effort of hauling by those at the top, chipping by me to free his chest, and much wriggling on John's part, he suddenly came free like a cork from a bottle.

Before I left I spent a moment looking around. John had most certainly been lucky, for ten feet to the right the crevasse was wider, it would not have jammed his chest, and appeared to have no bottom. He had spent about three hours in the depths, and oddly enough it was he who had kept up all our spirits by his courageous encouragement: only he really knew how firmly he was stuck and what his chances of survival were.

Back at base, after he had recovered from shock, it did not appear that he had suffered much; his hands were numb and un-willing to bend, but we attributed this to the long exposure to cold, and thought that it would soon wear off. We were wrong, however, for the ropes under his arms had damaged the nerves to his hands and wrists and left him with no control. It was nearly six months before he could resume complete activity at base and, for him, all chances for summer travel were gone.

I suppose of all the members of our base John was the only one who could have coped with the six months' inactivity in the way that he did. He never allowed himself to appear depressed, and if he was so, never let the evil germ spread to the rest of us.

I had seen a great deal of the inside of that crevasse and had several nights of sleeplessness, and ill-formed thoughts grew in my mind as I recalled similar touch-and-go incidents in the war. Incidents which left me with the thought, "Why was it him and not me?"—"Why am I spared and somebody else taken?" The division that the Good God places between life and death is often very narrow. I suppose that this is one of the reasons why life in Antarctica is so very stimulating. The stakes are high. It pays good dividends, but exacts heavy payment for the smallest mistakes.

Looking back on the incidents we were lucky to get away as lightly as we did. Probably our nearness to base was the factor which saved John, for from there we could get plenty of rope and plenty of people to pull. I don't think we had discussed fully enough the procedure to be adopted in case of accidents, and our knowledge of the many simple tricks of rope work which are standard practice in mountaineering rescues was woefully inadequate. If the accident had occurred among a party of four sledging far away from base I doubt if John would still be alive.

Even before that time we had been more cautious than most expeditions about not wandering unroped over glaciers. From then on, even in the safest of areas, we insisted on everybody wearing skis and being attached by rope direct to the sledge.

The reconnaissance trip to the north still had to go, so Reg Freeman took John's place and a few days later we were camped ten miles to the north of North-East Glacier looking down into Square Bay. We had travelled fast on excellent surfaces. It was a perfect night, clear and calm, with the pleasant invigorating feeling that crisp, cold, and motionless air can give. There wasn't much shelter for the camp in the wide valley, but after a good deal of searching we found a place where the snow looked softer and Bingham decided it "would do". We dawdled in the luxury of perfect peace. I was outside man and had time to watch the sun drop low in the West as Duggie prepared the tent. Then as we lay in our sleeping bags we left the tent door open, watching the dogs grubbing around for their last grains of pemmican, silhouetted against the last light of the setting sun.

Six hours later it was blowing a "fumigator", more powerful than anything we had known before. I am not philosophical enough to be a good sledging companion when held up by wind in the confines of a small tent. I suppose that the sensible attitude to take is to ensure that all possible precautions for the security of the camp are completed when it is first pitched and from then on to take the line: "I've done all I can do, the tent must do the rest." At that time most of us did not appreciate the sturdiness of those tents, and I found myself lying awake listening to the noise and imagining the worst, convinced that neither tents, pegs nor guy ropes could withstand the strain and survive. I would worry in my mind and the only method of stopping the worry was to go outside and see that all was well. The wind blew hard for thirty-six hours, gusting, we estimated, up to about 100 miles per hour, and once every two hours it was necessary for somebody to go outside to dump more blocks of snow on the tent or to put tea dregs on top of the tent pegs to refreeze them into the snow. Placing the snow blocks in this high wind was an art in itself.

Early in the morning of the second day, the barometer rose,

and in a matter of minutes the wind had gone, and the world was calm and peaceful once again.

We had a rapid breakfast and went outside to survey the scene and see what damage had occurred. The whole snow level of the glacier had dropped by about eighteen inches and had gone out to sea in the form of drift. The tents were standing high above the snow level, on pedestals so to speak, surrounded by the remains of our snow blocks now cut into fantastic shapes.

Two boxes of dog pemmican, of fifty pounds each, had been uprooted and blown forty yards downwind and the sledge, still with a dog tied to it, was a hundred yards away tipped on its side. Gone was the smooth, hard snow of the trip out, and instead it was cut into sastrugi, ridged like weathered sandstone or miniature Grand Canyons, and looking for all the world like a choppy sea that had suddenly frozen.

No longer was sledging to be comparable to travelling in a modern car on an asphalt road; it was more reminiscent of a runaway pony trap careering diagonally down a flight of steps. We completed the reconnaissance down the glacier on foot and found our route completely barred by a wide belt of crevasses. The day was still young so we packed up camp and started up the glacier for home. It was a day that I will long remember, and one of the most memorable of my two years.

Two things are essential when handling a sledge under rough conditions: to keep it upright and to keep it moving. Steep-sided trenches must be crossed at right angles or one runner will drop and turn the sledge over, rather on the lines of a car running its wheels into a ditch. Bingham was a delight to watch as he handled the sledge with the consummate ease of long experience; sometimes running behind, and then checking it momentarily with the brake before swinging it, just as it reached its point of balance, through a right angle so that it came to a line of snow drift head-on. The front of the sledge would rear up and buck like an unbroken colt and he would with a deft movement of the handlebars twist it round and drop it neatly and still upright into the dip beyond.

The dogs, well out in front on their long traces, revelled in it, for the broken surface made life for them ever interesting. It was no longer a dreary haul, chasing the tail of the dog in front. We raced against time and still had ten more miles to go with only a few more hours of daylight left.

The sledges themselves took a terrific hammering, twisting and turning as if trying to shake off the load that they were forced to bear. But as we came down to North-East Glacier the surface became smoother and our pace increased. It was dusk as we ran down the last steep slope to base and nobody saw us arrive.

At base on my bunk I found a signal from the Admiralty telling me that I was ineligible for permanent commission with the R.N. as I was two months outside the age limit. I noted in my diary: "I am glad the decision is not mine to make for I might well have stayed on and taken the easier course. Now at least it means that I can be enterprising and lead my own life." What a contrast it seemed between an Antarctic base and the rigid rulings of My Lords Commissioners in Whitehall, who by a stroke of the pen could control a man's future. It seemed queer in many ways to be thinking in terms of the distant future and a career, for in the remoteness of Antarctica one tends to live in and for the immediate future. Our reconnaissance had shown that the route to the plateau via Square Bay was no good. The signal from the Admiralty could be forgotten; our immediate commitment was to complete the plateau depot via North-East Glacier.

On September 3 we left again, Robbie Slessor as leader and five others: Mike Sadler, Mason, Joyce, Freeman, and myself. We took with us seven hundred yards of rope, and enough rations to last a month and travelled in a day to the old depot at the bottom of the steep slope. The weather was perfect and we were optimistically full of hopes to be back at base with the job done within a fortnight. In any case we were carrying a small wireless set and Mike reckoned to keep contact with base two or three times a week. We had a week of reasonable weather and worked about ten hours a day so that by September 10 the depot load of 110 cases was on the top of "Sodabread slope", as the first slope had now been named.

The rope had certainly proved its usefulness, and three of us with one dog team would harness ourselves at the top end of the rope where it passed through the pulley block. As we pulled down, the sledge came up assisted by three more men and another dog team pulling up. With the load at the top we would reverse our positions and start all over again.

Working this way we could handle loads of about four hundred pounds on the slope of one in two and a half.

The weather was kind but by no means perfect. Much soft snow fell and hampered all our movements and day after day had to start with several of us on snowshoes, tramping a track for the sledge and the dogs to follow. In between the snowfalls the sky was clear and the still, sunny days made it all seem like the high Swiss Alps in springtime.

From the top of Sodabread slope a long haul of about a mile and a half led to the sheltered amphitheatre which we intended to use as our half-way camp and on the easier grade we reckoned to handle the loads on separate sledges unhampered by the rope. But the heavy falls of snow each night made progress very slow indeed so that on September 16 Doc Slessor decided to go back to base, where we could wait until the wind should harden the snow slopes and give us a surface on which work would go both easily and quickly.

We returned rather sadly with the job only half complete and the knowledge that we would be away again very soon.

We left again on September 19, but for a whole month the weather was against us and we spent twenty-four days lying in our tents listening to the wind and wondering just how much longer it could last.

We spent the first half of the month windbound at the camp site below Sodabread slope and worked away between-whiles lifting the load to the amphitheatre, and then on the 10th we were able to break camp and move our tents up to the amphitheatre camp site. Here the relentless wind held us again, and it wasn't until October 26 that the last box reached the plateau and the depot could be called complete. As a result the whole period is rather disjointed and lacks continuity; in my mind it was made up of a series of incidents, almost all of which were in some way connected with the wind. We spent the day after our arrival on Sodabread slope, hauling up the extra cases which we had brought with us, and felt so certain in our minds that the weather had changed for the better that we laid out the long rope in readiness for the next day. We were premature in our well-wishing, however, for the wind caught us, and when we emerged again after a week there was no sign of the rope at all. It took three full days to dig it out, buried as it was under seven feet of hard-packed snow. I remember once when we were working on the rope that Reg Freeman came cautiously up the slope gaining but little security from the slippery soles of sealskin boots. I was digging, like a roadman looking for a drain, and as he lunged forward to grab the lip of my hole he missed it, slipped, and then slid to the bottom of the slope, quite unable to stop himself; there was no danger and we laughed our sides out as he left us, but he had to repeat the weary climb all over again.

On many areas of the glacier the wind had been so strong that it removed all trace of snow and left the bare glare ice exposed. It was smooth and blue and fit only for skating. There was one such area just at the bottom of Sodabread slope and close to the camp. It looked solid enough for there were no cracks in its surface and we had walked across it unroped on frequent occasions. One day I saw Rory, my lead dog, in obvious difficulties with only his head and shoulders showing above the level of the ice. He succeeded in pulling himself out but I roped up and proceeded to investigate the area more closely. It was an enormous crevasse that was treacherously covered by a thin bridge of ice not half an inch thick. It widened out as it grew deeper and as Mike Sadler remarked, "If somebody fell down that it wouldn't be worth collecting him."

The lie-up days were not everybody's cup of tea. Joyce I know never liked them and seemed to consider them in terms of precious time wasted. I felt the same for the first few days, then, when I realised that I could dream the days away with a clear conscience, I actually enjoyed it. In a tent with Duggie the routine was very simple and required very little effort. Breakfast we timed for ten a.m., lunch was at twelve, tea came at two p.m., supper shortly after four in the afternoon and after that we would turn over and go to sleep again, or at best doze the night through until breakfast-time. We sometimes played strange paper games to pass the time, but the noise of the wind was too deafening to make conversation very easy. We read between meals and wrote letters and diaries, but couldn't afford to use the primus too much to keep the tent really warm. We had foreseen the lie up and had brought two long books each. Between us we had *Anthony Adverse, English Social History, Pride and Prejudice,* and *Alice in Wonderland.*

Neither physically nor mentally did we require the long rest that the enforced lie up gave us. We tended to doze fitfully with the noise of the wind and the tent as a backcloth to our thoughts. Dreams as a result were more vivid than ever before and one kept on repeating itself and is now firmly in my mind. The scene was a little brick courtyard in an Elizabethan village with the deep redness and warmth that their buildings have. It was overlooked by three tall chimneys of decreasing size, decorated with the royal plumes carved on the sides, and each was topped with a chimney pot that was shaped like the Imperial Crown. Inserted into the wall under a mullioned window was a stone plaque marked "T. Ashfield—Masterbuilder—1617". I have never seen the place in real life, yet such was the clarity of the picture that I am sure it is real; who knows but that one day in some remote English village I will really find it.

The peculiar isolation of the enforced lie up would only be broken once each day when one member of the party would go outside to feed the dogs and pay the briefest of calls on the other tents. As we lay in our sleeping bags a shout that was scarcely audible above the drumming of the wind would tell us that immediately outside the tent door we had a visitor. A bearded face would push its way through the sleeve and would ask if it could do anything for us. There might be a request to tighten a guy rope, to exchange a book, or to examine the upwind side of our tent to see that there was still sufficient snow to hold it down. A precis of the nine o'clock news from the night before would probably arrive on a slip of paper, and with it a request for a hank of darning wool because somebody had a hole in his sock. Then the head would be gone and the door would be re-secured and our own isolated life would continue.

If Duggie or I had to go out it would be a longer process, for we had to ensure that before the outside man left the tent he was well sealed up and utterly drift-proof; in high winds fine snow will find its way through the smallest of gaps. On one occasion I remember going out with my gloves imperfectly pulled up. When I returned twenty minutes later there was a neat bracelet of frostbite around my wrists. Outside the tent it wouldn't be possible to stand, and progress would be on all fours, one's head well into the wind. Sometimes even this would be impossible for the wind would drive one off course, sliding one across the slippery snow and it would be necessary to use a sheathknife or tin opener in each hand as claws to give something to pull on.

Each day every dog had to be visited and fed with its ration of pemmican and the whole camp had to be examined to see that there was no likelihood of the tents taking off or of equipment being removed by the force of the wind.

A visit to another tent would be quite an occasion and as one stuck one's head in through the door any questions might be asked, from an opinion upon some mathematical problem which was required to solve an argument to the name of a pub in some obscure corner of England.

As a visitor lying in someone else's tent door the contrast between one's head and one's feet would be extraordinary. Inside, with the primus just alight, it would be warm and sociable, while outside, with the wind running at something above eighty miles an hour and the temperature at zero, one's feet seemed to be in a different world. With the questions answered there would be a brief good-bye and a crawl to the security of one's own tent and the day's work was done. It wouldn't be long before the undressing would be complete, the drift snow brushed out of all the crevices, and one would be back in the warmth of the sleeping bag again.

One day I recall very vividly indeed. The blow that had continued for six days without ceasing suddenly stopped. We cautiously emerged from our tents. It was too late in the day to move the complete camp to the amphitheatre. In any case weather that had suddenly changed for the good was rarely trustworthy. However, Robbie Slessor decided that Duggie and I should lift our tent and see if we could move at least one camp load to the top of Sodabread slope and on to the amphitheatre camp. It was a long struggle pulling the sledge up the long ropehaul, for it was heavily loaded, and all the while we watched with distrust the windy wisps of cloud that formed at the plateau edge. Quite suddenly the fumigator was with us again. We anchored the sledge where it was on the crest of the slope, removed our two sleeping bags and rolled them down the hill back to camp, where we lived, three in a tent, for another seven days while the fumigator blew itself out. Robbie's wise decision to move but one tent at a time paid us well. If we had been caught with all three tents packed away on our sledges the game of re-erecting them in a seventy-mile-an-hour wind would have been rather hectic.

Then on October 9 we had one good day and managed to lift all our load to the amphitheatre camp-site which was only 1,200 feet from the plateau lip, but almost as soon as we had made camp the wind arrived and pinned us there for another ten days. On October 20 the morning broke bright and clear and the weather stayed that way for five complete days. We reconnoitred the last bit of the route to the plateau and by the 26th the job was complete. It had been a wearying thirty-six days with twenty-five days lie up inside the tent. Looking back, there seem to have been many even more disjointed incidents than those I have already recorded. They have no bearing on the main story but I include some of them just the same.

Tutluk, the bitch of Robbie Slessor's team, caught us unawares by deciding to have puppies. She was rather old and short-coated, and always reminded us of a muscular circus woman rather past her prime, dressed in tights. We hadn't the heart to let her have her pups in the open air so built a snow igloo as maternity ward, and each of us supplied an old piece of clothing for furniture. She promptly ripped these into shreds and threw them outside and in due course produced, with a certain air of disdain, a single fine black pup, in a snow hole of her own choice close beside her husband. We were not working her in harness at the time and one evening when we returned with the rest of the dogs from the plateau she had torn her way into Reg's tent and both she and her pup were firmly ensconced in Joyce's sleeping bag.

Mike Sadler seemed possessed of an uncanny sense of direction which often made one suspect that he must carry a compass that was connected in some way to his brain. We had been hauling the loaded sledges on the upper slopes leading to the plateau and were caught by a strong blow. The soft snow that lay around was picked up as drift and in a matter of seconds our landmarks were gone and our old tracks were invisible; camp site was a mile away. We followed Mike back, and with unerring accuracy he led us straight to camp. The weather really was thick; standing beside one tent it was quite impossible to see five yards away. I suppose his sense of direction was one that he had developed strongly working as navigator with the Long Range Desert Group in the war.

Joyce, as I have already said, hated the long days of lie up and was not prepared to dream the time away as the rest of us did. He finished his allowance of candles far too soon and though he survived at first by borrowing from us, he finally was lightless. With a cigarette tin and a pair of surgical scissors he and Reg Freeman fashioned a small paraffin lamp with a cotton wick, but it smoked abominably and covered the whole of the inside of the tent with a layer of fine black soot. The tent was quickly nicknamed King's Cross Station.

We listened each night to the B.B.C. news, and the results of the Nuremberg war criminal trials were coming out; we found ourselves trying to assess their value to the world's peace quite impersonally, in the same way as one judges historical events through the distance of time.

On October 26 the whole depot was complete and so we left for home and in seven hours we were there, enjoying the luxuries of warm water, sheets, and one of Ken's masterly suppers.

Establishing that depot had taken much longer than it should have done. Inexperience, caution, and the weather were the main reasons. The whole job from start to finish had occupied fifty-eight days of which thirty-six had been spent lying up in our tents.

Perhaps it had not been as badly done as we felt at the time. We had at least got complete confidence in ourselves and our equipment, and above all in our dogs and our ability to handle them.

CHAPTER 8

The First Antarctic Summer

THE base that we returned to at the end of October was very different from the place we had left in mid-September. The bitter winds that had kept us pinned in our tents for so long had swept the snow off the glacier and taken it down to the sea. The base hut was completely submerged in a huge drift, except for the upwind side which still remained clear; the engine house was entirely covered and only the wind charger tower and the exhaust pipe from the generator poking through the snow showed where it stood. The meteorological instrument screen on the top of the hill, which normally stood four feet above ground, now had to be examined on hands and knees, the dump of seals, which now numbered about fifty, was deep in snow, and it was a major excavation to extract one for distribution to the dogs.

Those at base had been busy indeed, and their efforts were very evident. There was now enough dog food on the island for four months, there was linoleum on the floor in the dining-room and the greenhouse was full of flowers and plants. The six puppies which we had left as wild youngsters were partially trained, and a good deal of work had been done inside the hut in the way of painting and sealing up of cracks.

Almost as soon as we had checked all our sledging gear and cleaned it up in readiness for the future, Bingham announced his plans for the summer. Seven of us were to leave in ten days' time for the plateau, and on leaving the depot would divide and work in two parties.

Bingham, Reg, and myself would leave Two Ton depot and attempt to work northwards up the western lip of the plateau while Robbie Slessor, Mike Sadler, J. Joyce, and Duggie were to try and work northwards on the eastern side.

Both parties set out together on November 8, and after a good deal of delay on account of snow and wind, we reached Two Ton depot nine days later. We left the depot very heavily laden, and after a good deal of relaying of loads we reached the high ground at about 6,000 feet, from where we had hoped to see both the east and west coasts of the peninsula. The seven of us were still travelling together and in the first day we made fifteen miles before we had to camp; the next morning when we looked out of the tents we were in dense cloud and visibility was nil. Four days of lie up followed, we watched our precious rations dwindle away, and then Bingham very sadly announced that for medical reasons he had to return to base. He had unwisely tried to exert himself equally with the rest of us, even though he was twenty years our senior, and had twisted his back. Robbie Slessor had soundly advised him to return before it worsened and Bingham reluctantly agreed with him. Reg Freeman and I returned with him, and we reached base just after midnight on December 4.

Once summer had started the whole tenor of life changed. There was always much more work and, mercifully, more time in which to do it. In the winter and spring the frequent falls of snow and the deep drifts tend to keep the whole place tidy. As soon as the snow around the huts becomes soiled, or the patches of snow around the dogs become littered with seal bones and droppings, a new fall of snow carpets it over, and the process starts afresh.

From early December until late February the continuous sunlight melts away the snow and, as it disappears, so all the debris of the year comes to the surface. Tools that have been dropped the previous autumn reappear; maybe a dog harness that I had left beside the snow shovel many months before would surface and I would remember how I had been called to the hut when the harness had been in my hand, and I had put it down where I stood. My stay in the hut had been longer than I expected and the snow fall had covered it up and forgotten it for me.

The first real signs of the approach of the summer thaw appear on the sea-ice. The familiar tide-crack where the floating ice meets the shore is no longer a harmless rift in the snow but becomes a major obstacle of the dimensions of Becher's Brook. Wherever a seal has lain far out on the sea-ice, rolling in its own filth, pools form and melt their way through to the sea beneath.

94

Few folk realise what a large part dirt plays in the melting of the winter's snows. Any dark object on the snow absorbs the warmth of the sun and, because it is dark, it re-radiates that heat and melts the snow in its immediate surroundings. Dark ash spread over the surface of a snow drift will make it melt away with far less trouble than all the shovels at base.

This same effect is magnified around base. The hut acts as a central radiator, as do the black tarpaulins which cover the food dumps; all around the level of snow starts to fall. Gradually the hard snow drifts become soft and sodden like a mass of wet undissolved bath crystals. No longer is it a simple job to walk around the tethered dogs, as feet sink down, leaving only the knees above the surface. The walk becomes a flounder where only a few days before there was a surface as smooth and hard as a concrete road. Streams start to flow, and the flow must be controlled. The water could easily find its way to the unopened crates of next year's food dump or underneath the hut, where it would refreeze in the shade. If left to its own resources it would cover everything with a layer of hard blue ice, just as had happened in the American workshops. John Tonkin became officer in command of public works, and under his direction we energetically chipped and dug. Our main drain was a channel 13 feet deep cut through the snow drift downwind from the base hut. It flowed for many months down into the sea.

We were able to achieve a pretty efficient water supply by knocking the tops out of some forty-gallon petrol drums, painting them black, and filling them with fresh snow each day. The sun's rays on these provided us daily with a hundred gallons of pure water which we could pipe into the kitchen tank.

The dogs, too, required endless attention. As each rancid and much-loved piece of blubber came to the surface they would delight in rolling in it, and their coats would quickly become coarse and matted and valueless for warmth in the cold of the winter ahead. The grease wouldn't comb out and had to wait until the next moult and each day it was necessary to tour the dogs and collect the rancid blubber and burn it on the sea-ice.

Dog feeding was no longer the pleasant job that it had been. The seal was soft and probably rancid, the sledge load of food would no longer run on the snow surface but would plough its way, like a boat in a sea-way, through the crystalline slush. Sometimes, if it were a clear cloudless day, it would be worth waiting for the brief period after midnight when the sun was low, when the slush would be frozen, the sledge would remain on the surface and run free. If it were cloudy and overcast the cold period would never materialize and it would be pointless to wait.

All the time we were casting far and wide in the search for seals for dog food. The bulk of the sea-ice was still there, and we knew that it is far quicker to collect seals by sledge than to wait until the ice was gone and do it all by boat. Like the snow drifts ashore the sea-ice had changed. The snow on the surface had melted and refrozen into large areas of fresh-water blue ice. Sometimes this was hard and firm, frozen solidly to the sea-ice beneath. Sometimes it would merely be a thin layer covering a pool several feet deep; sometimes the pool would have no bottom, for the salt-water ice beneath had also melted away.

Sealing under these conditions became quite hazardous, but enormous fun. Often John and I, or Ken Butler, would go four or five miles from base to collect a couple of seals which we had seen through binoculars and would load the five-hundred-pound carcasses on to the sledge. If we chose our return route well the sledge would ride over every hazard, but if badly, and this was usually the case, it might break through the thin ice of a surface pool and sledge and man would be dragged helter-skelter through a three-foot-deep bath, while the dogs in front pressed on dry-shod.

Often penguins would decide to visit us at our base, and the quiet of the evening would be spoilt by the excitement of the dogs. To the dogs the penguins were "just another meal", to the penguins the dogs were creatures that must be inspected. Many is the time that I have watched these quaint birds walk in and out among the dogs quite oblivious of their danger; sometimes halting a few inches away from the object of their curiosity, they would sway on their heels, like a man who is almost drunk, and, still just out of reach of the plunging dog, they would curiously and quickly smack the frenzied animal with a hard black flipper. Lizzie, the bitch of John's team, was the only really wily one, who could ensure a free meal for herself whenever a member of the black-coated suicide club came near. She knew the length of her

1)Very nasty conditions for plateau travel. Whiteout and drifting snow.
Safe progress is possible with well trained teams.Here John Tonkin has
the leading team with his lead dog Darkie.We drove some 15 miles that
day,steering a compass course like a ship and finished up only a few
hundred yards from our food depot.

2)M.V.Trepassey from St Johns Newfoundland.128 ft long with a crew of 14 plus up to 20 expedition members.Note the 20 foot scow for unloading which straddles the ship just aft of the deck house.

3)Approaching the coast with small bergy bits among the larger icebergs.

4) Unloading stores using a makeshift jetty. Note the heavily loaded scow and the complete absence of snow on the foreshore.

5) The sixteen foot motor boat was stowed on deck and completely blocked all access to the bows. The crates are full of sledge parts.

6) The hut made rapid progress. This was the sixth day after landing on Stonington Island.

7) the same view four days later. Compare this with picture 31.

8)An early reconnaisance in fine autumn weather gave us a view of the
steep route to the plateau.The final route led up the centre of the
picture and swung to the right over the icefall.
9)Mike Sadler sits at the edge of the plateau.The glacier is some 3,000
feet below.

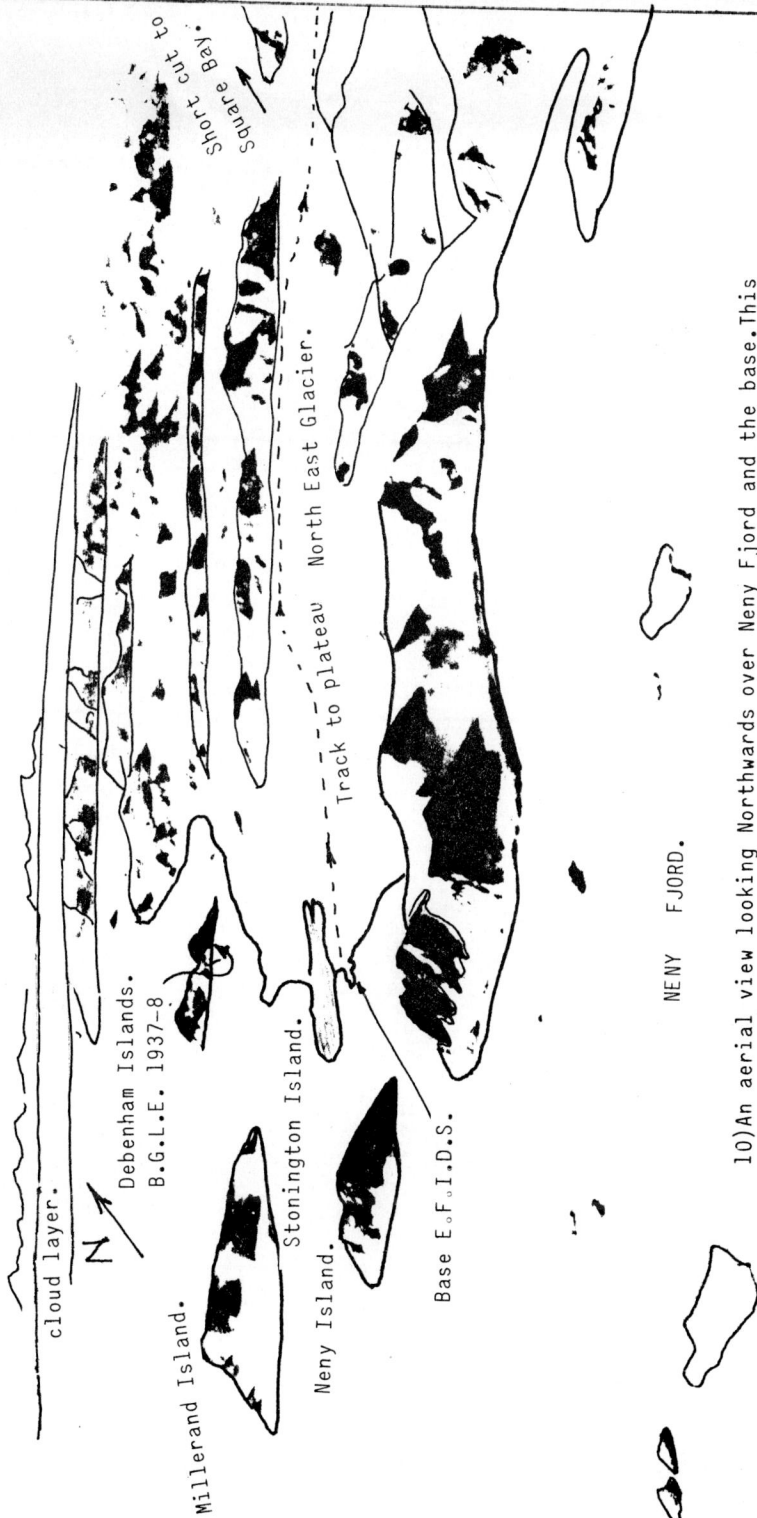

10) An aerial view looking Northwards over Neny Fjord and the base. This picture was taken in 1956 as part of an aerial survey of Graham Land. Adelaide Island which shows above the cloud is about 70 miles away.

11)The last 800 feet to the plateau was very nasty.A long traverse
above a mass of crevasses was followed by a steep haul with large badly
bridged crevasses at the top and bottom.Note the heavy windblown Sastrugi

12)Hoar frost instead of snow forms in the cloud on the plateau.It may
look very beautiful but the surface that results is about as slippery
for sledges as desert sand.

3)Sodabread slope(this was not it's real name) gave us 1,000 ft of height
ain with a mean slope of 1 in $2\frac{1}{2}$.In the first year before we had really
earnt how to handle huskies and had well trained teams we used a long
ope passing round a pulley block anchored in the snow.4 men pulling
own and two men and a dog team pulling up could handle a load of about
00lbs.By the end of our time with well disciplined teams we used 3 or 4
eams in line ahead and did without the rope.Problem then was how to
et the teams down again for the next load.

14) Taken through the tent door on one of the rare occasions when we saw the sun on the plateau. The sledge is upside down to prevent drifting over and the dogs are still grubbing round for the last morsels of pemmican.

15) Running gently downhill towards a visible plateau edge. In sunlight this was quite wonderful but bear in mind that the ridge in the background could well be the lip of a 3,000 foot drop which in whiteout conditions would be invisible.

6)John Tonkin and Dougie Mason setting up a plateau camp.We worked to a
very careful routine with a place for everything.In good conditions
making camp is easy but imagine it in a full gale and very cold and
routine becomes essential.After a blow the snow level could easily be
above the snoshoes.

7)Mike Sadler,Dougie Mason,Robbie Slessor and J.Joyce after 35 days in
the field.

18)Returning down N.E.Glacier after the depot laying journey.The route to the plateau goes round the icefall on the upper right hand side.On this occasion while we were untangling the dog traces three got off and ran back to base free.

19)Bouncer and Sister enjoy a well earned breather.Bouncer was my boss dog.Rover was the leader who only pulled to keep out of Bouncers clutches.

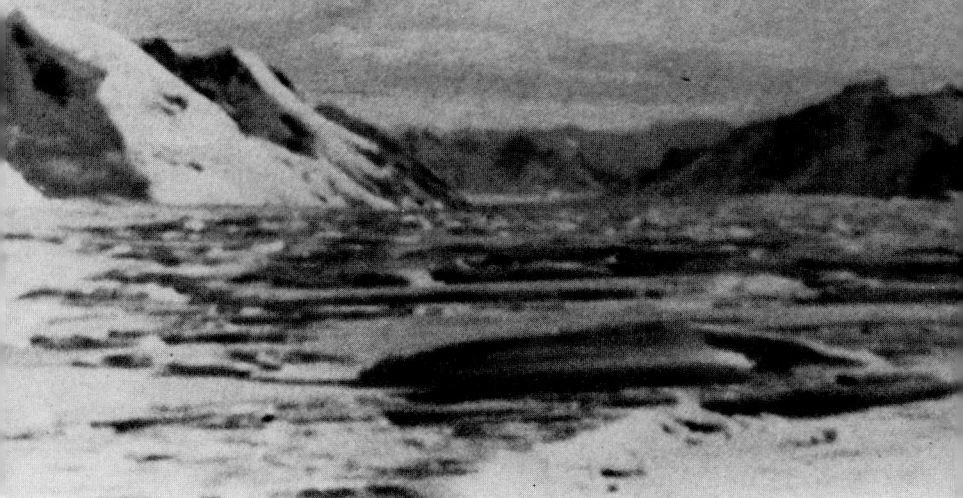

20)After a strong blow,the wind reaching perhaps 90 miles an hour the smooth glacier surface was cut into sastrugi up to 3 feet high.Sledging over this surface was not easy especially when running downhill.

21)Only once were we forced to set camp in the centre of a glacier where the wind was strongest.Holding a tent down was difficult and the continuous noise very alarming.In this camp about 2 feet of snow was blown away.we were forced into quarrying large blocks of snow and sliding them down wind onto the tent skirt.

22)Photographed by Dougie Mason on the East coast shelf ice.Hard snow and lack of wind gave splendid running conditions.Daily distances well in excess of 30 miles a day were often possible.

23)My nine dog team near base.It was a measure of some satisfaction to be able to pass the seal in the background without the team taking charge.

4)Low level aerial view of base taken in early spring.Note the long
shadows and the downwind snow drifts tailing away from the huts and rock
outcrops.The dogs were tethered on single chains and you can just see
the circular tracks by the hut.

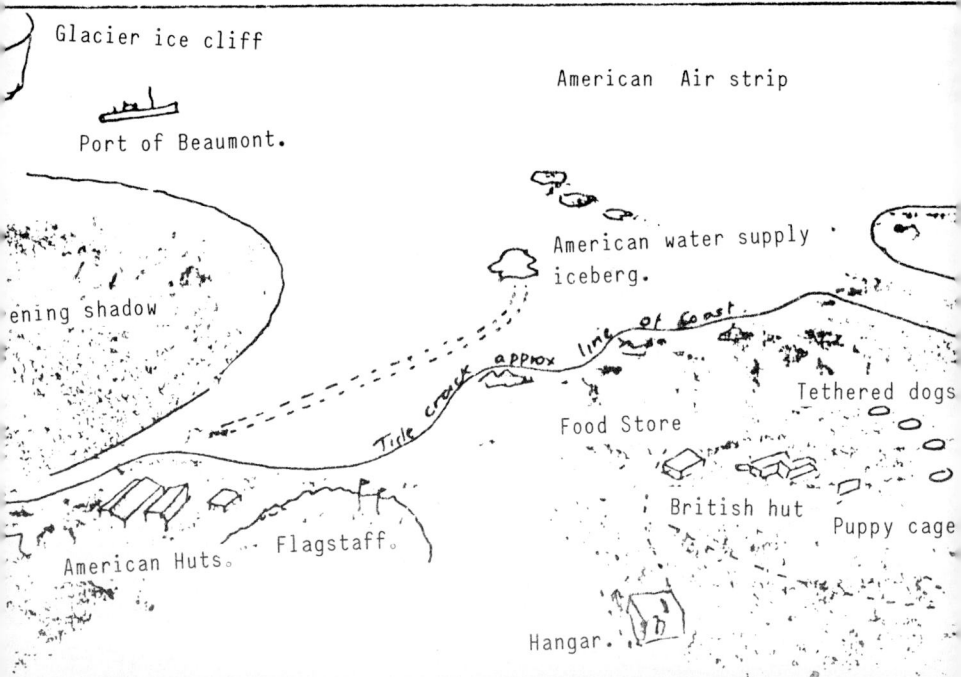

Glacier ice cliff

American Air strip

Port of Beaumont.

American water supply
iceberg.

evening shadow

approx line of coast

Tide crack

Food Store

Tethered dogs

American Huts.   Flagstaff.

British hut

Puppy cage

Hangar.

25)Building the hangar in 1947.The timber was rough sawn Pirana pine very solid and almost impossible to nail.The doors lifted out inwards in sections and we reckoned to be able to have the aircraft airborne within a hour of deciding to fly.Hangar design was a bit of a compromise as we had no timbers longer than 14 feet and needed a 40 ft span.

26) almost complete.

27)David Jones at work on the engine.The aircraft was relatively simple
to maintain especially with a dry hangar of it's own.It started very
easily by hand once the engine was filled with hot oil.

28)Ice cold Katy on the sea ice which was our airfield in front of base.
I suppose in retrospect this rather light civilian aircraft could be
considered as rather frail for these conditions.Working from a small base
it was probably the most we could handle.

29)Bernard Stonehouse and 30) Tommy Thomson 3 days after the plane had crashed and they were on their long walk home,not at that stage knowing if they would ever get there. These picture were taken with my camera which they left in a small depot which I later retrieved.It is a salutory thought that these could well have been the last pictures taken of them alive if the sea ice had not held or they had not been found by the American air search.

31)Typical puppy training
situation.Winnie always
had a mind of her own,was
prepared to pull hard in
almost any direction but
the right one.By start-
ing her with a team that
was trained she soon
learnt that it paid
to pull in the same
direction as the rest.
In the end she became
a good worker.Enthusiastic
but still stupid.

32)Looking Eastwards over N.E.Glacier.Cloud shadows on the glacier surfac[e]
prevent one realising it's real extent.The Plateau is about 15 miles away
and the crevassed areas inland are not visible.

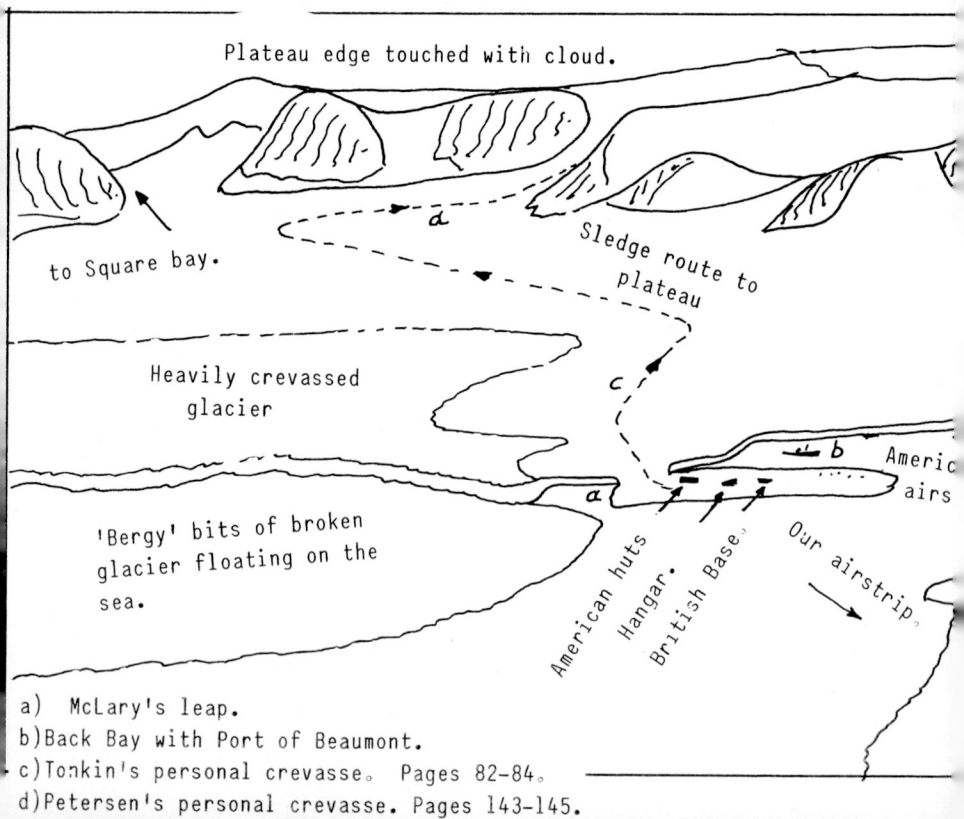

Plateau edge touched with cloud.

to Square bay.

Sledge route to
plateau

d

Heavily crevassed
glacier

c

b

Americ[an]
airs[trip]

'Bergy' bits of broken
glacier floating on the
sea.

a

American huts
Hangar.
British Base.
Our airstrip.

a) McLary's leap.
b)Back Bay with Port of Beaumont.
c)Tonkin's personal crevasse. Pages 82-84.
d)Petersen's personal crevasse. Pages 143-145.

33) The base hut in early spring.Melting has already started.The lean to on the right of the notice board was built during the second winter and included a bathroom.Compare this picture with picture 7.The sea in the background was well frozen.The windcharger on the main hut roof almost took off in high winds.The maximum wind speed recorded was 94 knots.

34) Later in the year the snow melted back from all dark objects.By this time it was crystalline and dirty.All sorts of interesting things lost months before came to light.Note the sealskin stretched on the roof. Fuel is being struck down to the generator by the party in the background.

35)8 Men,6 sledges and 43 dogs hauling up Bill's Gulch after the meet up with our visitors from Hope bay 400 miles to the north.We rarely saw good weather like this on the plateau and made a long day of it.13 miles and 5,000 feet of height gain was followed by two days of superb weather.We reached base and watched the plateau cloud over for nearly a month.

36)Mountain glaciers on the East coast spill out to form the shelf ice. We spent some days reconnoitring this area in the hope of finding a way through.   This is no place for man or dog travel. 2 miles from left to right.

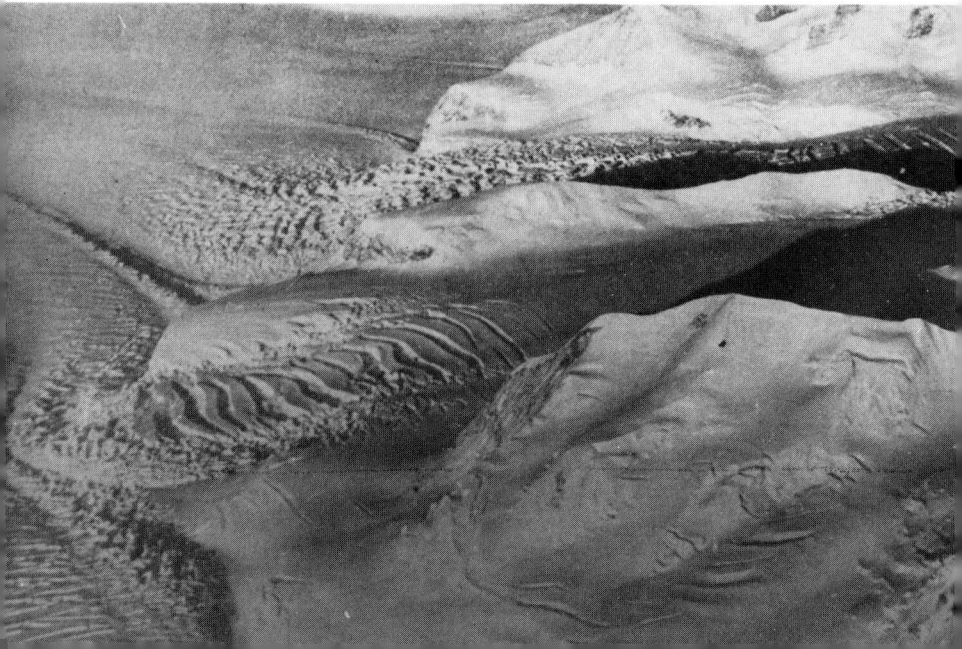

7)Though our nearest penguins were 12 miles away they sometimes came to
visit us as the sea ice disappeared. They are as graceful in the water
as they are comic ashore.

8)In the Autumn before the sea had frozen an American walked backwards
over this ice cliff as he was laying out a guy rope for a wireless mast.
He survived the cold ducking and afterwards this place was always known
as McLary's leap.

39) Typical evening scene at base. Terry Randall(wireless)David Jones(air engineer)Reg Freeman(surveyor)Ken Butler(leader second year) and Dougie Mason(Surveyor)Note the flowers on the table and the bunks open to the main living room.It was an agreed custom that if one was in one's bunk one need take no part in the hut conversation.

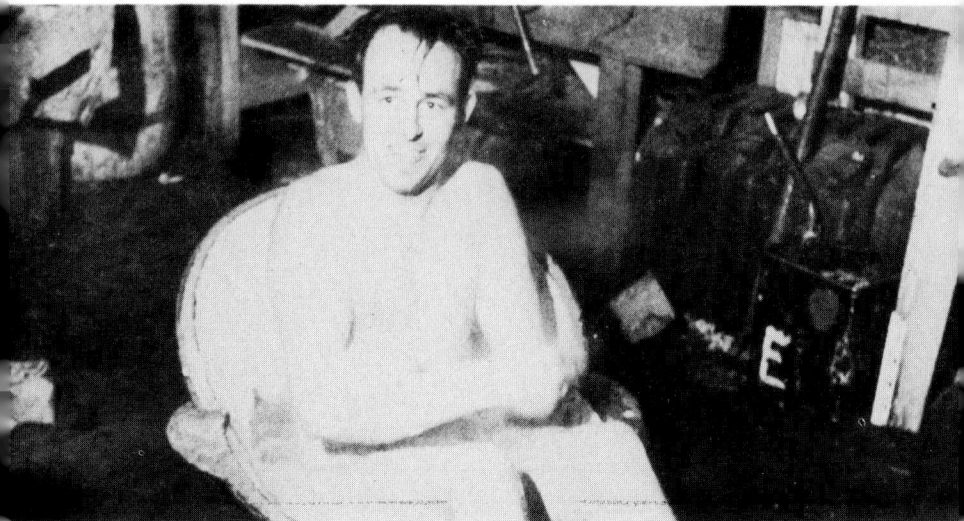

40) John Tonkin. Baths were strictly by rota when the base was full.The bather was responsible for keeping the base water tanks topped up with snow and for heating his own water.The workshop doubled up as a bathroom and the cans in the background did not contain fuel!

41)Excercising a dog team on the sea ice was full of surprises.Here we
meet up with three americans.Nelson McLary,Don McLean and Mrs. Jennie
Darlington wife of one of the American fliers.

42)At Base in the spring as the snow melted much debris appeared.Here
Sister and Bouncer are very dirty but happy.In the second year when the
sea ice was slow to melt we tethered them 'at sea' and shifted them
around .

43)One night when I went outside the base hut in my pyjamas I met 'George' and introduced him into the sleeping hut.The result was chaotic as everyone thought that I was having a fit. Normally the first warning of a penguin visitor would be bedlam among the tethered dogs.

44) At the end of the second year the hut was overcrowded. Four of us took off for 10 days climbing. This superb 1,000 ft spike was climbed by the right hand ridge. We climbed by day and listened to the London 'Proms' at night.

45) This was the largest team that I ever drove. There are 11 dogs and the pinnacle is the dark shadow above the third pair.

46) The party before we finally left. From Left to right.At rear.Ken Mcle
Reg Freeman,John Francis,E,W,K,W. Next row.John Tonkin,Frank Elliot,
Dougie Mason,Dave Jones,Bernard Stonehouse,Ray Adie.
In front.Terry Randall,Ken Butler,Mac Choyce,Tommy Thomson ,Doc Butson.

47) Returning sledge party with the incomers from Hope bay.From left to
right.E.W.K.W. Mac Choyce,R.Freeman,Ken McLeod,Tommy Thomson,Ray Adie,
Frank Elliot,Don McLean and George di Georgio.

48) I took the 'Pilot' to the American Icebreaker U.S.S.Edisto by dog team.Here the ice was about three feet thick.The icebreaker had little difficulty in ploughing through it at fast walking speed.

49) The 'pilot' went aboard by rope ladder over the bows.Bouncer treated the ships bows in the manner that all dogs treat strangers.

U.S.S.Edisto found an excuse to return to our base after escorting the
American ship out to sea.Here she breaks a channel for the John Biscoe
the relief ship that replaced Trepassey.

51)The U.S.S.Edisto escorts the John Biscoe out of Marguerite bay.

chain and would lie seemingly unconcerned until the penguin carelessly came within her circle. An inch inside and we knew that Lizzie wouldn't need a meal for a day or two.

One night I couldn't sleep and had wandered outside in my pyjamas to watch the midnight sun creep across the spires of the southern mountains when I found a curious "George" (penguins seem to answer to that name), making off with a rusty steel bolt. I picked him up and brought him back to the hut and slipped him in through the kitchen door. He swore at me, and cursed again, and the hut woke to life with a bang. Ken was convinced that I was having an epileptic fit, and Bingham thought the same. George retired to sleep, grumbling like an old gentleman, underneath John Tonkin's bunk.

The part that I remember most about that period was the utter timelessness of life. We worked hard whenever there was work to be done and with only five of us at base and no regular duty cook, we ate at irregular hours. Often when we sat down to supper we would find that the time was eleven o'clock at night, and we had to tune in to the B.B.C. to find out the date.

Then, to complicate matters, in mid-December we heard that a private American expedition intended to re-occupy the American huts and was expected to arrive in early February; our relative peace was to be broken. I don't think that I realised at the time how essentially good our travel equipment was, and my first reaction was one of interest tinged with pleasure. I suspected that when they arrived we could put away much of our gear and modernize our methods. I was to be sadly disillusioned.

Many of our excess stores had been neatly stacked in the dry American huts throughout the winter, but in the spring they leaked badly where the canvas covering had ripped off in the wind and the ice in the lagging had started to melt, and we had to sledge them all back over the hill to our own area. We tidied and swept the American huts and tried to make them look welcoming and habitable to the new arrivals.

Christmas came, with only mild celebrations, for we were waiting until the sledging party should arrive. I know we had a Boxing Day that was a *real* Bank Holiday with no voluntary jobs to fill up the day. Three of us lay sunbathing on top of the food store dreaming of the sea shore at home and wishing for a warm swim.

We re-formed the Antarctic Swimming Club, with qualification for membership simply "to have swum in Antarctica". Ken, I think it was, fell in first, while he was watching for seals at a crack in the sea-ice. Willie went to his rescue and stepped too close to the edge and automatically became the second member of the club. As far as I can remember we had no further members that year, though I know I qualified three times in the year that followed. We spent a good deal of time in the last few days of 1946 preparing for the official base Christmas. John, as usual, dealt with the cake, this time a monster of fourteen pounds, and we made a very professional job of icing it with a miniature sledge as decoration.

The veal and ham pie was decorated with the F.I.D.S. crest, a penguin rampant toasting sausages beside a coke brazier, and a Christmas pudding was made, abiding religiously by Mrs. Beeton, except that penguin eggs replaced the hen eggs that her recipe required. We were having glorious weather all this time, a strange contrast to the bitter snow and cold at home that the B.B.C. reported every night on the news; we had almost cloudless skies for days on end. The hut was incredibly warm and no fires were lit. Windows were kept permanently open, and with almost twenty-four hours a day sunlight the greenhouse plants simply had to grow. A box full of purple pansies with bright yellow centres seemed strangely out of place, lettuces grew ready for the table in a few weeks, mustard and cress in a matter of days. Sometimes we spent the evening quietly fishing through a hole in the ice, catching weird fish with jaws like a pike and bodies like a whiting—and ate them cold, with fresh salad.

On January 8, while I was making breakfast, I looked out of the window and saw black specks high up on the glacier: the sledging party had returned.

We had been waiting for them for days and all rushed out to meet them. I made an enormous omelette of fresh penguin eggs and we heard the story of their journey over the breakfast table.

For them it must have been a very infuriating trip, full of frustration. Since we left them on November 29 they had covered only 200 miles and of the forty-seven days away from base thirty had been "lie up", waiting for the plateau weather to clear. They had travelled essentially with a purpose; their job was to survey, and to do that they had to see the country through which they passed. Once on the plateau, day after day was the same, cloudy and overcast without shadow and with nothing visible more than a few hundred yards away. J. J., as geologist, had scarcely seen a rock outcrop, let alone been able to obtain a specimen. There were a few clear days, however, and Mason had been able to fill in at least some of the blank spaces on the maps of that area and had learnt some of the difficulties of the type of survey that Graham Land required.

They were all fit, very snowburned and weathered and, though they had lost a good deal of weight, the rations had proved adequate. I say blithely that they all returned, all, that is, save two of the dogs, Wolf and Razzle. Both had played truant at Two Ton depot and refused to leave the plateau. A week later Razzle, fat and well fed, returned alone the fifteen miles to base with a trace of a smile on his face, and a "no knowledge of Wolf" expression in his eyes. We never discovered Wolf's real fate. Did Razzle turn cannibal, or did he fatten at 6,000 feet on the tonic of leisure, fresh air, and sun? We would never know.

We celebrated Christmas on January 11, and we started to consume the enormous cake which was John's masterpiece. Ken Butler had kept all our special telegrams until that day, John made some coloured paper hats, we shaved and became civilized, put on our tidy suits, and the party was on.

I, as cook, was rather busy in the galley that day and so my memories of Christmas seem to centre around what we ate. I remember mixing up the rum sauce for the Christmas pudding and taking a spoonful into Ken's wireless cabin for approval. He pronounced it "a bit lacking in rum". I adjusted that point so that when we finally lit up the pudding in the traditional style, the rum sauce caught fire.

In many ways, however, it was a sad Christmas, for Bingham told us that on medical grounds he was leaving us when the ship called and was relinquishing command of the base, and later the whole of F.I.D.S., to Ken Butler. It was, I know, a bitter blow for him and a very sad blow for us as well.

Surgeon-Commander Bingham had not had an easy job, for

we were, as a group of men, a good deal more independent by nature than might have been expected in any normal expedition. As a result of the war we were both used and willing to accept much wider responsibilities than he was prepared to let us have. In war far too many of us had been leaders, and it was extremely good for us, though sometimes irksome, to be led. It was only in the year that followed when we found ourselves able to travel and explore as we pleased that we realised the true measure of the debt we owed him.

What in actual fact was the result of the year's travels from Base E? I suppose geographically we had not achieved very much; we had reconnoitred a route first discovered by the Americans in 1940 and had put it adequately on the map; we had achieved a frustrating journey on the plateau without mishap. We had learnt the continuous necessity of reconnaissance on glaciated country and of insistence on keeping close beside the sledge; we had learnt, too, the necessity of keeping accurately to previously reconnoitred routes if safety were to be maintained. We had learnt how to camp and live in comfort, how to handle dogs, and cope with heavy loads. All these points, though we never realised it at the time, were to bear fruit in the years that followed. But beyond all these material points we had, I think, gained something far more important and less tangible. We had sorted out our relations with one another. It is quite impossible to live for long in a tent with someone else without getting to know many of his inward feelings, and in so doing, to know anp try to eradicate one's own irritating habits. Duggie Mason must have often cursed me inwardly for my habit of asking questions and supplying the answer in one breath, or for never having the patience to let other folk do the things the way they liked.

Bingham had, so to speak, been both instructor and examiner, and we had now passed the entrance examination into the school of polar travel. He was satisfied with our progress and felt able to leave us to fend for ourselves.

CHAPTER 9

Arrivals and Departures

TOWARDS the end of November the *Trepassey* had arrived in Port Stanley from England and after a very brief stay she had pushed on to Deception Island to visit and re-store the base there. We were very relieved when the report came through that all was well with Featherstone at Base B, for he had stopped broadcasting in September and we were sure that there had been some form of accident. We were right, for their living quarters, the old whaler's barracks, had been burnt flat one September afternoon and such was the fierceness of the fire that virtually nothing had been salvaged that was of any use. They had moved to another building, and when the *Trepassey* arrived four veritable castaways were on the foreshore to greet them.

Fire is the great dread of the Antarctic leader, for it is so ruthless in its destruction. At Base E we had taken a great deal of care to sub-divide everything into separate dumps so that the disaster of fire would not leave us utterly without resources.

Throughout December *Trepassey* was kept busy calling in at the northern bases. She carried several passengers, among whom, in the capacity of Colonial Office adviser, was Mr. James Wordie who knew the Antarctic well, for he had been the geologist of Shackleton's *Endurance* Expedition.

On the way from Hope Bay to Laurie Island the *Trepassey* must have passed close by Elephant Island, and Mr. Wordie's memory must have gone back just thirty years to the first time he had seen that spot. I wondered whether they went close enough for him to see the old boat shelter which they had erected on that exposed and desolate northern shore, or whether the ice conditions had forced them further northwards just as had happened to us the year before.

At Hope Bay they landed the three other passengers. David

James had returned for a brief spell to act as adviser with a small photographic unit that was taking background shots for the film *Scott of the Antarctic*. It was good to be able to exchange brief messages with him as he moved into his old haunts at Hope Bay.

At Laurie Island, which had gone off the air only a week after the last visit of the *William Scoresby* the previous year, all folk were well, and their wireless silence had been due to a generator fault, the repair of which was beyond their resources. It is a great tribute to "Mac" Choyce, their leader, that they all volunteered for a further year's work in the Dependencies. Laurie Island had not proved the most suitable of bases, being difficult of access and rather too far east to fit in with the weather observations of the rest of the Survey, so the hut was evacuated and a new one erected on Signy Island on the western end of the South Orkneys, where a new base of four men, under the energetic leadership of an Australian physicist Gordon Robin, was set up.

"Mac" Choyce was moved to Hope Bay as meteorologist and, though none of us knew it at the time, he was due to sledge 600 miles to Marguerite Bay within twelve months.

Trepassey returned to Deception Island, picked up stores and fuel, and then worked southwards to Port Lockroy where the base was to be closed down and the stores and members moved to the old B.G.L.E. hut in the Argentine Islands.

"Dick" Burd, the navigating officer of my old destroyer *Relentless*, was due to take command of this new base and I had a long yarn with him on *Trepassey's* wireless.

It was a weird thought when I remembered that the last time I had seen him was in the Red Sea, sweltering in the heat of a following wind, trying to work out ways and means for him to come to Antarctica. In the Argentine Islands the dory was still where we had left it, tied to a rock by a piece of light line, but of the hut that the year before had stood ten yards away there was no trace. Theories were put forward of tidal waves and high tides, but none of them rang true. In this time of tangled Antarctic politics it seemed to me, to quote an Irish inquest verdict, to be an "act of God, under very suspicious circumstances". This lack of hut did not affect plans very much as the ship had plenty of timber on board, and in thirty-six hours a new hut stood on the site of the old; however, purely by chance a day later a foreign warship paid a friendly visit.

In Marguerite Bay we knew that the *Trepassey* was unlikely to reach us before the middle of February, and there was still a great deal of work to be done before she arrived. The base party was changing considerably. Robbie Slessor was not staying on the second year, but was due to take up some specialist appointment at home; Mike Sadler was to leave us and go to Hope Bay as surveyor and navigator; Willie Salter had not renewed his contract of service and had plans for work as a schoolmaster somewhere in England, and Joyce was due to go home to work up his results.

The loss of the Deception Island hut meant that each of the remaining bases were asked to sacrifice a portion of their surplus equipment in order to restart it as a going concern, and this involved us in digging out all our dumps of stores and recrating portions of them for onward shipment to the new Base B.

The summer thaw around the American huts was exposing enormous piles of equipment debris. We organized a large-scale drainage system just as we had done round our own buildings, and tried to lead the water into Back Bay, and spent many, many hours trying to put the area around the American base into something like a shipshape order; all this extra work was sandwiched in between the normal goings on of an Antarctic base.

Our dog food was now secure for the rest of the summer, for since our return from the trip to Square Bay we had collected about seventy-five seals and stowed them, skin side up, on the foreshore. We certainly had the quantity required, though the quality was rapidly deteriorating in the summer sun. We fed everything to the dogs. The more rancid the meat the better the dogs seemed to like it and we fed every part of the seal to them. Old Snipe seemed to revel in demolishing a complete seal's head, cleft in two with an axe, and would leave only the teeth as evidence of his meal. Dog feeding was still an arduous game in the soft waterlogged slush, and we became quite expert at hurling lumps of seal, after the style of bombardiers throwing hand grenades, to the waiting dogs. On one occasion, as I threw, a splinter of rancid seal bone dragged across the ball of my thumb and cut it cleanly to the bone so that Robbie had to stitch it up.

Such is the germ-free nature of the Antarctic that it healed without trouble in a matter of days.

Then, right at the end of January, the sea-ice in the wide spread of Marguerite Bay really started to move, and Bingham was able to tell the *Trepassey* that she could sail south to relieve us.

On February 2 all the familiar icebergs were gone and the sea was clear of floating ice as far as the eye could see; once more we were on an island, and our isolation was complete. We scrubbed the hut out from end to end, completed the final details of our many technical reports, and wrote in the last lines of our letters home; on the 5th, just as the last part of the tidying up was complete and the last crate for shipment to Base B down on the foreshore ready for loading, the *Trepassey* came round the corner of Neny Island, blew a welcome on the siren, and dropped anchor fifty yards off shore, right in front of base.

It was strangely good to see the old ship again and to learn all the news from the old hands. We had our first visitors for eleven months and they did noble justice to our cream-filled brandy snaps, our hot Scottish drop scones, and fresh sponge cake.

Captain Shepherd had left and Captain Burden was now in command. He was a sealing captain from St. John's, Newfoundland, and from all reports it was quite obvious that he never felt at home unless his ship was well surrounded and protected by pack-ice. There was a new mate, and an ex-minesweeper captain, who in private life was a working member of a small family concern of craftsman shipwrights near St. John's. Under his guidance there was an air of sound seamanship on board that had never been there the year before. By evening on the 6th all the cargo was ashore and on the 7th, as it was dead calm and windless, the huge crate containing the new aircraft was floated ashore on a raft made from forty old petrol drums; with the aid of a large block and tackle made fast to an anchor well back from the beach and the cry "All hands", it was literally walked ashore, where it was rolled up the beach on old American oxygen cylinders. The ship reloaded herself with the stores for Base B, took on fresh water and some ballast, and was ready to leave by the evening. As dusk fell on February 7 she lifted her anchor and was gone.

Somehow I had found her whole visit to be an incredible

dream. We had longed to see her, to read our mail, to hear first-hand details of the world outside, yet when it came to the point we were so busy that we had little time to do more than make a vague start on such things. It took several days to realise fully that the dream was in fact a reality. Folk who we had regarded as permanent inhabitants had gone and there were new folk in their place. We all missed the imperturbable Robbie, for now it was a different voice that answered to the cry of "Doc".

I had moved my bunk and now slept where Robbie had been; it was cosier and more private than my old one and there was a corner in which to hide away. The evening after the ship had gone I retired to bed and read throughout the night to finish my mail. It was peaceful, and only the sound of the others asleep broke the silence. For the first time since I had been away I felt really isolated, for in my family so many personal things had been happening, and I could only be a spectator in spirit. Both my brother and sister were married to folk that I didn't know; there were builders in the house and my mother had had her sewing-machine done up at my expense. Our old sexton from ten years before had rejoined the family, and my uncle had at last returned from service abroad to occupy the Somerset house which we, as children, had loved so much. I felt impersonal, and yet I longed to be there.

Just before the ship sailed the mate had brought a case ashore for me, marked in gay print "For Christmas only". No one else had had a Christmas box and I fell to wondering just why this was so. Perhaps it was because as a family, with parents as missionaries abroad, we had always expected to be apart, and as result we had made Christmas parcels a special feature in our family ties. Opening the case brought tears to my eyes but I didn't mind. All the odd-shaped little parcels popped out to greet me gaily, and momentarily made the 8,000 miles that separated us disappear. There were coloured paper and sprigs of holly, crocus bulbs and a gay woolly balaclava, a new Viyella shirt made by my mother and even a parcel marked "For your birthday 1947".

The ship had gone, there were new folk to welcome, and there was work to be done. Doc Butson replaced Robbie Slessor as expedition doctor. He was a keen mountaineer and strong skier. His chief notoriety seemed to have been in Pernambuco where he had been popped in gaol for changing into bathing trunks on the beach. Apparently this is quite illegal in Brazil and he did not know of it. Dave Jones was an engineer from the R.A.F. who was to service the new aircraft. He was a Yorkshireman who had been shot down while serving in a bomber and spent three years as a prisoner of war in Germany. He took over John Joyce's bunk beside the fire. Tommy Thomson was to be pilot of the new aircraft; he had been a member of the Fleet Air Arm and had served much of his war with Swordfish aircraft in anti-submarine work from light aircraft carriers. He was married, a Scot, and had been with a firm of London rat-catchers before joining us. Ken MacLeod was a Falkland Islander and had just finished a year at Port Lockroy with Mike Hardy. He joined us as a general handyman and took over a bunk from John Tonkin, who moved up to the window in the bunk Mike Sadler had vacated.

Bernard Stonehouse, aged twenty, joined as meteorologist and moved in to Willie Salter's bunk with its incredible array of dials and automatic weather indicators. He was a bit of a dark horse in terms of his past and it was only as we got to know him in the course of the year that we realised that already he had lived a pretty full and active life. Though he was officially meteorologist he would turn his hand to anything, was a zoologist in all his spare moments, a competent pilot when required, a seemingly idle, but in fact a thoroughly efficient cook, and was possessed of a sense of humour only equalled by Dave Jones's or John Tonkin's.

As a base, however, we could afford to waste no time, for the days were already becoming markedly shorter. There was still time for an autumn journey which was planned to go northwards again from Two Ton depot, a route the Americans had used in 1941 on the coastline. But before this journey could start all our efforts were required to put the base in order for the coming winter. We were determined to eliminate all dumps of stores under tarpaulins and to house everything in properly sited semi-permanent buildings. From now on we decided that the continuous effort of digging out our supplies of coal from Reg's coal mine, or mining under a ten-foot snow drift for spare wireless parts, which had been a feature of our first year, was to cease.

Already the small engine-house had been connected to the

front porch by a long passage. The *Trepassey* had brought wood in plenty to build a hangar for our new aircraft, but there were no planks longer than eighteen feet. The Auster aircraft's span was forty feet and the wings wouldn't fold away. An Irish Parliament, a discussion in which no one listens and everyone airs his views, started over the hangar design as we drank a mid-morning cup of tea. As might be expected there were no conclusions at all so in the afternoon Dave Jones and I started to level a site seventy yards away from the hut, northwards and downwind. In our own minds we had a vague idea of how we would build the framework and thought that the details would probably sort themselves out as they cropped up.

The general principle, however, was to build four roof spans 40 feet wide, which might or might not collapse when loaded. If we gave them enough intermediate supports they would probably stand up, and, with any luck, when the time came to fit the hangar to the aircraft, we could saw away a few supports and both the roof would stay up and the aircraft would go in. The whole plan worked out very well and eight days after the job had started, the aircraft was removed from its crate, assembled, and fitted into its new house.

Only two of the internal supports had to be cut away to make room for the aircraft, and rumour has it that when we did so, far from collapsing, the roof rose up two inches: such was the value of my structural engineering training!

The hangar was completed on February 18, and the base was sufficiently in order for us to start thinking of travels once more. In the evening, however, a Chilean frigate, the *Iquique*, arrived and we were literally invaded, albeit in a very friendly manner. As I explained at the start, this area of Antarctica has a truly international flavour. We, as British, claim ownership of and administer the whole of this area, but neither Chile nor Argentina will recognize this claim and try to replace it with claims of their own. The arrival of a foreign ship in British territorial waters results, to quote *The Times*, in an extraordinary Gilbertian state of affairs. Ken, as British Government representative, presented a written official protest to the Captain of the *Iquique* as the Chilean Government representative; who at the same moment delivered a written protest to Ken; by the same messenger there also arrived an invitation from the ship's officer for us to go aboard for dinner and pictures that evening.

Five from the base left for the ship in our pocket-sized dinghy; the weather was far from smooth, so that after only a few yards' rowing discretion took the better part of valour, or maybe Ken remembered his initiation into the Antarctic Swimming Club, and they turned back. Half an hour later *Iquique's* boat arrived to take them on board. Leave to go ashore was given to the ship's crew and in a few short hours all our winter's work of tidying up was forgotten. The American huts were stripped from end to end; the proverbial bull in a china-shop was nothing by comparison. Boxes that had stayed happily unopened for seven years were smashed, unexposed film was opened and strewn around like paper streamers, in the snow outside. A locked case of surgical instruments was emptied save for a few old needles. The American sledges, never I admit of much practical value, were removed and used by cheerful sailors as toboggans down the crevassed glacier behind. I suppose logically the contents of the American huts were still American, even if while we were at war they had set up their base on what we considered British soil, yet by the accepted code of Antarctica the unused equipment of expeditions is always left for use of those who follow. This wholesale and wanton destruction by a passing ship's company was unfortunate, and after all our hard work, difficult to accept. It seemed probable that a similar visit had been the reason for the state of the American huts when we first arrived.

While the Chilean crew were ashore it had been quite impossible for us to act as watch-keepers for everything on the island for we were very busy guarding our own property. I remember finding three shivering sailors squatting round a fire of wood shavings in our newly built hangar quite oblivious of the tank full of petrol in the aircraft not ten feet away.

It took us several days to clear up the mess and only on February 22 were we able to examine our sledges, renew our dog harness, and prepare in happiness for a journey.

CHAPTER 10

The Autumn Reconnaissance, March 1947

THE summer journey that Robbie Slessor had led had proved one thing quite conclusively: it was not possible to do a survey of the east coast by remaining on the plateau and looking over the edge, for the continuous cloud made both survey work and travel well nigh impossible.

John Tonkin was selected, therefore, to lead a party consisting of Mason, Butson, and myself with the express aim of finding a practicable route off the plateau to the eastern ice shelf. We were to try and locate Bills Gulch, the route that the Americans had found in 1940, which we knew led down into Mobiloil Inlet, and we would then work northwards on shelf ice to see how far we could get.

Already the days were getting shorter and the sooner that we could get away the more daylight we would have.

We started to prepare on February 22, and were ready to leave by the 28th.

It was a busy week, for with the experience of the previous year's travel there were changes in the equipment which we wanted to make; we had learnt under Bingham's tuition to use the equipment we had brought, and now felt that we were justified in some minor alterations. There was also an immense amount of work in the general overhaul of part-used gear. The tents that had been used throughout the previous year were carefully examined and where there were signs of chafing or wear numberless small patches were sewn on or stuck on with rubber solution. Sticking on patches like this proved excellent for the smaller repairs but it was always necessary to hammer them into place and drive the solution well into the body of the material. We decided to fit loops to the corners of the snow flap which could be used with pegs when camping in windy weather.

We had scarcely used skis the year before and had always used snowshoes, uncomfortable though they were. This year each of us dug out our own skis from the pile of unsorted stores in the corner of the hangar and fitted some new moccasin-type ski bindings that had come down with *Trepassey*.

We discovered some crampons (spiked footgear) which we adapted to fit our soft boots to enable us to manage better the steep Sodabread slope.

The sledges came in for considerable work. Some of the cross-pieces had broken due to faulty seasoning of the wood, and had to be replaced with spare pieces from the 1934 B.G.L.E. sledges which we had brought from the Debenham Islands.

We wanted something more permanent in the way of a brake for running down steep gradients so fitted ropes which could be slipped beneath the runners and looped over a wooden toggle on the opposite side of the sledge. Under Commander Bingham we had learnt to lash the sledges round and round rather on the style of lashing up a long thin parcel, but had always found it a long, slow and rather tedious business, so we replaced it with a series of loops along the side of the sledge which could be picked up alternatively by a single short rope. The process of modifying the equipment starting from a well-tried beginning had in fact started.

Personally, I always enjoyed the period of preparation for a journey, provided I had plenty of time and a definite target date to work to. There was invariably some small detail which in the past has been forgotten, or never been thought of, which required attention. Every evening filled up with endless small jobs. The rubber straps of the snow goggles might require renewal and the nose pieces had to be re-padded to prevent the chafing that had occurred on previous trips. The various notebooks that we were to use in the field required special covers of waterproof material which would keep them clean and dry, and there would be some addition required in their lay-out to make theodolite observation easier in cold weather. We made up some more oversize chamois leather gloves which could be worn outside fingered woolly ones, and altered the theodolite tripod to make it collapsible and usable with both camera and plane table. Every item required thought and ingenuity, and any suggested changes would start

off the most cheerful of arguments that were continued mostly
for the sake of arguing.

John, just as the Commander had done the year before, retired
to the office with a complete list of the stores remaining at Two
Ton depot and emerged an hour later with a table of the items
that were to be carried on each sledge; he aimed at taking reasonably heavy loads up to the plateau, leaving the depot with forty
days' food for man and dog with the party, and wanted to return
to base not later than April 20. We were to take the small Army
battery-driven transmitter for further trial, and, of course, the
small lightweight wireless receivers which had served us so well
in the previous year. We were to take three teams of dogs, each
team seven strong, and he estimated that we would start our
journey from the depot with 750 pounds of load on each sledge.
He intended to take his own team, which had been the Commander's the previous year; Duggie had inherited a riotous
bunch from Doc Slessor which were ruled over by the brothers
Nigger and Nero, and I was to take my own crowd which Bernard had now christened "The Orange Bastards" in doubtful
honour of three rather idle reddy-brown dogs, Rory, Red, Rhu.

The front and rear sledge were to be entirely self-contained and,
for convenience in relaying, the centre sledge carried only food
and expendable stores.

That at least was the general scheme that John wanted to adopt
once we had left the plateau depot.

The job of reaching the depot at all was in a different category,
and for that reason all the resources of base were at our disposal.

Reg Freeman, who had now acquired the nickname of Grand-
pa, offered to come to the plateau with Tommy and Ken Mac-
Leod as support party, and they would bring with them all the
dogs that remained at base.

At the very last moment, however, Dave Jones replaced
Tommy, whose finger had swollen and become poisoned. Dave
had an enormous sense of the absurd, and as he stuffed his clothes
into his kit bag the night before we left, he told us how he had
"got his job" with the expedition. When he had left England
by air at the end of November he was under the impression that
he was to be some sort of Air Attaché in the Falkland Islands;
yet here he was, three months later, inside the Antarctic circle to

service and maintain an aircraft which could not fly because it had no ski, and preparing instead to chase a team of husky dogs up a snow slope and to sleep on a glacier in a tent.

The journey itself is best described from the pages of my diary, and I propose to quote it word for word except where some detail needs more careful explanation; where I do this brackets are used.

March 2. We left base very late, at 10 a.m. to be exact, in spite of promises to ourselves to make an early start. The summer's rest has helped the dogs enormously and I have never seen them pull so well. We reached camp E (at the foot of Sodabread slope) in just five hours in spite of our comparatively heavy loads.

The dog droppings of the spring and summer journeys acted as signposts all along our route. In some cases where the snow was stained yellow and refrozen into hard ice, tall pillars had formed where the glacier around had melted away. As we navigated up the very featureless glacier, Darkie, who was in the lead, would spot these old favourite lamp-posts from far away and all the dogs would pull harder than usual with the added excitement. (We had rather a rude expression for this method of navigation, and for the sake of propriety I will refer to it as Hit and Miss.)

Ken Macleod came in to-night for a social evening and chat and we made an extra brew of cocoa for him. We are risking a change of weather during the night, and the tent door is wide open as I write. The sun setting over base makes North-East Glacier seem easy and short, and it is hard to realise that it is over twelve miles away, as the snow petrel flies, to Stonington Island.

March 3. We are in camp at the amphitheatre after a long and tiring day. We used the long rope on the steep haul although it took Duggie and me nearly two hours to dig it out from the ice where it was so firmly embedded. The dogs are in such excellent spirits, compared with last spring, that we could have dispensed with the rope entirely. We have left Reg, Dave, and Mac at the lower camp and so there are just the four of us here. It is calm and overcast to-night and I think it will snow heavily before the morning.

March 4. It did snow heavily as we feared it would, and this morning there was about two feet of it, and it was still falling when I left the tent. It was quite obvious that it would be wasted effort to make tracks for the plateau. We couldn't communicate with Reg and hoped he would realise our decision. At 10 a.m., however, he arrived with the other two, having snowshoed all the way from the camp 2,000 feet below. It is typical of his superlative conscience and nobleness of heart that he did so; if only we had a small wireless we could have saved him all this effort. John decided, in recognition of his efforts, to have a go at reaching the plateau. We broke camp and after about two hundred yards of floundering in the deep snow it was obviously no good going on so we repitched the tent and sent the other three back to their camp at the bottom of Sodabread slope. This afternoon, though it was still snowing, we walked, four abreast, on ski and snowshoe, up to the plateau depot and back in the hope that at least some of the track would be still available for to-morrow. (We brought snowshoes on this trip especially for the purpose of making a track for the sledges in deep snow on the way to the plateau. The 200 yards' travel represented the smallest day's journey with full loads that we ever achieved in the two years we were in Antarctica. The effort required is, I think, inversely proportioned to the distance; a thirty-mile day, for instance, usually means excellent surfaces and relatively little effort.)

The deep crevasse on the edge of the plateau where the high snows start to break away into the head of the glacier is now much wider than before, and the snow bridge over which we will have to cross is very unstable. The sides of the crevasse are quite smooth and vertical for the first 200 feet and we could not see bottom.

March 5. It blew quite hard last night and the surface improved considerably as a result. We were out of tents at 7 a.m. and John decided to take the sledges up one by one to the plateau, and not to use the rope hauling process at all. We finally reached the plateau with the first sledge at 11.45 and rarely have I ever been so tired. In spite of the concerted efforts of the seven of us and a very willing dog team, the load was just too heavy and we weren't wise enough to reduce the load and do it twice. I was quite prepared to call it a day and leave the other two sledges at the amphitheatre, but after an hour's rest we felt better. Dave was in excellent spirits and was satisfying his thirst by mixing neat concentrated orange juice with snow and pretending it was an ice cream. John decided to walk his team back to the amphitheatre camp and to try hauling one sledge up with two teams in line ahead. The difference was unbelievable. We brought Duggie's sledge up 1,200 feet in forty minutes and the dogs never flagged at all. The only reason for halting the sledge was because we ourselves were breathless and couldn't keep up! We turned round at once and came down with Duggie's team to collect my sledge, which was even heavier than the last, and took it up to the plateau in the record time of thirty-six minutes. The support party left us at 6.15 right at the edge of the plateau and we then hauled our loads over to the depot, which was completely snow-covered, with only the tip of the flag showing. We camped about 9 p.m. The first trip has taken more out of us than we realise and I for one know that I am tired and seem to have strained my back. We owe a lot to the support party who have just returned to camp; they climbed 2,000 feet in deep snow yesterday, just because they had superlative consciences, and to-day they have climbed an aggregate of nearly 5,000 feet, half of which was behind a loaded sledge. We can, thanks to them, leave relatively fresh to-morrow. This game of combining teams in line ahead has taken the bug out of the route to the plateau. I can visualize next time coming up with three or more teams together and enjoying the climb.

March 6. It took most of the morning to dig out the depot and sort out our loads which seemed horribly large when we finally put them on the sledges. Snow conditions are not as good as we had hoped so John decided to leave the tents standing and to take about two-thirds of our total load forward to the highest point of our route, five miles ahead and 1,000 feet higher. Doc and I skied down towards the edge of the plateau in the evening to try and get a view of the area around base. The view was superb. Alexander Land, about 100 miles away to the south-west, was clear and the whole expanse of sea was dotted with enormous icebergs and streams of pack-ice that cut it into channels and made it seem like an archipelago. There was a grand sense of detachment from the lower levels of North-East Glacier, and it reminded me rather of flying in an aeroplane. There was the definite sense of sitting at the edge of a table 6,000 feet high with the world spread like a patterned carpet at one's feet.

March 7. It has been a most excellent day. We picked up the extra loads from the highest point of the plateau by 11 o'clock and went on with full loads. John was of course in the lead and had to make the tracks. He was pulling just over 700 lb., and Duggie and I could follow in his tracks with about 850 lb. each.

We made about thirteen miles and are now camped at the head of a long wide glacier which must, we think, lead down to Bills Gulch. The word "gulch" seems a misnomer, for my idea of a gulch is a narrow rocky ravine in waterless California, not a wide glacier that seems to slope faultlessly to sea-level 5,000 feet below. John and Duggie used the skis for the first time instead of snowshoes and were astonished at their resulting freshness. If they had snowshoed the same distance I dread to think what they would feel like to-night. Ken had just come up on the wireless to say that Reg arrived back last night at 6 p.m. after an incident-free journey down North-East Glacier.

It was a very cheerful broadcast indeed, and I find myself looking forward to the next one. John made contact and sent back a telegram for me for Father's birthday.

March 8. Just after we had camped the wind increased and stayed with us throughout the night. We were all very stupid to-day and all must share the blame: we were lucky to get away as lightly as we did. At 8 a.m. the wind had dropped, it was calm and clear, so John, Duggie, and I roped up and started to walk down the hard windblown glacier surface to see if we could locate the American route down to the ice shelf. The distance seemed to be about three miles and we kept on thinking that the next few hundred yards would "give us the answer". Gradually the valley narrowed; we passed through an area of smooth snow that was dotted with snow mounds that looked like gigantic haycocks and which on investigation turned out to be the tops of enormous bridged crevasses; but then quite quickly the smooth surface of the glacier gave way to a stretch of jumbled ice, quite impassable to a team of dogs and only possible for a party of adequately equipped mountaineers. We turned round to return to camp and realised that we had failed to notice the rising wind, which was now dead against us, and found that instead of three miles we were something over six miles from camp. It took us three hours to get back to the tents, with wind increasing all the while. The drift snow started to lift from the ground before we got home and life was beginning to be really unpleasant. I have now stripped off all my clothes as they were sodden with perspiration, and am writing this lying naked in my sleeping bag while they dry out at the top of the tent. If the wind had been just a little bit stronger, enough to raise the snow sufficiently to blot out the tents at thirty yards I expect we would be still wandering around. It was a bad error of judgment. The Good God looked kindly on our mistakes.

(Sadly enough we were within 600 yards of the ultimate route to the shelf ice but had entirely missed it in the jumbled mass of ice at the lower end of the glacier. Missing this route was very unfortunate for if we had found it then it would have completely altered not only that journey but the rest of the year's travels, and the whole future policy of the expedition.)

March 9. It is blowing like blazes outside and has done so ever since we returned to our tents last night. Visibility isn't much more than twenty yards. John decided this morning that as we were on known ground—the autumn trip had passed this way—we need have no fear of walking over the edge of the plateau and, except for the discomfort, there was nothing to stop us from travelling.

(I will break this diary for a while here to explain the difficulties of this plateau travel. The plateau corresponds in many ways to an enormous Christmas cake; a huge layer of rock many thousands of feet high, spread generously with a layer of icing two or three hundred feet thick. In some places there are long slanting routes off the edge, or running trough-like from the centre of the cake, but in general the whole area is bounded by vicious cliffs and the smooth snow drops away without warning into the shelf ice 5,000 feet below. The plateau is the meeting place of the weather from the Weddell Sea and the open water weather to the west of Graham Land. It is almost always blanketed in cloud, which precipitates as snow and heavy hoar frost. In thick cloud shadows hardly exist; it is all whiteness ahead; and there is nothing to give warning of the edge of the table. Obviously if the area has been adequately surveyed there is no difficulty in steering a course that keeps clear of the edges, but if there is no such survey, and the country is all new, then it is only foolhardy to continue.)

It wasn't very easy breaking camp this morning for the wind was very strong, but once we were under way it was dead behind us and we made excellent progress. Travelling was in fact almost pleasant.[1]

Duggie knew from his autumn journey that after about eight miles we would be at the head of another glacier so we stopped with seven miles on the mileometer and made camp. It is the first time we have put up tents in a good strong blow and it took nearly two hours before the camp was complete and we were both in our sleeping bags.

The wind makes the tent too noisy for sleep at the present.

March 10. I managed to sleep last night in spite of my doubts. We had set the tent up very badly in yesterday's wind, and the sides sagged with the weight of snow on the outside. Duggie's shoulder was acting as a tent prop this morning and my head was hard up against the side of the tent, the air-space between the tents was gone, and I could feel the hard snowdrift close against my scalp. The wind died down during the night, and when we emerged from our tents this morning visibility was perfect and we could see that there were still six miles to go to the next glacier. The surface has been excellent all day but the glacier which we wanted to reconnoitre stayed full of thick cloud until late this evening when there was no time to do any reconnaissance. As a route it doesn't look promising for, just where it spills on to the ice shelf, its wide expanse is narrowed down between two rock faces less than half a mile apart, and that will mean very heavy crevassing. (Obviously a glacier three or four miles wide that flows smoothly downhill will be terribly rough if it is suddenly restricted, just as happens when a placid river is narrowed into a rocky gorge.)

March 11. Snow all day, with visibility about ten yards and no question of reconnaissance at all; it would have been pleasant enough travelling if our conscience had let us, but we must stay and have a look at this glacier. To cheer us up John lent us the wireless receiver from the other tent and base came through very clearly. Apparently the American party are expected at

[1] The frontispiece photograph was taken on this occasion.

Stonington Island in the next few days, and the *Trepassey*, with the Governor on board, is due a few days later.

March 12. Snow stopped at 10 a.m. and we got away at once on the reconnaissance. The glacier was exactly as we had expected. In its lower reaches it is one of the roughest I have ever seen anywhere, definitely no route in fact. The camp, however, is well sited from a survey point of view and there are good views to the east and north which will tie in with previous work. Duggie spent the afternoon surveying while I took down his readings inside the tent. After supper it was very quiet and peaceful and we have been reading *Alice in Wonderland* aloud to each other.

March 13. Last night was rather disturbed as my dog, Brother, decided to chew himself free and to wander around. He only does this if somebody has been bullying him and I suspect old Bouncer, though I haven't caught him at it. Brother is very lame in one foot and it looks like a broken bone; it obviously isn't poisoned. We made only eight miles in total distance but had to travel fourteen miles in the process. The surface was excellent at first but rapidly worsened, and we finished up by relaying the loads up a long gradient. It is the first time that the night sky has been clear since we left base, and Duggie is busy outside with the theodolite trying to get a star sight. It is fine, calm, and very cold; every now and again I hear some fine Army language as he tries to revive his frozen finger-tips, or breathes too hard and covers the eyepiece of the instrument with ice.

(In still, cold weather it is quite a game to get one's eye near to the business end of any form of telescope, for as soon as it gets close the vapour round the face condenses on the glass and forms an opaque layer, which is most easily removed with the tip of a soft pencil. Progress with the observation is very slow as a result.)

As we were eating John made wireless contact with base and shouted across that the American party had arrived, and then added, as an afterthought, they have brought women with them. I think he is pulling our leg; it is a cheerful thought, however, but I hope it is actually untrue. I think they would make life too complicated.

March 14. A most excellent day in which we made a good fifteen miles on fine snow surface and, once again, we are at the head of a long glacier running down to the east. John Tonkin has somehow hurt his foot and is limping badly, but refuses to give himself a break from the arduous job of leading. With his team in front he has to concentrate very hard on driving his dogs on a compass bearing and cannot give himself the rest that we, as followers, are able to achieve. Towards the end of the day Brother improved and his paw now seems quite all right again. He must have sensed that we had been considering his destruction if he got much worse.

March 15. Snow fell all day, and we could not do any reconnaissance. It fell very quietly and lay thick upon the tent, and slid off in unstable avalanches every time we shook the cloth. Late this evening John contacted base again and confirmed the disquieting news that the Americans have indeed brought women-folk: two among twenty-one men. Duggie rather wryly produced the story of the Marx brothers telephoning from a medieval castle in which they are imprisoned, and pleading for help from the outside world.

"Here we are, seven men and two women—send us five more women."

Ken also told us that he had learnt from the Americans that the Bills Gulch route was close to where we had turned back on March 8: we must have missed it and are all rather sorrowful as a result.

March 16. Perfect conditions for travel and we should have made about fifteen to twenty miles, but after only three miles we reached the top of a wide and very promising glacier completely covered in cloud. We cannot reconnoitre it in cloud, and equally well cannot pass it by. So we camped very early and played liar dice with the tent door open, watching for the glacier to clear. By 6 o'clock the cloud was gone, but it was too late for a reconnaissance so the other two came in from their tent and we had a very hilarious social evening with more liar dice.

March 17 and 18. Two days continuous lie up with high wind and driving snow; Duggie fed the dogs to-day, otherwise neither of us have left the tents.

March 19. It cleared quite early and stopped blowing so we skied down towards the glacier. It was an astonishing trip, for at one moment it all looked quite easy and we were plotting our route along the glacier ahead of us and the next we realised that our path was barred by a 2,000 foot ice cliff that up till then in the shadowless light had remained quite invisible. Standing on top of the cliff we saw that the route below was quite impossible: the lower stretch of the glacier is crossed with wide regular crescent-shaped crevasses so evenly spaced that they seem to form a repetitive pattern, and then the glacier narrows down and flows in a horrible jumble between two steep rock cliffs. It took hours to dig out camp after we returned from the reconnaissance and we only made seven miles this afternoon, driving directly into a rapidly rising wind.

March 20. It has been an all-day lie up with the wind at a steady force 7 (about 40 m.p.h.). Duggie and I started to play paper and pencil games to pass the time, and I find that I am doing well if I can beat him one time in five. No wonder, he is a one-time Oxford scholar. Ken came up on the air and talks with enthusiasm about flying up to see us on a visit. It would be most excellent to see him, but I don't think he quite realises the dangers of this country. Travelling in it, as we are, we do appreciate the extreme ruggedness of everything. I only hope he isn't serious about it. The tents are half buried in snow and Rover has pulled all the whiskers off his tail, by freezing it into the snow and then standing up too fast.

(Oddly enough under these conditions even though the tents become almost completely sealed we rarely suffered from lack of oxygen, and I think this was due in large part to the fact that the tents stayed pretty well dry in the low temperatures which we were experiencing. Some years later I discovered, to my cost, that with tents made of exactly the same material in wet climates, oxygen starvation presents quite a problem. As a precaution, and also because of the relative darkness inside our double tents we invariably burnt a candle which would flicker and die long before lack of oxygen affected the primus or was dangerous to ourselves.)

March 21. Same wind, same place; all-day lie up.

March 22. The weather eased up after noon and we got away at about 2 p.m. We are almost at the centre of the plateau and I really get the impression of the weather from the Weddell Sea fighting it out with that from the west and Marguerite Bay. To-day the good west coast weather won after a long struggle, and we have been rewarded with some perfect views westwards

to Adelaide Island and over the inshore fjords. We camped at
6 p.m., rather to my disgust as I felt like going on.

March 23. The weather worsened during the night and didn't
clear until 10 a.m., when we harnessed up my team and went on
a reconnaissance; suddenly it closed in, and we navigated our
way back to camp with visibility scarcely ten yards. We had
left Doc in camp as he had a slight attack of snow-blindness so
Duggie and I decided on our return to ask him and John in for
a yarn and "a change of scenery". These social evenings are
excellent for morale and to-night we made up some oatmeal
flapjacks, equal parts sugar, butter, and oatmeal, as a luxury
treat.

March 24. All day in the tent with a strong wind blowing. Lie
up continues. John's bitch has unexpectedly come on heat so we
can expect a week of disturbed nights with restless dogs. He has
tethered her round the back of his tent with Darkie in the hope
that the other dogs won't see her. I suppose his motto is "out of
sight out of mind". Duggie produced some mathematical problems which involve calculus that have kept us busy all day, and
made me realise how rusty my brain now is. In the evening I
worked out a series of graphs of possible sledge loads against the
numbers in a dog team, and related them to the number of days'
travelling that a sledge can do on its own reserves. I am sure it
would pay to carry slightly larger teams than we do, say nine
dogs with the same load, and to assume that the greater distance
that they will travel per day will counterbalance the fewer number
of days in the field. (This was a system which in the following
summer was adopted for the 1,200 mile journey.)

March 25. As a sledge party we learned a lesson to-day, and
very nearly a disastrous one at that. Early this morning, at long
last, the weather cleared, so John, Doc, and Duggie started with
an empty sledge and one team to do a reconnaissance of the
glacier. It was perfect weather with bright sun and no wind. The
snow was hard and the sledge left only intermittent tracks as a
result. At 2 o'clock, as I lay in the tent, I noticed the wind had
got up, and by 2.30 was blowing about thirty-five miles an hour;
the visibility was about ten yards. I knew roughly the route by
which they had left, and so collecting all the rope in camp, I
strung it out in a continuous line across the line of probable return.

There was little else that I could do until dusk when a light outside the tents would help. I lay in my sleeping bag, thinking every ten minutes that I could hear them returning. At three minutes past seven, just when I was about to warm up the wireless batteries, and wondering what I should say to them at base, I heard voices, and the weary wanderers returned.

John's greeting was typical, that "he was glad he wasn't me". He knew that the worry of waiting could sometimes be worse than the struggle to return. Apparently they had wandered too far from camp and had failed to notice the weather deteriorating behind them. The seven miles return, dead into a head wind, which the dogs would not face, didn't help them to steer an accurate course for home. They set course so that they would pass camp on their left. Then when the distance on the sledge wheel corresponded exactly to the distance out, they turned left and after several sweeps joined together by a long rope they picked up the camp. It was but a small thing that gave them the clue; a piece of toilet paper blown from the camp site told them to turn up wind, and in a few yards the dark tents came out of the murk.

For once it is very, very good to hear Duggie's snores coming out of his sleeping bag.

(It is quite an art to reach camp in conditions such as these. Once they had turned round and knew what conditions were like it would have been stupid to aim exactly for the camp: for once the distance on the sledge wheel tallied with that of their route out they could never know if they should turn right or left. There is the same problem when heading for a certain point on a coast line from far out across the sea-ice with nil visibility. It is essential to aim to one side of the objective so that you will know which way to turn when you hit the coast. I have often used the same principle when mountaineering in fog at home.)

March 26 and 27. It blew all day yesterday, but to-day the wind has dropped and only the fog persists, and so in fact does the lie up. Duggie and I seem to have worked up an excess of paraffin and we have been able to keep the primus just alight all day and to write letters and read. This is bestial weather and it doesn't give us a chance. A stampeding noise outside the tent in the afternoon made us look outside, and we found John careering around for exercise. He was complaining of stiffness and hospital sores so we suggested that he rub his bad spots with the medicinal brandy that we carried.

March 28. Wind has been high all night and stayed so till well into the afternoon and when the weather finally cleared we had not enough time left to make it worth travelling, or even to do a reconnaissance; we got out of our tents and made all possible preparations for a quick getaway to-morrow.

We heard to-night that *Trepassey* and *Fitzroy* are both at the Argentine Islands and are expected at base on the 30th.

March 29. It is Mother's birthday. To-day we all repeated the reconnaissance of the 25th, but this time packed up our full sledge loads and took them with us. As a reconnaissance everything has gone well. We stood on the south side of a huge east-west glacier trough which we could follow throughout its length, and it was quite obviously a good and safe route from plateau to ice shelf.

The weather was clear but overcast; there were no shadows; and at one stage the slope ahead seemed to run gently into the valley a few hundred feet below. It was getting steep and it was senseless to lose height without sledge loads, so we stopped and proceeded on foot. Almost without warning the slope ended and we found ourselves standing on the very lip of the plateau; the glacier that had appeared so close below was 2,000 feet away at the bottom of a huge ice cliff. In poor visibility with even less sun and no shadows it would have been only too easy to drive right over the top, after the style of the Gadarene swine. We retraced our steps and pitched camp thirty yards away from our camp site of this morning.

March 30. Almost an excellent day. We made fifteen miles homewards on a fine windblown surface which would just support the sledges. Red was sick all along the route to the delight of the other dogs and the general disruption of my team. John's rear dog, Mutt, was very lame, and we stopped for his sake. For the last five miles we had had an astonishing surface which looks very good but pulls like desert sand.

(This surface is always disheartening to meet. It seems to occur when there has been a high wind to consolidate the snow followed by a fall of a form of snow which is almost gritty and is only formed under certain rare conditions of weather. This lies on the hard surface of the windblown snow like sand on a concrete floor, and the sledge refuses to slide. Icing the runners sometimes helps. Actually on this trip so far we had met a fair variety of snow surfaces. One of the best, and typical of plateau travel, has been after several days in cloud when all the precipitation has been in the form of crystals of frost.)

March 31. Lie up all day again with the usual drift, cloud, and hoar frost. Ken came up on the wireless. *Trepassey*, with Bingham on board, and *Fitzroy* are both at Stonington Island, with more stores, more mail, and the aircraft ski.

April 1. A good fifteen miles run which finished up with a long one-mile drag uphill. I got terribly far behind, and with no one ahead to watch Rover became very discouraged. By the time I had reached the camp site John and Doc had their tent erected. We stopped early so that John could get his batteries really warm to give him a good talk with Bingham, but there was no call from base at all. It is all very worrying as it isn't at all like Ken to forget a schedule. It is a beautiful night again with a temperature of minus 15° and a golden strip of cloud lying behind the peaks of Adelaide Island. We can see over the lip of the plateau to the north and look right down into Laubeuf Fjord. Duggie is outside on the theodolite, and by the frequent "damns" I guess that it is much colder than I thought. Inside the tent is relatively warm, and I am booking the angle readings for Duggie as he shouts them to me from outside and writing my diary in between-whiles. John is obviously still drying his clothes, as there is a small cloud of condensation resting motionless over the peak of his tent. Sister, curious as ever, is sitting up watching Duggie and the theodolite. All the other dogs are sound asleep.

(This star sight forms the check-point on the method of exploratory survey that we used. In general, the method corresponds to navigation at sea. A traverse, or series of straight-line zigzags would be made, using a bicycle wheel behind the sledge for distance and a compass for direction. Obviously both these measurements were subject to error and every forty miles or so an observation could be made on the stars with a theodolite: this could give a position on the earth's surface, accurate probably to half a mile, and would provide a check on the previous traversing. Throughout the traverse, Mason would be making compass observations on the country around and would plot these out at night in the tent. Everything would, of course, be replotted when he reached base. He used two aneroid barometers for height recording and by a series of corrections, some official and some products of his ingenious mind, he was able to gauge his height to within a couple of hundred feet throughout the journey.)

April 2–8. Six days of continuous cloud; wind and visibility nil. We have been inventing numerous games to pass away the time. Spillikins, using matches, proved popular; then John came in because he had forgotten how to prove Pythagoras and wanted assistance. I managed to beat Duggie at a paper game called Battleships, at which he excels. If I beat him one time in ten it is a remarkable achievement. There was no sign of base on the wireless.

April 9. It was clear when we left our tents this morning, and we had a glorious ten-mile run to a camp site overlooking Bills Gulch. Theoretically I was the last man in the party, but we were all racing each other down the safe snow slope in line abreast and the dogs loved the excitement. Later, when we had dropped back into line, I was taking off my skis alongside my sledge intending to ride in comfort, when suddenly my dogs started on their own, and I had a mile chase after them on my one ski before the others noticed, stopped my runaway team, and waited for me. I reached them weary both with laughter and exertion.

April 10. We did a complete reconnaissance of Bills Gulch and discovered a safe route running close under an ice fall and leading right down to the shelf ice. At present there is still a lack of snow to cover the crevasses and the whole route needs care and caution, but when the spring comes and the winter snows have filled up the holes it will be safe and docile. It was only half a mile from where we had given up just over a month ago. We contacted base to-night and discovered the cause of the long delay since we last made contact. *Trepassey* had caught fire on the night of the 31st, and the whole base had been involved in repairing her damage and getting her ready for sea.

April 11. We set course for home to-day and covered nearly eleven miles, most of which was climbing. This camp is probably half a mile from where we were on March 5.

April 12. We made fabulously good time to Two Ton depot

on a glorious surface. I think the dogs knew we were making for home, and raced each other for the fun of it. During our midday halt for lunch we heard the sound of a summer wasp and the Auster appeared, a hundred feet up and obviously looking for us. The snow was perfect for landing, so we signalled the wind direction and Tommy brought her down beautifully. Dave had thoughtfully brought up some luxuries, some pineapple and beef stew, and Tommy produced a bag of mail. In ten minutes Dave restarted the engine and they were gone. For us there was a long downhill run to Two Ton depot where we are now, and I had the untold luxury of sitting astride the sledge, reading letters from home that had been written barely a month ago. To-night I feel very distended with a tin of beef stew inside me; while the prospect of a tin of pineapple for breakfast is magnificent. It is quite impossible to describe the delight that this last mail of the season has given. It was a lovely day anyhow with the long views over to the west, but to have such a day completed by a delivery of mail, while still seventeen miles away from base, is something I wouldn't have believed possible.

April 13. I am writing this at base after a horribly rough journey back from Two Ton depot. This morning we dug out, counted, and re-stacked all that was left there. Then with ropes twisted around our runners we made the dogs pull us all the way past amphitheatre camp to the top of Sodabread slope. Here conditions had changed considerably since the trip up, for on the steepest section the snow had blown right away and exposed hard, blue, shiny ice.

John, acting on our advice, and rather against his better judgment, pushed his sledge over the top of the slope and, relying on his brake, took it quite straight. We didn't see what happened, but he must have lost control and turned the sledge over rather than letting it over-run his dogs. We heard a crash, and when we reached him he was twenty yards beyond his sledge and thoroughly concussed. Doc examined him and coaxed him down to our old camp site at the bottom where we wrapped him up warmly, propped him up on Duggie's sledge, and brought him down as a stretcher case to base where we arrived at 6.30. He should be all right in a day or two, and apparently no serious damage has been done. Here life seems very civilized. We now eat off a polished table and use table-mats. My hyacinth bulb has come out and it sits in a bowl in the middle of the table.

That was the end of the autumn journey. As a journey, in terms of mileage covered, it had been incredibly poor, for we had covered barely 200 miles in forty-four days. Of those forty-four days we had only been able to travel on nineteen. Yet I think that to the base as a whole it was one of the key journeys of the two years. We had found the route down to the east coast ice shelf, pioneered by the Americans in 1941, and had put it properly on the map, and we had, thanks to the support party, laid low once and for all the bugbear of the haul to the plateau.

We had, too, enjoyed and appreciated the delight of John's leadership. He was an incorrigible optimist, ever cheerful, ever ready to ask advice, yet never flinching from taking a decision himself, and with it the responsibility of failure.

Though we did not realise it at the time this was the only major journey in which John took part during his time in Antarctica. Now that its importance can be assessed in retrospect it is one of which he can be proud to have been the leader.

CHAPTER II

American Neighbours

IN THE six weeks that we had been away an immense amount
seemed to have happened and we were hungry for news as a
result. Shortly after we had left there had been friendly visits
by Chilean and Argentine warships who, as before, quickly sent
the official "protests" against our presence in their territorial
waters and followed them up with invitations to dinner and
pictures. These visits, sadly enough, were even more disastrous
than the visit of the *Iquique* in February, and the American huts
were reduced to a state far worse than that in which we had found
them a year before. In March, without warning, the American
ship *Port of Beaumont* arrived and anchored in Back Bay. The
leader of this expedition, Commander Finn Ronne, who had
been present at the evacuation of the American base in 1940,
seemed ill-prepared to believe a word about our efforts to tidy
up the American huts, and their subsequent looting, and preferred
to send highly sensational reports back to the American press
accusing us of all the damage. His very aggressive attitude about
our having trespassed on American property mirrored most
admirably what we in Britain felt when we heard in 1940 that
the Americans had set up their base close beside the Debenham
Islands at a time when we were occupied with total war.

At the end of March the *Trepassey* and *Fitzroy* arrived, bringing for us the precious aircraft ski and an old army Nissen hut.
On board was the Governor of the Falkland Islands paying an
official visit and he sportingly stayed a night ashore in the relative discomfort of the base hut. Commander Bingham had
reoccupied his old bunk for the night, and Back Bay must have
seemed quite full with three ships lying at anchor.

Both the Governor and Commander Bingham had seen Finn
Ronne and stressed the British point of view and repeated again

and again exactly what had happened with the American huts. It was many months before the state of aggressive neutrality eased off.

Then, on the very night that she was due to sail, the *Trepassey* had caught fire and it took the combined efforts of the *Fitzroy* and the *Port of Beaumont* to put it out. By now the season was rapidly closing in and there was a frantic four days while the mate of the ship, the craftsman shipbuilder Mr. Stone, repaired the damage and made the ship ready for sea.

When we arrived back at base only the *Port of Beaumont* remained lying at anchor, close inshore, in the shelter of Back Bay. There was smoke coming from the chimneys of the American huts, and there was an assortment of strange dogs tethered near their base; otherwise there was little sign of life.

Finn Ronne in one of his conversations with Bingham did us the honour of stating that our hut was so clean and new that it could not possibly have been lived in for more than six weeks, and he implied to the American press that we had in fact occupied the American huts throughout the winter. To a discerning eye such a statement was obviously false for around our house the snowdrifts of a full winter were still visible; the remark, however, spurred us on to fresh efforts to keep our house in order and to maintain it spotlessly clean. At this early stage I think Ronne must have felt very embittered with our presence, and seemed to have decided that we, as individuals, would contaminate the members of his party; he put a ban on all social intercourse between bases, so that was that.

On our part, curious though we were to meet the "Folk over the Hill" we decided to let the matter rest and knew that time and the friendliness of Antarctica would soon sort it all out.

We ourselves still had an immense amount of work to do: the "Folk over the Hill" assumed the status of gremlins: the story of the two women seemed a mere myth for nobody had seen them, so we kept ourselves to ourselves and worked like beavers.

As I said before, we aimed to erect enough in the way of buildings around our house to store every bit of equipment that we held on Stonington Island. We wanted to make the base itself as self-contained as was possible so that there would be a minimum need to go outside in the winter's winds. We fitted the Nissen hut that had come down with the last trip of the *Trepassey* on to the end of the workshop building and mounted it on stilts about four feet high to provide us with a covered basement in which we reckoned to house a full year's supply of coal. A passage-way from the old back door linked it to the main hut, and this was carefully fitted out as a storage space for ski with special clamps to hold them on to the wall.

Reg Freeman and Ken MacLeod designed some massive shelves for the Nissen and barely a week after starting to erect the hut we were bringing in the stores and filling the place up. Reg, with his innate sense of orderliness, became quartermaster and ruled us with a rod of iron; everything was meticulously arranged. There were shelves of photographic and survey gear; a series of fitted chests held the medical equipment. There were racks full of tins of corned beef, or dried onions, Quaker oats or dried eggs, all arranged with the precision of a grocery store. Odd articles such as sides of bacon, hanks of rope, scrubbing brushes, or broomsticks, hung from hooks in the ceiling and the whole place had the atmosphere of a village shop.

At the far end of the Nissen, with great pride, we erected our own privy, a hygienic two-holer made after due reference to that American classic *The Specialist*.

Bernard Stonehouse, in a way which we never quite got used to, would disappear day after day without saying a word and then finally announced, over a cup of tea, that he had built a laboratory for himself leading off the new passage that connected the hut to the engine shed.

We still, of course, had a full year's rations in a hut fifty yards away from base, and with it was stowed our emergency supplies of coal, paraffin, and clothing. The hangar was now used as a store-room for all the sledging equipment.

Those were the main outside structural alterations that we carried out; inside the hut we were just as busy. Bunk space for the eleventh man was made by removing the wireless equipment from the wireless room and putting it into the porch and making the empty cubicle into a private cabin for Ken. He then evacuated his bunk and Terry Randall took it over. The latter was our new wireless operator who had arrived down in the *Trepassey*, after having left England by air at the end of February. He was a tall

The Stonington Island base hut at the end of the second season

Yorkshireman, only eighteen years old, who had served as a Naval wireless operator.

Our pride and joy, however, was the new bathroom which Ken MacLeod had made by enclosing a space at the end of the Nissen hut. He had used an old forty-gallon drum tipped on its side as boiler and built around it a fireplace from the bricks that we had magpied at Deception Island the year before; not content with that, he had erected proper drying space around the roof.

In the kitchen region very little was altered. We did, however, arrange a special chute for semi-dirty water. In the first year we had always thrown our used water on to the snow outside the back door, and as the summer thaw came on we were left with a hard, slow melting mixture of washing-up water and snow. We decided to get rid of all our water into the rock rubble underneath the hut where it could drain away and disappear. We built a large funnel into the hut wall, near the back door, and all washing-up water went down it. Every month or so there would be a shortage of teaspoons and we would have to climb under the hut and collect them from the rocks beneath. The odd teaspoon in the washing-up bowl could be so easily missed by the hasty washer-up.

In the hangar there was a great deal of extra space alongside the fuselage and behind the aircraft wings, so Doc Butson, Tommy, and I converted one corner into a fine workshop designed exclusively for the maintenance and construction of sledges, and on the opposite side, where we had dumped all the sledging stores before we left in March, John Tonkin sorted through and stowed the stores which belonged essentially to the travel side of the expedition. The sleeping bags and tent, primuses and new dog whips all belonged here, and it was in this space that we reckoned to prepare our equipment for a journey in the field.

By mutual consent we had changed the daily routine considerably and we seemed to have much more time for work as result. Breakfast was still at 8 a.m. but there was now a break at 11 for morning coffee or tea. Lunch was at 1 o'clock instead of the old time of noon, tea took place at 4.30. Supper was postponed and now occurred dead on 8 p.m.

Saturday morning was always reserved for what we called

barrack-room sports, for we stopped all other work and scrubbed the hut out from end to end and tidied up all the outhouses. This was Reg Freeman's idea and was extremely popular, the base remained very much cleaner as result and we also achieved much more leisure. In the previous year, for instance, it had always been necessary to clean the workshop out meticulously every evening for it was also the bathroom, but now, with the thought of Saturday's Sports in our mind it could be left a little less tidy during the week.

Sunday was utterly changed. Breakfast was not until 9 a.m. and the cook of the week was expected to precede it by an early morning cup of tea for anybody who was awake. The day itself was always considered as a voluntary day in which we all, except for the essential jobs such as dog feeding or weather observations, could do what we liked. We could ski on the nursery slopes or lie on our bunks all day with a clear conscience.

On April 27 I was cook, and we felt we were entitled to have a party to celebrate the completion of the base for the winter. We could look around and know that all the "store-humping" for the year was past, and now, if the wind and winter should hit us, we could feel utterly self-contained. There was one more major change in routine. The Friday night party was a thing of the past. We had all found in the previous year that it wasn't easy to accept "a drink on Friday" as a hard and fast fact. There were many days when it would have been preferable on the Thursday or the Sunday, after some strenuous activity, or at a moment of general depression due to bad weather. So we decided to leave the row of four bottles, that represented the month's ration, on a shelf in the living room and to leave it to the individual to decide when he wanted his tot. It was a most happy arrangement, and as result, on the average about once every ten days, gay spontaneous parties would start at moments when we all felt the need. It was also a tribute to the happy atmosphere in which we lived that the unlocked bottles were never abused.

One such spontaneous party I can recall well, when Tommy and Dave decided to make up a hot rum punch. It seemed an excellent idea, and one by one we all filtered into the kitchen to assist, John to add his lump of cinnamon and I, maybe, a dollop of fresh butter. By the time the brewing, mixing, and tasting stage was over we had finished the whole lot, and the row of unfilled mugs on the sitting room table bore witness to our intentions.

The situation that existed between the Americans and ourselves was too artificial to continue; so finally one day John and Ken dug out some specially ironed shirts, creased their trousers, and went on board the *Port of Beaumont* for supper. Finn and most of the expedition were still living on board; the sea was still unfrozen and they had always to be ready to move ship if the weather became unkind. The two of them came back early, and John confirmed that the story of the two women was certainly no myth.

A few evenings later Tommy and I wandered over the hill to visit the six Americans who were living ashore, clearing up the huts, and making them ready for the others. They could not have been more welcoming, and we asked them over to supper the next day. They were all so full of enthusiasm about life and obviously a little sad that Finn had been so firm about lack of intercourse between the groups. They, as an expedition, were "dry", and when we served buttered rum after supper it proved an excellent ice-breaker. Two people stand out as result of that first visit; the first was a tall Russian-bearded individual named Bill Latady, who was probably the most competent and experienced explorer-mountaineer in both camps. He described most things as rugged, and this is the word that best described him. The other was Bob Nicolls, a geological professor from Tufts College, Massachusetts, who had lived for and loved Antarctic literature. He had an infectious enthusiasm for everything that he turned his hand to, and seemed in his friendly American manner to know all the explorers of the past by their first names.

We heard tales of the exploits of the *Port of Beaumont* as they steamed south, of complete circles made by the ship with the wheel hard over, and the scientist on watch sound asleep, and of the llamas that they had bought in Valparaiso from the zoo to assist in their Antarctic travel problems, and how these were killed and eaten by the dogs on the way south.

There was another party on May 1 which was Bernard Stonehouse's twenty-first birthday and John had really gone to town with the birthday cake. We presented Bernard, officially, with the keys of the front door and Ken gave him "his parental consent

to keep late nights without having to ask for special dispensation."
It is interesting to note that he was by no means the youngest for
it was over two years before Terry Randall celebrated his coming
of age.

The evening became more and more fun, and it only needed
a suggestion from John that "he hadn't had a good rough-house
for ages" to start us off with the most riotous schoolboy rough-
and-tumble that I had known since the days before the war.

On May 6 we had our first cold spell with temperatures down
to zero and the sea started to freeze. The winter had started and the
sense of isolation that comes from living on an island was soon
to stop. The *Port of Beaumont* looked pretty secure so all the Americans moved ashore and left the ship to look after itself. With
Finn Ronne ashore Ken was in a position to pay one or two
friendly visits and gradually the barrier was lifted and the Americans were officially allowed to talk to us. No longer did we have
to meet like wicked schoolboys in places where Finn couldn't
see us and furtively exchange news and views. The Americans
learnt to drift over to the hut on the flimsiest of excuses and soon
did without those. The 4.30 tea-time was of course a meal entirely outside their routine, and we could always expect three or
four very appreciative guests. I always had the impression that
they really did appreciate our efforts to keep our hut clean and
a sense of civilization in the air, and this in itself was one of the big
reasons why they liked to come.

We now, as I have said, ate off a polished table that Ken Mac-
Leod had made from wood that had been left over from the
hangar, and used table-mats cut in hexagons from odd pieces of
naval linoleum. The constant supply of hot water meant that we
were able to keep remarkably clean and except where beards
were being grown intentionally we still adhered to the "shave at
base" routine.

Gradually we were able to piece together the history of the
American Expedition and the general extent of its programme.

They had left Beaumont, Texas, in the middle of February
after endless unavoidable delays; they were very late in the season
and had to hurry south as result. The ship itself, the *Port of
Beaumont*, had been used in the war as a form of boom defence
vessel that had been built of wood by a shipyard which was

unable to build in steel. It was solidly made and, mechanically, very complicated; in spite of this, by using scientists in the engine room and on the wheel, they had managed to find their way most successfully to Antarctica. On deck they carried three aircraft, two in pieces for re-erection in the field and the last, a light Army spotter, known as the L.5, was kept ready on deck fitted with floats for use among the pack-ice if reconnaissance proved necessary. They also carried three ex-Army tracked vehicles, known as Weasels, designed essentially for use in the snow, and these they proposed to use in their travels.

The thirty huskies that had been bred in New England at Wanalancet had been sent to the ship just before it sailed, but such was the hurry of departure that they were never inoculated. By the time they reached Valparaiso only about nine had survived and Ronne had had to make up the numbers by combing the streets of Santiago for strays. It was a motley collection of rag-tag and bobtail that were tethered in the snow outside the American huts. A spaniel-cum-corgi lay alongside a very English-looking sheepdog, and a strange brand of whippet looked miserable as it watched the huskies revel in the cold weather. The Santiago zoo offered two llamas from the high Andes and a large supply of hay to keep them for the winter but, as I have said, both of these had been killed and eaten by the dogs on the way south.

There had never been any intention to bring the women-folk further south than the last port of call, but it hadn't worked out that way, so that the leader Finn Ronne and the senior pilot Harry Darlington both had their wives with them when they arrived at Stonington Island.

In aircraft they obviously were very strong, and the main exploratory aim of the expedition was to explore the east coast of the peninsula southwards by air, to put it on the map with continuous strips of air photographs, and to discover just how far south was the extremity of the Weddell Sea. The twin-engined Beechcraft was the photographic plane, and the Norseman was the all-purpose load carrier. For journeys on the ground they were not really so well off. The three Weasels were well-proven and most excellent vehicles for shore-based work in the Canadian Arctic but little was known of their performance on sea-ice or on crevassed glaciers.

In dogs they were obviously very weak indeed and as far as I recall, by including the newest pups and any Santiago dogs that vaguely resembled huskies, they could run one team of fifteen, but it was neither convincing in performance nor size.

Their scientists had a very wide programme indeed. Andy Thompson hoped to maintain a full year's seismographic observation. Petersen was investigating cosmic ray radiations, and shared the weather observations with Larry Fiske. Bob Dodson, who had been secretary of the Harvard Mountaineering Club when Bill Latady, whom we had met a month previously, had been President, was lined up to do the survey work when he wasn't busy training dogs.

The senior pilot was to be Harry Darlington, an ex-Naval Lieutenant-Commander who had spent a year with Finn Ronne at Stonington Island in 1940, and had been a member of the very creditable sledge journey down southwards on the east coast. It was his wife "Jinny" who was to be with them for the winter. The other two pilots were Jimmy Lassiter and Chuck Adams, both U.S.A.A.F. captains, who had spent much of the war as pilots on the Burma supply route, and were now filling in time before taking permanent jobs as personal pilots to an Indian Maharajah. Jimmy Robertson, from near New York, was the air mechanic. There were many others, and as time went on we were gradually able to work out where they all fitted. From the start, however, it was impossible to miss the ship's Captain, Ike Schlossbach, one-time submarine captain and officer in Wilkins' sub-polar submarine *Nautilus*, three times member of Byrd's various expeditions to Antarctica, and a veteran of at least three Arctic winters. He also flew aircraft, had his pilot's wings, herded cattle on his own ranch, and looked, and loved to act, the part of a rascally sea captain of the sixteenth century.

Finn Ronne himself was the son of Roald Amundsen's sailmaker in the *Fram*, and had two Antarctic expeditions behind him; one in "Little America" and the 1940 one at Stonington Island. He had had a long and continuous battle to put his expedition in the field at all, and it was enormous credit to him and his friends at home that he was able to get away as well as he did.

In general the Americans therefore were very strong in field scientists and in aircraft, while we were strong in dogs and

moderately experienced travellers. It was obvious that some form
of active co-operation would be essential.

Ken had a series of interviews with Finn Ronne, and made little
progress in this respect until just before mid-winter's day when
he agreed in principle to "co-operation".

Finn had put in an immense amount of work planning a very
long sledge trip which was to go southwards on the west side of
Graham Land and to King George VI Sound and then strike east
to Mount Tricorn, about six hundred miles from base on the
Weddell Sea coast of the Graham Land peninsula and about 74°
south; he suggested that this party, which was to be air sup-
ported, should include a British observer with a large team of
British dogs. Ken on his part suggested that a British party with
an American observer should travel via Bills Gulch to the
Weddell Sea and work as far southwards down the east coast as
was possible with limited air support. When once the sledge
parties were at their furthest south Finn would fly the Beechcraft
southward to the limit of its safe range, photographing as he
went, and hoped to be able to reach the southern tip of the
Weddell Sea before he would have to turn back. As a comple-
ment to this proposed east coast journey southward Ken decided
to ask a party from Hope Bay to sledge down the ice shelf from
the north to a rendezvous on the east coast where they would be
met by a guide party from Base E who would escort them back
to Marguerite Bay by way of Bills Gulch. In this way he expected
to survey a continuous strip of coast almost 1,000 miles long.
This broad plan was a generous compromise on the part of both
expeditions and showed the extent to which the good will had
by this stage been developed.

We drifted over the hill to the American huts quite frequently
by now and saw how they had sorted themselves out. The havoc
wrought by the Chileans and Argentines had been eradicated,
most of the stores had been landed from the *Port of Beaumont*,
and the place was now warm and welcoming. Finn Ronne and
his wife, Jackie, had taken over a small shack set apart from the
main building, the same lone hut that he had occupied in 1940;
Harry Darlington had partitioned off a portion of the main living
room with light plywood, and his wife had made the place gay
with bunting curtains from the ship's flag locker and bright-

coloured wall paint. The two separate buildings at the back, the workshop and scientific hut, had been joined to the main block with a covered passage so that they too, as a base, were pretty well self-contained.

Mid-winter's day was most definitely the end of our period of estrangement, and we were entertained to a magnificent meal of fried chicken and mushrooms, sweet corn, grilled steak, fruit salad, and ice cream and we in return asked them, in groups of seven, to join us for a typical British Christmas meal, followed by a social evening enlivened with buttered rum and liar dice.

Throughout the winter, while Ken was organizing plans for the summer co-operation, life went on as usual, and the second winter seems in memory to be made up of whole series of unattached incidents. On May 18 Nelson Maclary became the first American to join the Antarctic Swimming Club. He had walked backwards over a 40-foot ice cliff as he paid out the wire stay for an aerial mast. Everyone could see it about to happen and yelled at him to stop, but he didn't realise the shout was for him and kept on walking. He was found, up to his neck in icy water, cautiously balanced on a submerged rock by his toe muttering to himself, "I guess I know now who those sons of bitches were shouting at."

Bernard was proving an exceptionally versatile meteorologist, and quickly organized his routine to give him spare time for many other things. He sent up weather balloons, unheard of the previous year, and established a liaison with the American "climatologist" Larry Fiske, by which they would cover one another's weather schedules if either wanted to be away from base.

Doc Butson had brought with him a series of scientific tests in which we were to be guinea-pigs. One I recall vividly had to be done before getting up, and I woke one morning to find him standing over me holding a form of miniature gasworks into which I had to breathe and pretend to enjoy. His other cruelty was to make us immerse a forearm in a basin of ice and water for fifteen minutes while he plotted a graph of our blood pressure. Somewhere in the test came an injection of adrenalin which oddly enough put me right out.

Tommy took over pup feeding for a fortnight. He had seven lively little brutes enclosed in a large pen. They gradually learned

139

Marguerite Bay

F.I.D.S.   R.A.R.E.

The sketch on the menu for the mid-winter's day, 1947, dinner of the Falkland Islands Dependencies Survey and the Ronne Antarctic Research Expedition

Kevin Walton

Gary Rundell   Bernard Stonehouse

Menu

Chicken Broth

Steak Pie
Potatoes

Brussels Sprouts   Green Peas

Loganberry Blancmange   Trifle

Stonington Sixbury

Cheese   Biscuits

Coffee

Who broke my last No. 9?
C.W. Kevin Walton

Stuart Jones

A reduced facsimile of the author's own menu card. The drawing refers to the fact that due to the scarcity of needles he tended to monopolize the sewing-machine to ascend the sides of the pen, where they would pause for a moment before tumbling off into the outside world. All learned except one, who always got stuck with his fore-paws only over the top. He looked for all the world like a "football spectator" and was usually named such.

We had one or two dog casualties which demanded operations. Hugh acquired a twisted stomach which Doc cleared successfully, but Hugh was a timid creature and lacked the will to recover. Doc kept him going for many days with saline injections, but in the end he died. Bouncer, my king dog, was always in trouble, for keeping the unruly orange dogs in order was an all-time job and he was always being wounded. He must have had twenty stitches in him before the winter had finished and spent one long month with his torn ears covered by a leather head bandage.

The American party had brought with them a cinema pro-jector and generously asked us over twice a week to see their films. Invariably I took advantage of this weekly exodus and would volunteer to stay as fire-watcher in our own hut, where all was so peaceful and quiet. Bill Latady would sometimes come over, to sew or talk or stick in photographs, and I began to piece together the wide experience of his adventurous life. His ability to turn his hand to anything, and to do it better than anyone I knew, always astonished me.

The luxury of the bathroom was soon found to be worth while except in one respect. Under certain conditions of weather the chimney would not draw and it would be almost impossible to light the fire at all. Various solutions were suggested, but I think the best was one where we pushed a pressure blow-lamp through a hole in the side of the chimney and started a convection draught. Most often, however, we lit the fire by the age-old method, some paraffin, apply a match, and retire rapidly. If the embers were still hot there would be a slight but harmless explosion, which emptied the soot from the chimney and all would be well. I was busy on the fire one afternoon, and unknown to me Ken was experimenting with a new system of fire-lighting, which involved looking down the chimney from the roof. I applied paraffin and a match and went outside to admire the smoke that I knew would be pouring out, only to find a by no means silent cross between Paul Robeson and Little Black Sambo eyeing me wrathfully from the roof. Ken had taken the full charge of soot straight into his face.

There was one lengthy and less spectacular job which occupied us a good deal in the second year, and that was the local survey. Reg Freeman undertook this and set about it with the thoroughness we associated with anything that he did. He established a concrete survey post on the rocks to the east of the base hut and modelled it on the best ordnance survey lines. He formed a pillar of concrete, cast inside ten-gallon drums, and anchored the whole thing with steel rods to the living rock. It was cold when he was laying the concrete, and each night he could be seen with sacks and bales of straw wrapping his pillar up for the night with a miner's safety lamp as a hot water bottle. The question of sounding out the harbour came into the survey as well. Normally this would probably be done by the boat when the sea-ice had gone, but for us this was impossible, and instead, while the sea-ice was still thin, he plotted the frozen sea into squares, and we would all go and help him chip his way through and sound for the sea bottom.

On June 29, by way of a tonic and to speed up our recovery from the celebrations of mid-winter, I went over to the Debenham Islands with a large group of Americans so that they could see the B.G.L.E. hut. It can rarely have been so crowded. There were fifteen of us sitting round the room, eating our mid-day meal of hot soup and sausages. The lively ghosts of the original inhabitants must have been agreeably surprised to hear the appreciations of their home in a woman's voice.

It was a glorious evening as we returned, absolutely calm and clear and so cold that we had to run behind the sledge to keep warm. The new-formed ice was still smooth and hard, and the four teams raced for home one beside the other instead of tail to tail, somehow sensing that it was only half an hour before feeding time.

The second winter seemed to come to an end very quickly, and it wasn't long before we were beginning to count on the fingers of one hand the days until the sun should return. It was time in fact to start preparations for the year's journeys that were to be the climax of the year's work.

CHAPTER 12

A Crevasse Rescue

FOR us the preparations for the summer journeys were clear-cut. They were material preparations that involved sledge building, rations, and methods of lightening loads. But for the Americans it was rather different. Their equipment was much more varied, and they had still to know its limitations. A few days before the sun returned, Ronne decided to take his party for a toughening trip into the mountains. I should, I think, make it clear that our attitude to travel method seemed to differ widely from his. Our method of training for our first trip was to study and abide by the exact details of those who have travelled before; whereas his seemed to be on the lines, "Give them a tent and some gear, they will soon learn". The result was I think that in the field the Americans probably lived more uncomfortably than we did and, oddly enough, carried heavier loads in the process. About July 17, a party of eight Americans with all the available dogs left Stonington Island to establish a camp somewhere near Two Ton depot, and to leave Petersen and Dodson there to do some cosmic ray research at the first sign of the spring sun. In a very short space of time they reported by wireless that they had arrived on the plateau. The weather up to then had been kind, and they could be justly proud of their efforts. However, the next morning a full gale hit them; it was in just the same place as this that one of the tents had blown to shreds in 1940. They were not much better off this time. The Alaskan type Army bell tent, which I had shortened for them, was not man enough to stand the strain and partially collapsed. A light-weight yellow nylon tent stood the test, but was far from windproof, and the third tent was a twin brother of one that had blown away in 1940. We would hear them talking on the wireless each night and they sounded cold and miserable. One night the weather cleared, so they left Dodson and Petersen, took the dogs, and skied back to base in the dark. To us, with our intimate knowledge of the crevassing of North-East Glacier, this seemed madness even though they were better skiers than we were, and looking back I think our attitude was over-cautious. Conditions for Petersen and Dodson became worse. The tent they were in collapsed and started to tear, and the whole place filled with drift, while the other tent, like its twin in 1940 , blew to shreds. Cooking was impossible, and it was very, very cold. In the early afternoon of July 25 there was a break in the weather, so they decided to make tracks for base seventeen miles away. On the steep snow slopes that led to the bottom of Sodabread slope, it was hard to use ski in safety, and when they reached the more level glacier at the bottom Petersen was too tired to manage them properly. They had no route plan which would take them clear of all crevasses, and in any case with Ronne as guide on the way up they had cut all the corners, and it seemed reasonable to do so on the way down. In the dark the area around them seemed hard and safe so they unroped. Twenty seconds later Petersen was wedged 120 feet down a crevasse. There was little Bob Dodson could do except mark the hole, fix it with compass bearings, and ski back to base. At 10 p.m., while everyone was at the movies, he burst in and told us all that "Pete was down". Quickly rescue teams were sent out. The first, led by Bill Latady, went on foot to try and locate the area, and an hour later we followed with two sledges, pulled by our best two teams, carrying all our safety equipment. By now it was a clear night, and there was not a breath of wind. Away across the glacier I could hear the vanguard of the rescue team, consisting of Bill Latady, Bob Dodson, Bob Nicolls, and Ike Schlossbach, who was tail-end Charlie at the end of 120 feet of climbing rope.

At 2 a.m. we thought we were in the right area. John lost a dog down a crevasse and managed to save the two others who had fallen in at the same time. Finally, by sweeping across the glacier roped together in a long line, we located the hole, and using a torch we could see Petersen wedged far below. It was a shocking area in which to have been in daylight for the whole place was riddled with deep, badly bridged crevasses. We adopted a drill that had been discusssd many times since the rescue of John

Tonkin. The sledge was up-turned over to form a bridge, a pulley block was fitted underneath, and in a few short minutes Doc Butson, who had volunteered for the job, had been lowered into the depths and was able to report that Pete was alive, and remarkably well. An hour later, after a good deal of chipping of ice, Petersen was out on the surface and wrapped in a sleeping bag inside the tent. For Doc Butson it must have been eerie in that crevasse, for we were lighting it from above with a Naval signalling lamp; it was all very blue and the hoar frost crystals on the side glittered like diamonds, yet in a crevasse sounds have no echo, and all is still and lifeless.[1]

It was still two hours to daylight, and it was cloudless and bitterly cold, yet we were not prepared to cross those crevasses again in the dark, so we shivered our way to the dawn. By 10 a.m. we were all back at base, and the nightmare was over.

Petersen had been extremely lucky; few folk fall 120 feet down a crevasse, spend twelve hours down there, and survive, let alone survive almost unharmed, yet he had done this in Antarctica. That he was unhurt was a miracle, that the night was clear for our search was an act of God, which might not happen again. Was the accident necessary? Basically it was lack of judgment on the part of Pete and Dodson, and they would I know agree with me; but their decision had been made under duress, in conditions which need never have arisen. To use a tent whose duplicate had blown away in similar circumstances seven years before was unwise, especially when other well-tried tents were available. If any of the three tents had survived, the long chain of events which so nearly ended in disaster would never have started. It is only by attempting to analyse such accidents that we can hope to avoid them in the future. Basically, the mistake was not of their own making.

For me the rest of August was extremely busy. I was trying to complete all the sledges that would be wanted for the long journeys, before the end of the month. Tommy and Doc would often come up to the hangar, and we would spend a happy day lashing up new sledges or repairing partly used ones. Altogether at base we must have had nearly twenty sledges which were in use, and continuous maintenance was required. There was a tendency,

[1] A year later Dr. A. R. C. Butson was awarded the Albert Medal.

and I was as much an offender as anyone, to seize the first sledge that came to hand, whenever there was a hauling job to be done.

On one occasion a freshly killed seal was brought in and a new sledge covered in oily blood. To use that sledge on a journey without careful cleaning would cause havoc, for hungry dogs find seal-smeared wood very appetizing! As a result we started to name the sledges and turn them over for keeps to their future owners. Horrible Herbert was a very low ex-Army one that was used for seals. Slippery Sam was shod with stainless steel and ran well in wet snow. Tigger, the Jabberwock, and Winnie-the-Pooh were due to go on the long trips.

My job as British observer in the long American sledge trip meant that I had to spend a good deal of time in their huts sorting through the equipment that we were due to take. Bob Nicolls was to lead the party, Bob Dodson and Art Owen were to be surveyor and dog driver respectively, and I, though merely observer was the only one who had ever sledged before!

Every time the question of equipment came up I had to analyse the item. Should I be party to taking equipment, the 1940-type tent which had failed on the plateau for instance, which quite obviously wasn't worth taking, and in so doing wreck all chances of completing the journey? Should I use a sledge that had twice broken on local trips, purely because it was American, in preference to my own which I knew? Should I use "windproof" clothes which experience showed were not windproof, and as a result endure a journey of misery and discomfort, or should I take my own?

I think that before we were due to leave I had managed to reach a compromise between my own sense of security for the party and my sense of obligation to Ken to try out American equipment and ideas. Bob Nicolls always took these problems very seriously and every item's merits and demerits would be discussed for hours. I finally insisted on planning to take my own sledge and my own tent, and I made it clear that, if in the course of our journey any items failed I could replace them with my own, which were to be carried as spares for general use by the whole party. In rations, dog food, and method of camping I would abide by their ways. I made one mistake, and that was in assuming that I could find somewhere "instructions" similar to ours, which could act as a guide to American travelling methods. Nowhere did there seem to be a screed, corresponding to ours, which could state clearly "This is how it was done before".

The American dog team which was to go on the west coast trip numbered fifteen, and Ken had promised that mine should number eleven. I managed to train Winnie and Joe, a couple of rather frightened pups, to run with my team, and as a last pair had a fine old stager named Snipe with the laziest dog at base, Roger, running beside him. Almost every afternoon I would take them out on the ice, often with Harry Darlington's wife Jinny as passenger. After a mile or two I would turn the whole team over to her and walk back to base to go on with my work. She obviously enjoyed it and it saved me a great deal of time, the dogs enjoyed it, and I was always very grateful to her. The team always behaved: maybe they enjoyed hearing the words of command in so feminine a voice.

The American dogs, however, were not doing so well. Always there seemed to me to be too much advice and too little practical help. Bob Dodson and Art Owen put in untold work with them, and often I would arrange to meet their team with mine out on the sea-ice, well out of sight of base, to see if they would pull better when following in my wake. I think one of their difficulties was their lack of whip. If a dog misbehaved all that they could do was to walk in among the dogs and wallop him in person, while the others tended to cringe away, wondering when their turn was coming. We always found that with a long whip a dog that is slacking can be reminded immediately that he has been noticed. I have heard folk say that a whip is cruel; as we used it I know it wasn't. It rarely touched the dog, and in the main it was the sound that reminded it of its duty. Another thing that their dogs never seemed to learn was to jerk as a team when the sledge was stuck. Instead of jumping forward on the command "huit", as ours did, and lunging into their harnesses, they would all leap vertically upwards, with no attempts at a unanimous forward jerk. Commander Ronne disapproved of our habit of tethering our dogs out in the open all the time, and early on built an enormous underground shelter covered with canvas. We called it "Dog Heaven" and his dogs lived there in warmth and luxury, bedded in the hay that had been bought for the llamas. As a result they never had the benefit of watching other dogs work in the way that ours did.

Quite naturally too their general driving trace was based on the centre trace method that is so necessary and popular in North America. The complete set of traces and harnesses for the fifteen-dog team was a complicated and heavy affair, and it was slow and wearying to assemble.

The Americans always carry their sledge loads inside a canvas tank, so I had to make one for my sledge. It seemed to have much in its favour, for our loads, though both secure and flexible, often looked like a travelling tinker's cart.

Tommy and Dave meanwhile had been having most excellent results with the Auster aircraft. The ski which had been brought by the *Trepassey* had proved an enormous success and the addition of a small tail ski in place of the skid was immediately successful.

Tommy and Dave obviously aimed to run the aircraft with as little fuss and bother as possible. They knew how much reliance we were placing on its performance, but realised that if we had to spend long hours in the cold slipstream hanging on to a wing tip waiting for it to take off, or helping to manœuvre it in and out of the hangar, we would rapidly come to dislike the aircraft intensely. The fact that we had a hangar from which we could operate gave us an enormous advantage over the Norseman and the L.5 over the hill.

If the weather looked at all possible for flying, and Tommy quite rightly would only fly in settled conditions, Dave would put the four-gallon drum of engine oil on top of the kitchen stove to warm. He and Tommy would wander up to the hangar and free all the doors of ice, and remove any drift that was necessary from the way of the skis. Often the hangar doors would be half covered with snow, but it didn't matter because they all opened inwards and as it was a high-winged monoplane it was easy to dig troughs through the drift as ramps for the landing ski and then haul the aircraft out with a block and tackle. Dave would then do all the necessary daily checks, and by that time the decision to fly would have been made, and the oil would be warm. With warm oil in the tank two or three swings of the propeller would usually start the engine, and after a few minutes' warming up Tommy would be ready to take off.

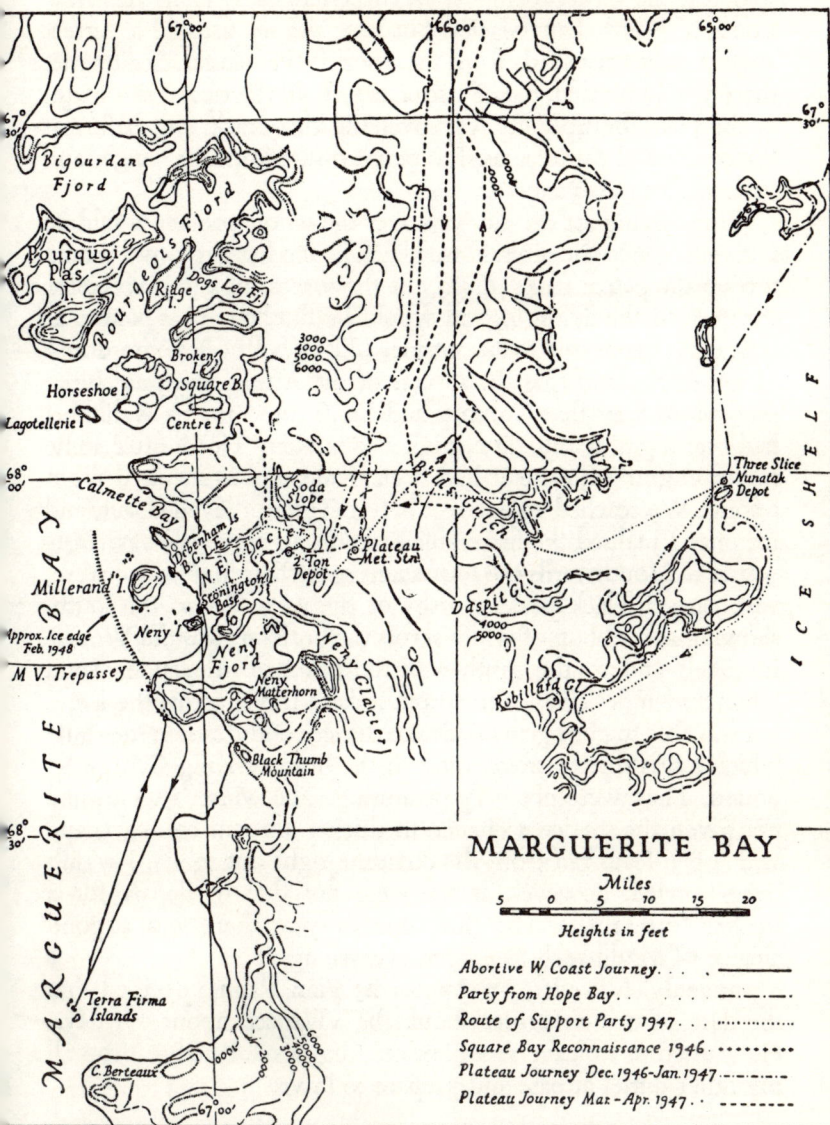

MARGUERITE BAY

Miles

5   0   5   10   15   20

Heights in feet

Abortive W. Coast Journey . . . . ————
Party from Hope Bay . . . —·—·—·—
Route of Support Party 1947 . . . ············
Square Bay Reconnaissance 1946 ·●·●·●·●
Plateau Journey Dec. 1946–Jan. 1947 ·–··–··–·
Plateau Journey Mar.–Apr. 1947 · · – – – – – –

Bigourdan Fjord
Pourquoi Pas I.
Bourgeois Fjord
Dogs Leg F.
Ridge
Broken I.
Square B.
Horseshoe I.
Lagotellerie I.
Centre I.
Calmette Bay
Soda Slope
Debenham Is.
B.G.L.E.
N. E. Glacier
Stonington I.
Base
2 Ton Depot
Plateau Met. Stn.
Millerand I.
Neny I.
Approx. Ice edge Feb. 1948
M.V. Trepassey
Neny Fjord
Neny Matterhorn
Neny Glacier
Black Thumb Mountain
Terra Firma Islands
C. Berteaux
Dashit G.
Rubillard
The Gullet
Three Slice Nunatak Depot
ICE SHELF
MARGUERITE BAY

3000 4000 5000 6000
4000 5000
2000 3000 6000

67° 00'
66° 00'
65° 00'
67° 30'
68° 00'
68° 30'
67° 00'

A detailed map of the Marguerite Bay area of Graham Land showing the
various journeys undertaken during 1946–47

Before the sea-ice formed it was necessary to fly from the lower slopes of North-East Glacier, but later the sea formed a perfect airstrip only fifty yards from the door of the hangar. Sometimes there would be a couple of assistants to hold the tips of the wings as the plane bumped its way over the tide-crack, but before it finally crashed Tommy used to taxi it down from the hangar and back without assistance.

When flying for the day was over the whole process would be reversed. Once the aircraft was back in the hangar Dave would top up the petrol tanks, drain out the warm oil and, except for completing the flying log, all would be finished. That picture at least is as it appeared to an outsider like myself. I have no doubt in my own mind that the success of the Auster was due to the meticulous way that Tommy and Dave cared for its welfare. I had one flight at this time, high above Neny Fjord, after some minor engine adjustment had been made, and it required flight testing. We reached 10,000 feet before Tommy levelled out, and for once I realised the incredible scale of our surroundings. Eastwards and southwards the mountains seemed as high as we were, vast, jagged, black peaks worthy of the Alps. Far to the south, showing as a ribbon of white across the horizon, was the Wordie Ice Shelf and to the south-west the peaks of Alexander Land a hundred miles away seemed but a day's travel across the ice.

I was able to get a general idea of the ice conditions on the route which I was due to travel over to the head of King George VI Sound. They were not very promising. The winter's winds had not given the sea-ice a chance to thicken up and compact, and wide open leads ran from the coastline right out to sea. I wasn't over-worried, however, as we were not due to depart for a further fortnight, and at this time of year there was a good chance of a cold spell to harden everything up.

Suddenly, however, on August 25 Finn Ronne decided that the date of our departure should be advanced about ten days. He wanted us to leave at 2 p.m. on August 28. I had to drop all my other duties at base and prepare to leave.

CHAPTER 13

The West Coast Journey that Returned

FROM the time that I had been appointed as observer to the west coast journey, I was allowed to take an active interest in the operational details that were to cover that trip. In mid-July several of us had been over to Commander Ronne's private shack to see the plans for the journey sketched out in the form of a chart on a large piece of paper. Briefly they were these.

A sledge party of four, of which I was to be a member, with twenty-five dogs and three sledges would leave base on September 5, and were to travel southwards on the sea-ice to the head of King George VI Sound.

About ten days after the party had left base the Weasels were to follow pulling loads of aircraft petrol, fuel, and sledge rations and would, all being well, have caught us up by the time we were ready to find our way on to the high level ice of the sound itself.

We, being a more mobile party, would prospect the way up on to the sound and the Weasels would follow, and then, between us, we would relay loads down the full length of the sound to the point where it turns to the west, some 150 miles further south. The Norseman, would, by this time, have flown a good deal of equipment southwards as well, so that a large cache of aviation petrol, food, and dog food could be established at a point corresponding to the furthest point south reached by Stephenson on the fine exploratory journey he did with the B.G.L.E. From here the sledge party was to proceed alone over the plateau with twenty days' food to arrive at Mount Tricorn, which was on the east coast some 200 miles away, and they would there receive further supplies by air to help them continue the journey southwards. They would be in the region as a rescue party for the proposed flights by the Beechcraft to the southern tip of the Weddell Sea; the sledge party would then return by the same route back to Stonington Island, a round trip of some 1,400 miles. I couldn't help admiring the way that the operations chart had been plotted out. Commander Ronne was always able to calculate the cost, in terms of petrol used, to place a gallon of petrol or so many pounds of supplies at any point on the route. For example, he knew that it would cost seven gallons of aviation petrol to put 15 lb. of rations at Mount Tricorn, or, again, four gallons to put the same weight at the southern end of the sound. We in our base tended to plan too little and it was a change to see it taken to the other extreme. But in the light of Commander Ronne's previous experience in Antarctica I often felt he had left out one point, that Antarctica is quite unpredictable. Our brief experience of this area of the Antarctic was that it had a distinct will of its own. As an adversary it never stopped fighting; if it was beaten in the first round when wind and blizzards were its weapons, it would change its tactics, and a strategic shift of the sea-ice or a sudden rise in temperature at the crucial moment would put the best laid plans in the dustbin. Commander Ronne knew, too, that as a party we were, in general, thoroughly inexperienced; and though I felt at the time, and still feel, that the rate at which he reckoned the sledges would march was not unreasonable, yet it could only be maintained by a very strong party, with well-trained dogs and good conditions. The Weasels, too, were quite unpredictable, and too much reliance had been placed on their performance in view of the fact that there was considerable doubt if they would perform in the local travel conditions at all. Little was known about their behaviour over bad sea-ice or among areas of crevassing, and their fuel consumption was based entirely on guesswork. I managed to keep most of these doubts to myself, and put all I had into making the preparations for the journey as successful as was possible, for I knew it would probably be the biggest chance that I would ever have.

All the preparations in August had gone well. The Weasels had been carefully converted by Larry Fiske and were now fitted with saloon bodies with bunks. Trailer sledges had been prepared, using some old sledges from the Debenham Islands, lashed side by side. Larry Fiske had gone to endless trouble to sort out his cooking gear, and to work out all the details of life with a Weasel as both transport and shelter. The unreasonable advancement of our departure date meant that all these preparations had to be hurried up. In spite of this by August 28 both the Weasels and the sledge party could be considered more or less ready. We, the sledgers, consisting of Bob Nicolls, Bob Dodson, Art Owen, and myself, were to leave on the 28th and Larry Fiske with Walter Wood, the ship's navigator, stood by to follow later with only one Weasel and about a ton and a half of load.

As far as I could see, John Tonkin was unlikely to get a chance of leaving base again, for Ken had decided to take command of the east coast party himself, so I obtained permission for John to accompany us for ten days with his team of dogs to help us carry our heavy loads.

I felt that his moral support for that period would be quite invaluable, and the relative experience of the whole party would be greatly increased. We delayed a day to give him a chance to get ready, but Commander Ronne insisted that at 2 p.m. on August 29 we must be ready to leave. I couldn't understand the purpose behind his adamant inflexible decision to send us out on a 100-day journey in the early afternoon, for it was quite obvious that with sunset at 4 p.m. we would not get much further than Neny Island before we would have to camp.

On the night of the 28th I put the point to Commander Ronne that an afternoon start was quite absurd, and he very unwillingly agreed to allow us to leave at crack of dawn on the 30th on condition that we staged a dress rehearsal of our departure on the 29th for the benefit of the photographers. The dress rehearsal gave me an immense amount of inward amusement, for I knew that once we were in the field my team would have to take the lead, as the American dogs refused to pull without another team ahead of them. The photographs taken during that dress rehearsal reversed this procedure, for they showed my fine team following the Americans out across the sea-ice and round the offshore point until we were lost to view, and I could pull out to the lead, unnoticed in the vastness of Neny Fjord.

In one thing I was very lucky, however. Ever since the 25th I had asked for a reconnaissance flight southwards along the line of our proposed route, but for various unconvincing reasons the aircraft were always busy elsewhere. It seemed to me to be a wise precaution, just to give us an idea of the actual ice conditions that we could expect. Tommy agreed with me, but was very busy with the Auster flying ration boxes to the plateau and felt it was an American commitment. On the morning of the 28th the cloud ceiling was 5,000 feet so he couldn't fly to the plateau and decided that this was his chance. He popped me into the back of the Auster and took me for a long reconnaissance flight southwards, well below cloud level, along the first seventy miles of our future route. Ice conditions were better than they had been during the previous week. The leads that had crossed our proposed track were now gone, but open water was a lot closer inshore than I would have wished. If there was a good blow from the east it looked as if the whole lot would go out to sea.

The story of this journey, and why we had to turn back, is best told from my diary.

August 30. Left at 10 a.m. with John Tonkin and Nelson Maclary in company to help for the first ten days. They have a nine-dog team with Darkie in the lead. Bob Dodson is running fifteen dogs and I have my eleven. John has 600 lb. of food; Bob and I both have 900. Bob Nicolls fell through the sea-ice just before lunch when he took off his skis to go to the assistance of John, whose dogs were swimming in slush. He doesn't qualify for the Antarctic Swimming Club because he wasn't wet above the waist. We are camped at the Refuge Islands, five miles south of Red Rock Ridge, and had a heavy haul for the last three miles over ice only one and a half inches thick that was caked with salt. The tent set-up is not as I should like it, and certainly isn't as good as it appeared when we tried it last week. (I had had to put my foot down finally the week before, and in spite of Commander Ronne's wishes refused to take more than one of the type of tent that had been carried away on the plateau a few weeks previously.)

My own British pyramid tent is acting as a windbreaker, and the blue American tent, which has a sleeve at both ends, is connected direct with our entrance. At present all the cooking is being done in the other tent, while we live in luxury and dry our clothes. I haven't finished my pemmican to-night; it seems too greasy for me at this stage of the journey.

Lively, who is running in Roger's place, has an enormous poisoned cheek, but I lanced it with a pen-knife and drained off about half a pint of fluid before I came in.

August 31. This has been a sad day. We started so well on hard ice, and covered two miles in forty minutes with full loads when John's team started a fight and Jeff had his paw very badly bitten. John realised at once that he would have to go back to base and give Jeff a chance to mend up in time for the east coast trip, which starts next week. So he offloaded his sledge and put the extra on to mine. There were tears in my eyes when he left, I had been relying on him rather more than I realised for his cheerful moral support at the start of this trip.

He gave me all his Kendal mint cake and the rest of his tea, and in ten minutes the incident was over and he was gone. My sledge was now too heavily loaded, and though I could ride on the surface on my skis, the sledge continually broke through to the slush beneath. We had to zigzag through broken ice and camped after about seven miles. I managed to finish off my share of pemmican to-night, but the grease wasn't easy, and is still all over my palate.

(The American rations have hardly been mentioned yet. In terms of weight per day they represented about thirty-three ounces, and the main proportions were the same as ours. The whole ration is packed in thirty-day sacks with all the items either in tins, greased paper, or cotton bags. Pemmican is in $\frac{3}{4}$-lb. blocks, and is very much stronger than ours and a good deal more greasy. In taste it reminded me rather of Hamburger steak without the onions: biscuits were not unlike English scones, though rather dry and stale; they soaked out well when immersed in bouillon. I never succeeded in getting the exact daily figure, but I think it was:

Pemmican	12 oz.
Biscuits	5 oz.
Porridge	4 oz.
Butter	4 oz.
Chocolate	3 oz.
Klim milk	2 oz.
Sugar	3 oz.

Plus a whole lot of delightful luxuries such as dried fruit, bouillon cubes, boiled sweets, life-savers, and lemon crystals. As a ration it failed, I felt, by being packed in sacks, with inadequate protection against wet and weather. The pemmican ration at twelve ounces was too large in view of the fact that it was extraordinary hard to stomach. I had a sneaking feeling that it had a laxative as one of its seventeen ingredients, but could never get it confirmed by the American cook, Sig Gutenko. In any case it behaved as if it had.)

September 1. We only made six miles to-day with surfaces that slowly improved and visibility that rapidly worsened. We were quite unable to keep good direction because of the broken ice and continually had to change course to avoid open leads. We are camped on a large pan, about one acre in size and approximately twelve inches thick. Just as we tethered the dogs a seal came out, so I dispatched it and fed it to the dogs. We've been eating the heart fried in butter for supper. The whole surface of the snow seems to be floating on eighteen inches of salt-water slush and my hard-soled American ski boots are soaked right through. It is not surprising, since they don't reach above the ankles and we are often in slush up to our knees. This tent set-up is getting worse every night. It is quite impossible to get our tent warm because we keep opening the door to get our food from next door; Art Owen is quite obviously very hard pushed to warm and cook the meal for four of us in the other tent, and I rather suspect he is still sitting around in wet clothes. Travel conditions are not bad, yet I haven't been so uncomfortable when out sledging before: it is all so very unnecessary.

September 2. We made nearly seven miles to-day with my load still bogging down all the time. The others did much better in this respect than I did with their load of 1,100 lb. on two sledges one ahead of the other, for in their case both sledges remained on the surface: their dogs, however, are not doing so well. There seems to be no ability to jerk a sledge when it gets really stuck. Bob Dodson and Art take a fearful beating because the united jerk that is required comes from them, instead of from the dogs. I think I will discard my hard American ski boots at the earliest opportunity, I seem quite unable to get my feet dry and long for my own sealskin ones. Only ate half the pemmican to-night and feel very, very hungry.

September 3. We lay put with the wind gradually increasing and backing round to the east. As a result, lying up is rather an anxiety for we are in the area where a B.G.L.E. party was nearly taken out to sea and had to abandon their tractor in 1936. Dog feeding to-night was very hectic as the American tether came adrift and all fifteen dogs started a fight. The brickettes of dog food made from dog meal and seal oil started to crumble and to-night I fed my team with handfuls of crumbs distributed on a shovel, but they didn't enjoy it.

September 4. The lie up continues with increasing wind and strange shudders which must be the edge of the fast-ice being crushed. I discussed plans for a hurried evacuation of the camp if the ice starts to break up. My sledge is drifted right up since I was unable to unload its canvas tank and turn it upside down as is our usual practice. Bob Nicolls and Art Owen sound miserable. The wet has come up through their groundsheet and their bags are obviously very wet and cold. The single-layer tent gives them little protection in this driving wind.

September 5. The strange ice noises continued all day, and the temperature rose in the morning to plus 31° F. from zero. We are very comfortable in our tent, so Bob and Art have just been in to get warm and we discussed the problem of proceeding or not. I am convinced that we must go back, re-sort our equipment, and get the American dogs working as a team. Already I am having to overload my dogs because the others cannot pull their share of the load, and this is not right for the start of a 1,400-mile journey. Bob feels that our re-equipment problems can be sorted out when the aircraft arrives, but quite agrees about the dogs. Art made contact with base on the wireless, told them that we were coming back, and closed down before they could reply. He also made it clear that this was no place for Weasels to follow. Art passed in a fry-up of bacon a short while ago which was excellent. I'll swear this pemmican has a laxative in it. Life in that respect is rather uncomfortable.

September 7. Before we left the camp site this morning I walked round the fast-ice. It had shrunk in size by nearly half, and was about forty yards across. The crushing noise was, in fact, the edges of the ice grinding together, and Bouncer who was asleep on flat ice yesterday was up on a mound of crushed and broken ice this morning. We headed back towards Refuge Islands and the wind gradually increased. We decided to push on until we could camp on the islands for security, so that we could have a night's rest free from worry. Wind is offshore, at about thirty-five knots, and we made camp on the southernmost island in the dark.

September 8. The drift was still blowing from the shore when we left, and I set course for Red Rock Ridge. Both Bob and I wanted to turn further westwards but the compass quite firmly told us we were wrong. We stuck to the compass course and to our astonishment after five miles came out exactly where we wanted. Around Red Rock Ridge the ice was even thinner than on the outward trip, but improved in Neny Fjord where we came across Larry Fiske in the Weasel. Apparently Commander Ronne had sent him out to turn us back. We plugged on and arrived at base at four o'clock in time for tea.

We saw Finn Ronne that evening and pointed out the reasons for our return; he took it very badly, and later, in his book, he took pains to accuse me of being the reason for this failure, as I had "talked Bob Nicolls out of his resolve to go on". Whatever he may think, for me that decision to return was one of the bitterest moments in my life. For years I had dreamed and longed for the chance to do a long and efficient polar journey. This was my first, and probably my last chance. I had learnt from the experience of others that an inefficient journey is less than valueless. We had failed because we were inadequately equipped, and because of this we decided that it was unwise to cope with the condition of the sea-ice that our early departure gave us. When we turned back I suspected (and air reconnaissance later proved I was correct) that ice conditions southwards were worsening. Had we gone on we would have travelled without the modest safety factor that all experienced sledgers should expect.

It was a failure, but at the same time was the same sort of failure that makes a mountaineer turn back on a mountain, even though everything in him is wanting to go on. To attempt to put the blame for failure on any one of us shows, I feel, lack of judgment and understanding of Antarctic life and travel. The reason for our return lay deeper than that. I think it was tied up with the different point of view between Ronne's attitude to polar travel and ours.

I know I learned many lessons. I was the first member of F.I.D.S. at Base E to travel on the sea-ice and was painfully aware of my inexperience. Because of Finn Ronne's sudden decision to make us leave a fortnight ahead of schedule, we were too early in the season for safety, and the condition of the ice could have been seen by a cursory air inspection before we started. The decision to turn back compares well with the experienced B.G.L.E.'s return in very similar conditions in 1936. I certainly had learnt the limitation of sea-ice travel. In some ways I had profited for I had watched with admiration the way two sledges, one behind the other could be handled with heavy loads. I had initially admired, yet soon learnt to loathe, the sledge tank method of loading. I had learnt by the hard way the snags of poorly evolved rations and thoroughly inadequate equipment.

Of one thing I am very certain, that under the trying conditions I owe much to the kindliness and tolerance of the three Americans, to me, a stranger in their midst.

Our sad return meant an entire revision of plans for the summer journeys, and it wasn't long before they were produced by Ken and Commander Ronne.

The proposed 1,400-mile west coast journey was definitely abandoned and instead Commander Ronne decided to let Bob Nicolls and Bob Dodson do a much shorter geological trip southwards on the sea-ice to the entrance of King George VI Sound: this journey was to be relatively self-contained and the only air support that it would receive was a large depot 130 miles from base. Nicolls had asked to be allowed to spend a hundred days in the field, and his loads, as a result, would be heavy so Commander Ronne agreed to let them have a Weasel for assistance in the earlier stages.

For me my chance of a good journey was over, but I resolved to do all I could to give Bob Nicolls and Bob Dodson their chance on the next venture towards the south.

The events recorded in the next chapter delayed the start of this geological trip, and it wasn't until September 27 that I could implement this resolve, when Doc Butson and I left base for a fortnight in support of Nicolls and Dodson.

The support journey was a success, for although it covered much of the route on which we had turned back three weeks previously, the two Americans had revised their equipment considerably, had British tents and sledges, and were able to make much better progress.

It was one of the happiest journeys during my two years in Antarctica; conditions were never easy and the sea-ice was alarmingly thin in many parts. I felt strongly that it vindicated the attitude to polar travel, that only journeys which are adequately and sensibly prepared deserve to succeed.

CHAPTER 14

The Loss of the Aircraft

OUR return on September 8 and the abandonment of the 1,400-mile west coast trip meant that plans for the east coast journey had to be considerably revised. Now the party would consist of four with three sledges and twenty-seven dogs, and it would be covered by the whole weight of air support.

For this journey at least three depots would be laid; the first at the weather station which was soon to be established on the plateau, the next at Cape Keeler about 150 miles further away on the east coast, and the third in the region of Mount Tricorn. When once it was at its furthest south this party would act as rescue party if anything should go wrong with the long-range exploratory flights to the southern end of the Weddell Sea. The party were to travel entirely with well-tried British equipment, would use British dogs, and would eat British rations throughout. Ken Butler was to be the leader, Reg Freeman the surveyor, and the American members would be Nelson Maclary (Mac) and Art Owen. This meant that at least one dog team would have to be driven and managed by the Americans. Of all the "Folk over the Hill" Mac alone seemed prepared to handle our dogs in the way that we expected. He had endless patience with animals, and it was a delight to see the way he got down to the job of getting to know the Paddie Darkie team that would be his for the long trip. He seemed to sense how very sad John Tonkin must have felt at seeing his own team prepare for a long journey in which he himself could take no part, and was ever appreciative of their excellent and still improving performances. He would come over daily and take the dogs out for a ten-mile practice run on the sea-ice, and then help John feed them at the end of the day.

Plans for a weather station on the plateau had been in hand for a long time, for we felt that it might provide a very useful link between the weather on the east and west coast when the long-range flying started. Ken MacLeod was to be the British member and Wood (Woodie), an American Merchant Service officer, was to accompany him. By September 10, Tommy and Chuck Adams between them had completed the establishment of the station, and deposited a large depot of sledge rations alongside the tent for use by the east coast party when they passed through three weeks later.

Chuck Adams very nearly had a bad mishap, for as he left the depot for the last time he walked straight into the propeller of his aircraft which was ticking over to keep the engine warm. Luck was with him, and he stopped just in time and sustained only a two-inch cut and a bad headache.

Once this plateau depot had been laid the next job was to put in the second in the region of Cape Keeler on the east coast, about 150 miles from base. For this trip it was a case of waiting patiently until weather conditions seemed sufficiently quiet to justify such a long flight. The scheme was for the Norseman to be the load-carrying aircraft and for the Auster to accompany her. The plan was for the Auster to take off first and climb above base to a height that was sufficient for Tommy to see away across the plateau from where he could judge the weather conditions on the eastern side. When once this had been done the Norseman would take off and they would fly in company across the plateau to the region of Cape Keeler on the far side of the peninsula. Tommy, in "Ice-Cold Katy", as we had named our aircraft, would look for a landing, land, and then lay out a flight strip with flags and smoke flares to guide in the Norseman. One point, however, differed from normal, in that the Auster would only carry a minimum of safety equipment, and the bulk of this would be carried by the Norseman for parachuting to Tommy in case of emergency. The safety of the trip depended on both aircraft keeping close company and careful adherence to pre-arranged plans.

We were still having lunch on September 15 when Commander Ronne rushed over to say that the weather looked better and the Norseman would be ready for take-off in a few minutes, and all was set for the trip to lay the Cape Keeler depot. Twenty minutes later, in record time, Tommy, Reg, and Bernard were in the air in Ice-Cold Katy and climbed high over base to see if the far coast was free of cloud. They carried a small wireless transmitter for talking with the Norseman, and they would use it to base until the range became too great. In spite of the hurry it was not until two and a quarter hours later that the Norseman was airborne. Time was getting short, and Tommy had to decide whether to proceed without the comforting company of the Norseman, or to call the whole trip off. He decided to go on, and somewhere above the plateau Met station he reported by wireless that he was going to Cape Keeler and asked the Norseman to follow. At 7 p.m. the Norseman was back at base, but had seen no signs of Tommy. The weather closed in with a bang, the wind and drift got up, and we knew that wherever the Auster was, it would be an uncomfortable night for the three flyers. We slept listlessly, and all hope of flying at dawn dropped as the wind rattled round the hut and increased in fury. We had two full days of non-flying weather, which gave time to draw up a detailed scheme for search and rescue. There were several possibilities as to the whereabouts of Ice-Cold Katy. First, it had landed at the pre-arranged place and been missed, and, as the weather had worsened, Tommy had decided to stay where he was rather than risk the plateau crossing unaccompanied. If this had happened, the first flight to Cape Keeler would find him. Secondly, he had landed, been missed, and decided to return to base alone, and had been forced down by bad weather *en route*. Thirdly, he had force-landed on the outward journey with engine trouble between the Met station and Cape Keeler. This was not likely since he had plenty of height when he was above the plateau and could have glided towards base, besides which we had too much faith in Dave Jones to consider engine failure seriously. If it was the second possibility, the route of his return would be dictated by weather, and was unknown. On Thursday, the 18th, Lassiter and Adams had a full day's flying up and down the east coast to see if the Auster was still grounded, but saw no signs of them; that evening we could at least mark areas of the map as "searched". For the whole of that day the drift snow at the plateau lip was quite spectacular, for it was blowing in an enormous plume several thousand feet into the air. For the aircraft, taking-off was proving difficult for there was still plenty of wind at base, and landing

might easily become impossible in their absence. On the other
hand on the east coast it was calm and clear with bright sun. It
was decided as a result to form an advanced base on the east coast
from which the L.5 could make search flights unhampered by
the vagaries of the Neny Fjord weather.

On the 19th John Tonkin, Duggie Mason, and Art Owen were
flown across to Cape Keeper to set up a base and a wireless
station from which the L.5 could fly unhampered. By the end of
the day we were able to write off even more sections of the map
as "searched". On the 20th and 21st it was blowing hard on our
coast, but still clear and calm with John Tonkin at Cape Keeler.
Chuck Adams made repeated attempts to get to them across the
plateau, but each time was tossed back like an autumn leaf. Once
we watched him climb to 9,000 feet and head out over the
plateau and saw him drop like a stone in a downdraught at the
plateau edge and skim out only just clear of the rugged mountains. I couldn't help admiring those two American pilots, Adams
and Lassiter. They realised more than any civilian could what
were the hazards of flying in those conditions and yet were still
prepared to have a go. It was courage of the kind that knows
what it is in for and still goes on, courage of the finest and
highest type. Late in the afternoon of the 21st the weather eased
back, and I went over to Cape Keeler in the Norseman with
more fuel and camp equipment.

We scanned the country beneath as we flew and my memories
of that flight are twofold. One was the awful realisation that the
whole stretch of country was twice as rough as I had imagined
it ever could be, and I knew then what little chance Tommy
would have if things went wrong with the Auster in mid-air and
they had crashed. The other was a purely material one. We
carried in the Norseman forty-gallon drums of petrol and there
were three of us lying full length on top of them as we peered
out of the small side windows. As we climbed so the atmospheric
pressure reduced, and the ends clanged outwards with a noise
that reverberated round the confines of the aircraft and made us
all reach for the emergency door and our parachutes.

Once we had arrived, we set to and built an enormous igloo,
installed the wireless inside, and used the call sign "Radio City".
On the 22nd it was still clear and windless for us at Radio City,

but at base in Marguerite Bay the wind was stronger than ever before. There was no flying. It was depressing for us lying warm in our sleeping bags knowing that somewhere, we knew not where, but probably within fifty miles, Tommy, Reg, and Bernard were cold and weary and at the end of their resources. Dave, with more fuel and equipment, arrived at Cape Keeler on the 22nd to service the aircraft, and John returned to base to discuss plans with Ken; at midday to our horror the B.B.C. broadcast a report about the missing aircraft while the outcome was still unknown. On the way home, using rather a southern route, Jim Lassiter suddenly spotted Tommy, Reg, and Bernard on the sea-ice a few miles short of the Refuge Islands on the west coast, slowly making their way home. He landed and picked them up, but the way we received the news was quite dramatic and is best brought out if I quote from my diary.

"Dave and I were in the tent listening to the B.B.C., while in the igloo next door Duggie was talking to base and Chuck Adams cranked the handle of the portable generator which supplied the transmitter.

Almost at the same time as the B.B.C. announcer read the words, 'The aircraft is still missing', we heard the shout from next door 'They are safe!' Chuck apparently forgot what he was doing and stopped cranking and immediately leapt up to shake Duggie's hand, and Dave and I unashamedly wept for joy.

By 7.30 we had all been flown back to base, Radio City had closed down, and we could piece together the whole story.

There is no feeling quite able to describe the one that is in me to-night. It is more than relief for I know I had given up all hope of seeing them alive again. The word resurrection is part of what is in my mind."

Apparently on the fateful day they had landed at the rendezvous, but the Norseman had missed the smoke flares. After an hour they decided to go back to base. By this time the normal route over the plateau was quite impossible, for the wind was funnelling down the glacier and Ice-Cold Katy could not make any headway, so they had to turn south and cross the plateau, where it was lower, intending to drop to sea-level and iceberg-hop their way back to base. It was dark when they reached the sea-ice on the west coast so Tommy decided to land and as he did so he touched a piece of iceberg with the ski and the aircraft overturned. The small transmitter was put out of action and the receiver could only tell them the tantalizing news, broadcast hourly, that we were searching the one area in which they were not. They pitched camp in the rising wind and waited till the next day. The actual story of the seventy-mile tramp back to base can never be completely told. Their assets were only the clothes they stood up in, a small tent, two sleeping bags, an ice axe, an alpine rope, petrol primus, seven pounds of pemmican, and some odd sweets. There were also two cine-cameras, not their own, my Leica, a wireless receiver, and a tank full of petrol. Ice conditions were the same as they had been on the previous week—a thin breakable crust covering two feet of watery slush. They had no ski or snow-shoes and couldn't walk without breaking through. Every step was a flounder and a struggle. They rationed themselves to three ounces of pemmican a day and struggled on, with high winds, driving snow, and very low temperatures. On the 23rd a seal popped up and they killed it with an ice axe, and then as they ate it the aircraft spotted them and they were safe.

That the three fliers were safe was most surely a miracle, and though the rescue was carried out on a calm day, in perfect flying conditions, tribute must be paid to the skill and courage of the American pilots, Lassiter and Adams, who were prepared to fly and search in conditions that would have grounded any normal pilot. That Tommy, Reg, and Bernard themselves had the pertinacity to go on in spite of all, is in keeping with the great tradition of endurance in polar travel. But as before it was necessary for us to investigate the reasons for the accident and to sort out our mistakes.

The flight as planned was a long one for the Auster to do, but it had proved itself in the previous few weeks and we felt that as long as it kept close company with the Norseman it was a reasonable journey to plan and carry through. From the start, however, this main condition could not be adhered to. That unnecessary two hours' delay between the take-off of the Auster and the Norseman forced Tommy to make decisions that he should never have been required to make. After two hours' flying he was lower in petrol than he would have liked, and was starting out later in the day than he wished; he had to decide whether to call the whole flight off, or to accept the lack of safety caused by the Norseman's absence, and go on to Cape Keeler in advance. He went ahead, landed, and was missed, partly due to inaccurate rendezvous navigation and partly due to the light colour of the Auster which was no contrast to the snow around. The same two hours' delay gave the Norseman less time to fly around to look for the landing-strip and it had to return without spotting him. Plans had never been thought out to cover this situation; from then on with one aircraft grounded and the other unable to find it, movements could only be guessed at. That Tommy could listen on the small receiver to our frantic search, and hear that our guesses as to his actual position were miles off the mark, was cold comfort when he knew that there was still seventy miles to walk.

Luck must always play a part in Antarctic life, in fact the life would not be complete without it; but just as in the case of Petersen and Bob Dodson on the plateau, Tommy's decision to continue flying started a train of events in which luck was ever against him. And the situation, in which that fatal decision had to be made, could have been avoided, if the original plan had not been brushed aside in the hurry to take off. In the war the destroyer *Onslow*, in which I served, had the motto *Festina Lente*, and we often translated it as "Hurry up but don't be messed around". It is a pity that it wasn't the motto of Ice-Cold Katy.

Though we now had no aircraft of our own, we did learn several things which went down in our log of experience. We learned that no matter how sketchy safety equipment is, it must include some form of ski or snow-shoes above almost anything else. We learned that if a wireless transmitter is to be carried, it must be a powerful and reliable one (a thing which we didn't possess), and that a poor one is a liability. We learned that light aircraft can only gain safety from each other if they know the responsibilities towards each other from take-off to touch-down, and we learned once again the treachery of our brand of Antarctic weather.

CHAPTER 15

The Completion of the Two Main Journeys

WE HAD had our fair share of accidents and disappointments, and it was high time to start the two main journeys which were to be the climax of the year's work. The main southern party could not leave until the Cape Keeler depot was complete, and the Hope Bay party could not leave until their depot beside the nunatak on the east coast ice shelf was actually in position. The full story of these two well-executed journeys is not mine to tell, for I spent the greater part of the time at base. They are, however, the stories of journeys, the work well planned from the start, that left very little to chance, and their success provided an adequate reward for all our labours. From Base E the plan, in the first instance, was for Duggie, Ken, Nelson Maclary, and Don Maclean, the American doctor, to start from base in early October; Don, however, broke his ankle ski-ing and could not be considered, and after our return his place was taken by Art Owen. Ken Butler, meanwhile, had promised Commander Ronne to make his "picture by wireless" apparatus work so he arranged for Doc Butson to take his place for the difficult plateau crossing, and planned to change places with him by air at Cape Keeler. The party, which left on October 10, consisted of Duggie Mason as surveyor and in command, Doc Butson, Nelson Maclary, and Art Owen. Mason was driving John Tonkin's old team with Darkie in the lead, Doc took Ken's team and Mac had recently taken over the uproarious black and white team led by Nigger and Nero. They were excellent teams and the long rather lazy spring with plenty to eat and plenty of work meant that they were in excellent condition. The morning that they left was perfect except for a faint trace of snow drifting off the extreme edge of the plateau. Six hours later it was blowing a full fumigator and they remained tent-bound in our old camp site at the bottom of Sodabread slope. After three days, when they emerged at the end of the blow, they found the camp in a shambles; one sledge had been uprooted and was partly broken, several ration boxes had been burst open, and the contents strewn around. The smooth snow on which they had travelled up was gone, and instead it was cut and furrowed worse than they had ever experienced elsewhere. Duggie decided to return to base and collect a new sledge, and took Nelson Maclary with him. Within ten yards the sledge, like a fractious horse, had hit a snow-bank and had thrown Mac and he lay with a broken collar bone on the snow. He was put back in his sleeping bag; four hours later, at a time when we imagined they were on the plateau, Duggie and Art arrived back at base. For us there was a moment of distinct uneasiness, for a sudden return of this nature could only mean one thing—another crevasse episode.

The next day, on October 15, I drove my red team up to their camp with Andy Thompson, the quiet American physicist, and the partly recovered Don Maclean, and brought Mac back to base as a stretcher case lightly lashed to the top of my sledge; Andy remained to replace him for the trip up to the plateau.

It was a bitter blow to the party, and even more so to Mac, for he was an adaptable enthusiast, and had learnt to handle his dogs extremely well. However, Andy Thompson was a most excellent replacement; he was tall and whimsical with a wry sense of the absurd, probably the most intellectual of the Americans, and possessed of a reputation for physical prowess which might otherwise have passed unnoticed.

By the 17th they were on the plateau and at the depot, having used a combined team of about twenty-five dogs to pull the sledges up the steepest section. As soon as they reached the site of Two-Ton depot the cloud came down and they were left with a visibility of about ten yards. The name "Two Ton" was by then a misnomer, for there was very little of value left, and it was essential to get to the large depot at the weather station as soon as it was possible.

The route was known and free from danger, and in spite of the wind, the going was good so Dug hitched the tail of his sledge to the lead dog of the second sledge, and made the second sledge do the same, and happily drove Darkie, whom he couldn't see, on a set course towards the Met station. After the requisite number of miles they made camp, and four days later the weather cleared and the propeller of the Met station's wind generator was a few hundred yards away. But once again they had bad luck —Andy Thompson's knees gave out.

Andy could go no further and so remained at the Met station and Walter Wood took his place. The travellers picked up an enormous load of food, the portable wireless set, a lot of paraffin, and set course for Bills Gulch. At long last luck seems to have changed for they reached the ice-shelf very easily and from then on, in spite of the loads, made most excellent progress. Before they could set tracks for the next depot at Cape Keeler they had one job to do, and this was to lay a food depot close beside a prominent nunatak which was to be picked up by the party that would sledge southwards from Hope Bay. Until this had been actually put in position and reported by wireless, the northern party was not prepared to set out. With considerably depleted loads they made excellent progress and just nine days and 140 miles after leaving the plateau Met station they arrived at Cape Keeler.

Ken had flown in to replace Doc Butson, and "Smithy", an American surveyor, replaced Wood. This east coast depot had become quite a township with a permanent population of six or seven to fly or look after the various aircraft on their longer exploratory flights. From the sledge parties' point of view the handling of the aircraft seemed quite admirable. Whenever airborne they would keep contact with both the Cape Keeler advanced base and the party in the field and whenever they flew north or south over the sledge party they would land in and have a discussion. On one occasion, when the Norseman was flying a depot out, Lassiter landed and picked up Duggie so that he could site the depot where he wanted it to be 100 miles ahead of his camp and then returned him to the sledge party, who had travelled a further five miles south in his absence. If the sledge party wanted something they would tell us by wireless and some time in the next few days an aircraft would take it to Cape Keeler and from there it would be delivered to them in the field the same evening. Gradually a line of depots was laid southwards from Cape Keeler, and we knew that the line of retreat of the sledging party was always secure if by some obscure twist of circumstance all the aircraft support should stop.

The American portable wireless, the S.C.R. 694, was working most admirably under Ken's expert guidance, and by carefully selecting his frequencies and times he never missed a schedule in spite of the difficult conditions that existed. I remember on one occasion Finn tried to record Art Owen's voice from the furthest south position with the intention of relaying it back to the States.

For all this time the party had been travelling by night when the surfaces were hard, and had not missed a day's travel because of bad weather, an unheard of state of affairs on the west coast. At first the travel had been entirely on the ice shelf, but as they worked further south this gave way to enormous rifts, and they dropped down to the sea-ice where they were able to pick up fresh seals. In the meantime Ronne had been extremely busy; all the time that he was keeping the sledge party supplied he was leap-frogging his supplies of petrol and equipment further down the coast, using the Norseman and L.5 almost exclusively for cargo hauling.

With the Beechcraft he photographed as he went, and it was then that Bill Latady's winter work of setting up and testing the complicated Trimetrogon camera set-up really began to pay the dividends that we all learned to expect from so meticulous a craftsman. By the end of November the party was at Mount Tricorn, which was to have been the objective of the west coast party from King George VI Sound, and to their astonishment found it thirty miles out of position according to the 1940 American map. There was still plenty of food and time in hand, and so they pushed on southwards to "George Bryan Inlet", and waited there while Ronne passed over them to do his long-range exploratory flights to the southern tip of the Weddell Sea.

While the sledge party rested at their furthest south position Ronne, Bill, and Lassiter completed two very long flights, and as soon as these were finished the dog teams were allowed to turn for home.

The journey back was remarkable for the smoothness of its execution. Loads were light, and they had no difficulties at all in picking up their depots as they went. Each day we would hear of daily journeys of twenty-five to thirty miles in a total of six hours' travel, and stories of the fit dogs who thrived on their increased pemmican ration of 1¼lb. By early January they were at Cape Keeler and, striking a lucky gap in the weather, were able to cross the plateau as tirelessly as if they had still been travelling on the shelf ice. By mid-January they were back at base, with almost 1,200 miles of travel behind them in a period of ninety-one days away from base.

Compared with our normal journeys they were able to move very fast, for the aim of the trip was to provide a ground control for the air photographs and in that way to do a continuous and intricate strip ground survey. Duggie was able to produce quite a good map in spite of his rapid progress, and, in doing so, to correct the numerous mistakes on existing maps. From a material point of view they had done a good deal.

The method of carrying dog pemmican in canvas tanks had proved admirable, the more especially because the weight saved by not carrying boxes could be fed to the dogs in the form of pemmican and with this increased ration they never seemed to lose weight or fitness. The trick of icing the runners before each day's travel, which was a tip passed on by Finn Ronne, had paid very well for at the end of the 1,200 miles the runners were so little worn that they could have left at once and done the trip all over again.

Above all it showed what carefully worked out aircraft support can do to help a sledging party in the field. The wireless had, under Ken's guidance, become quite essential, and was by no means the burden that a badly handled one might become; it was an integral part of the success of the journey. The larger dog-teams undoubtedly made for greater mileages with far less effort; and the greater power up Sodabread slope, where they had used up to twenty-six dogs on a single sledge, was quite astonishing.

While this journey was progressing, we at base were very busy, for there was still plenty of work to do before we could go out on our last journey.

By October 20 Mason had established the depot near the Nunatak in Mobiloil Inlet on the east coast of ice shelf. He had been able to give us an accurate description of its location by wireless, and this we passed on to the Hope Bay party. There the news was being eagerly awaited, for all their plans for the year centred around the long sledge trip which was designed to link up with our work at Marguerite Bay. Until they knew that the depot had actually been established they could not leave, and each day they watched the conditions of sea-ice and snow around their base deteriorate. The party of four left Hope Bay at the end of October and were due to arrive four days after Christmas at the Nunatak depot. The job of those of us who remained at base was to cross the plateau and meet them, and then to act as a guide party back to Stonington Island.

Ken left us for Cape Keeler in early November, and Doc Butson returned about ten days later on the 22nd. He was thoroughly fed up and had longed to get back, for he had been living on the American sledging rations, and had found the pemmican even more indigestible than I had made it out to be. He remarked that he thought the weevils in the quaker oats provided a more reliable protein value than the pemmican itself, and told us, to our amusement that after four days' trial Finn Ronne himself had wirelessed back for some fresh frozen beefsteaks to be sent over.

There was still work for us at base. The local survey which Reg was trying to complete gave us endless excuses to exercise the dogs and to visit some of the very small offshore islands well out into the bay. Sometimes Bernard would come and dredge the small thaw pools for strange bugs and organisms and there was a small patch of grass, almost a yard square, which became affectionately known as the Neny cricket pitch.

Bill Latady came over with an English Driving Licence which had been his during the war when he was at Malvern with the American army, and asked for its official renewal by the British Magistrate. It was duly and quite officially renewed for the year 1948, though I am not sure what fee was charged, and I often longed to see the face of the licensing authority in England who, in 1949, must have been asked to renew a licence which read 'W. R. Latady is hereby licensed to ride penguins and seals solo, drive dog sledges, motor Weasels, and all other forms of polar transport". His driving licence number was Graham Land 1.

Doc and I went over to the Debenham Islands one evening to take some theodolite readings for Reg Freeman and to exercise my dogs. In the summer conditions this base seemed even more perfect than ever. We stood on the highest point of the islands looking down upon the hut. It was wonderfully sheltered by the surrounding crags, with everything handy for both sea or ice approach. No wonder Bingham loved the place.

At that time of year those long trips were always a great relief. There was no night and there was never any sense of hurry. If the evening were calm and pleasant we would stay out late and watch the sun as it dropped lower until it dodged behind the rock peaks on the south side of the fjord casting long finger-like shadows across the flatness of the sea-ice as it did so.

All good things have to come to an end some time, and at the end of November John and Reg had worked out our loads and the details of our last trip. We had two jobs; one was to meet the Hope Bay party at the Nunatak depot and escort them back to base, and the other was to reconnoitre a very promising glacier route which Mason had discovered in his various aircraft flights. If it were possible it would provide a long, gentle, and safe highway south and east from the area of the plateau Met station and it might well provide a better route to the ice shelf, entirely clear of the steep, difficult track via Bills Gulch. Four of us with sixteen dogs were detailed to take about one thousand pounds of food to the Met station, pick up Ken MacLeod, and Giorg di Giorgio, the Chilean member of Ronne's party who was now with him, and proceed from there to the Nunatak depot. There we were to leave a party of two, who would stand by to receive the party from Hope Bay and they would act as our wireless link with base, while the other four of us were to see if this new glacier was at all possible.

We left base on December 1, at about 10 o'clock at night and made very fast time to the Sodabread slope camp. The haul to the plateau went off very quickly; the sixteen dogs literally romped up with the half loads and we reached the top on the night of December 3 and set off for the weather station at once. Mac and Giorg di Giorgio had formed a very snug little abode for themselves under the snow. When we arrived the tent was under eight feet of snow and Mac appeared, after the style of Peter Pan, out of a hole in the ground covered with a trap-door. He had tunnelled quite considerably, as his demand for snow to melt for water had increased, and delighted in showing us round his catacombs. It was his hundredth day when we arrived and he had never missed a wireless schedule. We dug out and repaired the tent, so that when we left, the party was six strong, Reg as leader and surveyor, Tommy and myself as extra hands. Don Maclean, the American doctor, was with us to make up for the long trip he had missed when he broke his ankle, and Ken and Giorg completed the party.

As we reached the top of Bills Gulch I could see that conditions had vastly changed since our visit in the autumn. We had to decide if it was better to travel by sunlight when the strong shadows would show up the crevasses and enable us to avoid them, or by night when the crevasses which would then be almost invisible, but would be bridged strongly with frozen snow.

Reg had strong words with Giorg, for he would leave the security of the sledge and wander unroped to look over the lips of crevasses; he only came round to our way of thinking when he turned his sledge over and was pinned with his head over the edge of a crevasse for some minutes while Don Maclean photographed his plight.

We were on the ice shelf on December 12 and reached the Nunatak depot on the 13th, where we left Tommy and Ken MacLeod while we pushed on to reconnoitre the glacier.

To make the best of travel at night at this time of year takes accurate timing. There is probably not more than seven and a half hours in every twenty-four when the surface is hard frozen, and, as a result, it is necessary to break camp while the snow is still wet and slushy, and, as soon as it shows signs of hardening, move off. We never seemed to achieve this, and I have hard memories of the next few days trying to keep Rover on course in wet floundering snow at the end of a day's travel when I knew full well that if we had started a few hours' earlier it could have been avoided.

By the 27th we were back at the Nunatak depot, and satisfied that the new glacier route was quite definitely impossible. The Hope Bay party was due the next day, and we were doing pre-arranged nightly broadcasts on our portable transmitter to give them encouragement. In our absence Tommy had made up some sort of Christmas pudding, and we were all asked to partake of this luxury in his torn and rather smoky weather station tent. As he heated the pudding over the primus the plastic plate exploded and we were left to pick dollops of pudding from all over the inside with our spoons. The nights were pleasantly cold, but in the daytime, in the sun-warmed tent, I lay dressed in flannels and open shirt, dozing and dreaming of an English summer. We waited two days, distinctly anxious at the non-arrival of the party from Hope Bay, for we knew the difficulties of the plateau crossing, and were not very keen to leave them to do it guided only by our written instructions. However about 10 o'clock on the morning of the 30th our dogs seemed thoroughly restless, and far across the ice we could see approaching the three sledges. It really *was* a meet-up, unique, I think, in Antarctic history. For them there was the joy of knowing that the anxious part of their journey was over, and they had the sense of security that extra food brings to a sledge party far from home. For us it was the delight of anticipating our part in the job that was nearing completion. Further there was the pleasure of seeing new faces, having news to exchange, there were new folk to listen to old jokes and fresh jokes for us to hear. Mac Choyce, the same old humorist, carried ten cigars for just such an occasion as this; Reg produced a bottle of rum, and the weirdest of parties had started. Our nearest neighbours, from 500 miles away it's true, had paid us a social call; could you blame us, miles from anywhere, raising our glasses and behaving for all the world as if it were a day at the races?

The four of them obviously had had a tough journey. Frank Elliott, a north of England rock climber of considerable reputation, was leader; John Francis, who had come down with us all in 1946, was the surveyor; the incorrigible Mac Choyce was meteorologist, and lastly there was Ray Adie, a South African geologist. They had come with twenty-seven dogs a distance of about 550 miles entirely on their own resources. From their base, in early spring, when the sea-ice was still in perfect condition, they had laid out a depot 130 miles away. But at the start of their main journey, after a long period at base waiting for news of the establishment of the Nunatak depot, conditions were depressingly different. Soft snow covered rotten sea-ice and salt-water slush, and camps had to be found on the security of small icebergs. Luckily the conditions gradually improved and, later, their only delay was caused by the weather, which blotted out all the survey features and made John Francis's job so difficult. They were always having to decide whether to wait the extra day to fill in the blank survey sheet, or push on to the depot and to security. They arrived with but one day's dog food and fourteen days' man food at the end of the sixty-four-day journey. We had passed on some of the luxuries which we had brought for them, bacon, tinned pineapple, and beef stew. It wasn't as kind a gesture as we had intended, for the strange ingredients didn't mix well with the easily digested sledging rations. John Francis greeted us the next morning with a wry smile and remarked that the tin marked pineapple reacted as if it had been syrup of figs. Mac Choyce said he had been very worried on the way south for fear he might be "going round the bend" but he developed an unfailing method of checking up. He would lean out of the tent in the peace of the evening, put his fingers on his tongue, and whistle for a taxi. He argued that if one turned up it was certainly time you went home, so you could hop inside. He had also been working hard on a scheme to lighten sledge rations by using dehydrated water as an ingredient, and was prepared to talk anyone into the reasonableness of his idea.

We were still rather short of food and could only spare a day for the others to rest. We re-divided the loads and sledged back to Bills Gulch. We, at Base E, always had a haunting feeling that the folk at Hope Bay had always thought that we had exaggerated the difficulties of the plateau crossing, and the ease with which we reached the Met station surprised even us. At Hope Bay they had never learned to drive dogs on an exact compass bearing and, luckily for me, Rover was steering impeccably.

The last day to base was typical of the plateau. With visibility only a few yards and a strong wind, we left the deserted Met station for the last time. It was difficult to steer a good course as the snow was very rough, and the sledge was behaving like a skittish colt. I asked Reg to come and help to manage the sledge while I watched the compass. We watched our distance, using the sledge wheel and stopped where the remains of Two Ton depot should have been; we were not prepared to go further for we knew it was only two hundred yards to the plateau edge. The cloud lifted momentarily and not fifty yards away was the depot flag. Frank

Elliot was, I think, very impressed, while Reg and I were very surprised. Sledge navigation, though it should be accurate, is rarely as accurate as that.

The North-East Glacier was up to its tricks again, and was filled with thick cloud. We cautiously stayed where we were, put up our tents, and hoped it would lift. The cloud finally thinned a little so we pushed our sledges over the top with ropes round our runners, and made the dogs pull us down the zigzag route to the glacier 3,000 feet below. The last run down our old enemy Sodabread slope was one that I will never forget. I was leading the other teams and Tommy was riding jockey-wise astride my sledge. With 200 yards of the steep slope to go, the rope around the runners broke. We slid helter-skelter, jumping like a steeplechaser down to the old camp site at the bottom. We then turned and watched the other teams come over the crest, changing as they came from specks in the distance to individuals, and then into the glorious sight of a team at full run. The cloud above us was rapidly closing down so we hurried back to base, navigating as carefully as ever and hoping against hope that the cloud wouldn't envelop us.

The Americans turned out in force to see the ten of us arrive and gave us an enormous welcome. The sight of all the five teams that followed me off the glacier down the last fifty yards to the civilization and summer dirt of base was one I will never forget.

It had been a glorious last day to a year's sledging. We had crossed the plateau in the thick cloud to the site of Two Ton depot, where we watched the cloud around us disperse, exposing bank upon bank of golden cloud which filled the gap between us and Alexander Land and left the distant peaks pink and clear in the morning sun. We were above the world and the long sunset that turned into dawn as we watched left us breathless. In life's experience we all have a happy tendency to forget the bad moments and remember all the best. The glory of that last day's run is something that will ever live in my memory.

These two journeys were a fitting climax to the two years' work, and it is a good thing to summarize their achievement.

The northern party had travelled a total of 600 miles in seventy-one days, and before starting had travelled a further 350 miles laying depots. They had surveyed 220 miles of coastline which had never before been seen and had checked, and redrawn a further 250 miles which had been visited by Nordensjöld in 1902. The geologist, Ray Adie, had collected many specimens and had travelled many miles over and above his normal day's journey.

The success of the southern party was of a different order, for Mason's job was to travel fast and provide a ground control for the air photographs. It was a great success in terms of miles travelled, and as a demonstration of carefully co-ordinated sledging with aircraft support. Only when the time comes to publish the combined map will it be possible to assess the true exploratory value of the journey; in my own mind it should stand very high in the list of man's travels in Antarctica.

If the success of any journey can be measured by its lack of dramatic incident, and in many ways I think it can, both these journeys were of very high quality. Both vindicated the British policy of strict adherence to details of equipment, and our indebtedness to explorers of the past. Neither journey was overplanned and lacking in flexibility as a result, and the untold success of the dogs was due to the training we had received from Commander Bingham in the previous year.

CHAPTER 16

The Last Summer at Base

W E ALL arrived back at base on January 4, and found the place transformed. The summer sun was really doing its work, and exactly as in the previous year, everything outside the hut seemed dirty and unkempt. Inside, however, John and his party had been extremely busy and had divided the workshop in half, fitted it with extra bunks for the new arrivals, and having been warned by wireless of our return, Bernard Stonehouse had prepared a meal of proportions that might even have floored King Henry VIII.

It was, I think, the first time in Antarctic history that a base had increased in numbers in the course of a season, so there was much to show the four new arrivals and even more to talk about.

We had some highly entertaining arguments about dog driving, for the party from Hope Bay had adopted the single centre trace method which they swore by. We at Base E quoted the usual argument about not being able to jump wide crevasses with dogs harnessed to a single trace, and by way of clinching the matter, I took my team out across the ice to find out just how wide a crack it was possible to cross. Ray Adie came with me, and we had a thoroughly entertaining and amphibious afternoon. The net result was that I proved that a nine-dog team with a half-loaded sledge could easily cross a 6-foot gap, a 7-foot gap was just possible, but when I attempted an 8-foot lead I fell in and became a member of the Antarctic Swimming Club for the second time.

I often used to go over the hill to help Bill Latady to develop long trial lengths of aircraft film, which were to provide a check upon the general quality of the photographic survey. It was a pleasantly quiet occupation that demanded great care and the notice on the dark-room door which read "Films developing—

do not enter," meant that we were left in peace. He above all others had taken immense care with every detail of the aircraft's emergency equipment on the long flights, and knew full well the general inadequacy that the necessary weight limitations imposed.

I noted in my diary that "Bill seems very relieved that the long flights are over." In polar flying there is a tendency to forget that the country over which one is flying is rugged and unkind to strangers, and the excitement of the moment can easily lead one outside the range of common sense and sound judgment.

At least once, well out of wireless touch with base, he had seen plans altered in mid-air and known that such alteration would nullify the emergency rescue plans that represented their lifeline. I will always admire Bill when I look back at this time. He knew what risks he had been involved in yet never actually voiced a single criticism, beyond his usual stock phrase, "It was a bit rugged."

There was still some flying going on, for the Beechcraft was finishing its programme with one or two exploratory flights to the west, but they did not involve any photographic traverses, and the lighter loads that resulted enabled Jim Lassiter to land in several outlying places. They made a landing on Charcot Island and Commander Ronne, to our astonishment, announced that he had taken a very accurate sight during the half-hour that they were there, using a marine sextant in lieu of theodolite. I noted in my diary, "It shows how degrees of accuracy differ—it's like comparing a cheap alarm clock with a chrono-meter."

In polar work where the aim is to travel and survey among mountains the chance to do serious mountaineering is very slight, but on January 14 there were too many folk chasing too little work, so Frank Elliott, Doc Butson, and myself joined up with Latady and Dodson for a mountaineering holiday. We told those at base that our trip was "highly scientific" and promised to bring back any mosses and lichen that we could find on places of abnormal exposure above the 1,000-foot level.

We were climbing in a group of mountains to the south side of Neny Fjord, and the view from the local "Matterhorn" is one I shall never forget. It was calm and bitterly cold, and the air was clearer than I had ever seen it. Forty miles to the south lay the

Terra Firma Islands, which had taken us seven days to reach during the previous spring. Sixty-five miles away was Cape Berteaux, beyond which still lay the remains of the crashed aircraft, and right across the horizon stretched the mountainous coastline of Alexander Land, pink and clear in the rising sun. Northwards across the deep shadow of the Graham Land plateau could be seen the base, a man-made cancer in this beautiful land.

In retrospect this was one of the happiest periods of my time in Antarctica. Sledging field-work is so bound up with, and yet apart from, mountaineering. Many of the precautions used in mountaineering are used in the technique of sledge travel, and many more could be, yet almost all one's time is spent looking at, and, to the best of one's ability, avoiding, all forms of mountains. In Graham Land there is no time on a sledging journey for anything except survey, and this applied also to all the 'ologies of polar field work. Climbing must be sought after, and is enjoyed all the more.

CHAPTER 17

Good-bye to Marguerite Bay

WHEN we returned from our mountaineering interlude, we found that the *Port of Beaumont* was getting ready to leave and by the end of January, before the last of the strong ice had disappeared from around the ship, all the aircraft were hoisted aboard.

There was only one thing wrong with all these preparations for getting under way: the ship was still firmly held in the sea-ice and there was still very little sign of a general break up of the ice in Neny Fjord.

Among ourselves we had, I think, become resigned to the idea of spending yet another winter in Antarctica, and knew that though we had our own whims and ways we were united as a party and could do a good job if the third year really became necessary: we had adequate food, and could live much as we had already lived, but we wondered just how life would go on over the hill if they were forced to spend a second winter. Food, we knew, was short, but we could help them out, but we knew, too, that they were a divided crowd, and often in our visits over the hill we had been aware of hard feelings and personal bitterness. A situation of that sort couldn't survive the rigours of another winter and remain free from outspoken strife.

All these thoughts were forgotten when on the 18th we heard that there were two American ice-breakers, the U.S.N. ships *Edisto* and *Burton Island*, in the Antarctic, and that they planned to visit Stonington Island on the 21st of the month. They were on a routine cruise, filling in some of the survey gaps left by the vast American task forces of the year before.

It was quite obvious to us that if our ship the *John Biscoe* was to reach us at all she must turn south at once and take advantage of the presence of the American icebreakers in Marguerite

Bay; by herself it was quite clear that she would be unable to reach us.

We told them by radio and were distinctly heartened when we received a signal telling us that the *John Biscoe* had turned south, and was coming on at best speed.

Early on the morning of the 21st two sledges left base. We headed for the edge of the fast-ice at the entrance to Neny Fjord, and in the morning light we found the two American ships. They had already started to break a passage and were solemnly steaming up the fjord at four knots, pushing through the 4-foot ice as if it were not even there. They stopped when they saw us. We drove our sledges under the bows and sent our passengers, Ken Butler, Finn Ronne, and Ike Schlossbach on board, while the dogs played lamp-posts on the heavy steel stem and paid little attention to the hundreds of sailors who lined the rails.

Ike's pilotage instructions were simple. If the ice-breaker followed the line of red flags stuck in the ice the day before, deep water was guaranteed all the way. As the two ships steamed majestically up the fjord and broke a passage towards the *Port of Beaumont*, we sledged alongside and exchanged greetings with smartly dressed sailors leaning over the rails, and as I looked at the size of those ships I wondered just what our visitors would think of the smallness of our home.

That night we asked some of the ships' officers to dinner. We delved into our wine store and collected the last two bottles of whisky from the year's ration, and enjoyed the sociability of new faces and the luxury of fresh conversation.

They told us of their visit to Shackleton's old hut on Ross Island and of the excellent condition of the buildings erected by Captain Scott, of the general ice conditions, and the performance of their ships.

The visit was all too short; in the late afternoon of February 22, the ice-breakers took the *Port of Beaumont* in their charge and shepherded her out into the open sea. In less than an hour the ship which only a few days before had been firmly stuck in the ice was lost to sight.

In the rush and bustle of departure we seemed to have had little time to say the good-byes that a year together in Antarctica demanded. It was sad to see the Americans go. We had made many friends; they had taught us much, and the generous good nature of them all had sometimes overpowered us, who had so little to give in return. As they left the fjord we knew that their departure was for us the first sign of the end of our expedition life. I sat on the rock behind base and watched them go and tried to work out in my own mind just what difference their presence had meant to us as individuals and to the work of the Survey as a whole.

As members of a small Survey base we would, in the normal course of events, have had a very much larger share in the year's travels and activities; we had I suppose come down south with the intention of acquiring a certain skill in travel and scientific exploration which, for all of us, would lead up to a share in a worthy journey and enable us to prove ourselves; to many of us this dream was never possible. We had worked long hours on our much-loved dogs, and seen them lent like motor-cars to others to do the journeys we had longed to do, only to hear the borrowers admit at the end that they had been "bored throughout".

For ten long years I'd been planning my life to fit into the membership of an expedition such as ours would have been if the Americans had not been there. As the *Port of Beaumont* left I knew in my heart that I would have to come back to Antarctica.

We had, it is true, as a double expedition, made journeys of a length and quality that would not otherwise have proved possible and, if the co-operation which we had achieved in Antarctica could be continued at home, then these labours would produce a map with a standard of survey previously unknown in Antarctic exploration.

It was quiet after the *Port of Beaumont* had gone, and I was reminded of the peace in the first winter. Already the ghosts of the folk across the hill had left the island and the houses were bleak and dead.

In the evening we talked to the *John Biscoe* by wireless, and heard that she was lying alongside the *Port of Beaumont* for the night, and intended to be at the ice edge at dawn.

At first light we took out two sledges to meet the ship and watched her nose gently into the channel left by the ice-breakers the day before, but it had refrozen and she could make no progress, so we slipped on board, collected our mail, and hurried back to base. I took my letters to the highest part of the island at the foot of the American flagstaff from where I could see the Debenham Islands, and sat down to read them in the warmth of the rising sun. They were utterly different from the letters of the year before, for it would only be a matter of weeks before we would see those who were writing, those we loved and longed for.

Almost as if it had been planned, one of the American ice-breakers came back into the bay to make some scientific observation, and found it necessary to rebreak the channel for the *John Biscoe*. Soon after tea both ships were lying in Back Bay just where the *Port of Beaumont* had been twenty-four hours before.

In five short hours the year's supplies were lying disembarked in dumps all over the ice, so that by midnight the ship was ready to leave again.

I went up the hill for the last time to visit my dogs and to say good-bye to them. I think I was more sorry to say farewell to them than to anything or anybody else. They were enthusiasts for everything, and above all for work; they were real characters who had to be maintained as individuals, yet moulded into a harmonious whole that was never perfect and demanded from us a standard that was always just out of reach. I sat down at the top of the last snow slope that led down to the ship and to home, and discussed the world with Bouncer and Sister. They romped with me and licked my face, sloppy and sentimental as teddy bears. Sister was still the rampageous flirt that she always will be, and Bouncer the rather gallant country gentleman that he would remain till the end of his days. As we left we were sad, yet glad, for ours was not the lot of previous expeditions; we left our dogs alive and trained in all things, ready to help other folk just as they had helped us.

There were tears in my eyes when it came to say good-bye to the folk who were staying for a further year.

We left early on the morning of the 25th and watched Dave, Bernard, Terry, and Ray Adie as they waved us good-bye from the point. We lingered on deck to wave our last good-byes and to watch the last tips of the mountains that we knew disappear from sight, and only then retired to sleep: the sleep of the very, very weary—in body and in soul.

Good-bye to Marguerite Bay

Soon after leaving the sheltered waters of Marguerite Bay the pack-ice cleared away and we saw the *Port of Beaumont,* hull down to the west before we turned northwards towards the Argentine Islands.

Six weeks later, we were in England—Tilbury, where we landed, was grey and dirty, but it didn't matter for it was just as we had expected it to be, and the smoke of the old country was good to see. My thirty months' absence didn't seem to matter as I waved to my parents on the lighter alongside.

Once we got home, we talked into the night, and as I woke the next morning in my old familiar bed the time was 7 a.m. I really knew I was home, for once again I could sit on a chair in my mother's bedroom, warming my feet under the mattress, and drink my cup of tea, just as I had always done.

CHAPTER 18

Retrospect

EVEN though it is seven years since I returned from Antarctica I have tried throughout the book to use the thoughts and language that were with me then. Views and feelings were those of the moment; in many cases they have mellowed or matured after reflection. To have left them out or brought them up-to-date would have destroyed the completeness of the picture.

I have a feeling that readers will be disappointed that I have not painted a picture of hardships overcome, impossibilities achieved, or of comradeship that grew up in conditions of discomfort and disaster. They may well have expected a story that would compare with those heroic tales of early explorers, whose writings form such a gallant part of our national heritage.

Just as those men of the past have tried to write with truth as their guide, so have I. I have sought to avoid the romantic garnishings that some modern journalistic writers are prepared to twist for the sake of publicity from the every-day process of polar life. Except in the case of accidents, and we had our fair share of these, modern stories of discomfort in life and travel, or of the physical toughness that is required to overcome them, must in some degree be a measure of lessons unlearnt, of incompetence or of twisted truth on the part of the writer.

I have heard criticism levelled at the modern explorer that he makes life too comfortable and as a result his journeyings do not compare with those of days gone by. That in part is very true for a thousand-mile sledge journey to-day must compare in physical discomfort with barely a hundred miles of manhauling thirty years ago. The argument put forward is that with all the detailed knowledge of polar travel and methods of exploration, stupendous journeys measured in terms of miles travelled must now be possible. In my own mind journeys of two to three thousand

188

miles could indeed be carried out in Antarctica to-day. But to think only in terms of miles travelled is to include but a small part of the polar heritage that is ours.

In the line of Antarctic exploration the British can be proud of their achievements in recent years. From 1945–48 when I was with the Falkland Islands Dependencies Survey and in the two years that followed, nearly a thousand miles of new coast-line were put on the map, and successfully covered by geological reconnaissance. Three journeys of over a thousand miles each were achieved in successive seasons in which three-quarters of the participants were trained scientists. A hazardous journey across sea-ice in mid-winter was accomplished in order to observe the breeding habits of the rare Emperor Penguins and records that would have pleased the great Edward Wilson were obtained. Nearly eight thousand miles of travel were completed without accident in the field by people who surveyed as they went.

I have heard it said that from the purely financial point of view this country "does not deserve to have its heritage of Scotts, Shackletons, or Watkins", for private expeditions have never sailed without the shadow of financial worry hanging over their leaders' thoughts. It is equally wrong to suppose that the Government should pay for all adventurous undertakings just as it pays for our social services or for education. The spirit of venture can only be kept alive if everyone who believes in its worth is prepared to help financially when some worthy cause arises.

I don't profess that support of an expedition is a good financial investment for the donor; it will not bring in its regular profit, but on a long-term basis for an individual it does at least provide a means of identifying himself with the Elizabethan sense of venture for venture's sake.

I am often asked as I wander around the country, "Why explore?", and I am hard put to supply the exact answer. A well-known mountain writer and philosopher has said that an essential ingredient of any living nation is the spirit of adventure; that in part expresses my thoughts. I am all too often aware that many millions in our country can see no reason for exploration, unless it be to provide better material for the silver screen. I am aware too that a much smaller number have no need to ask, "Why explore?", for they can sense the answer, yet have no wish to participate. There are many people who would, had they the chance that came my way, go and explore and let the future take care of itself. In my own heart I feel that it is that sense of venture that keeps the nation alive and able to play its part in the world. It is not done for escapism or personal gain, but because some unseen force inside us tells us that the job is worth doing at whatever the cost and demands that the job be done well. It is that unseen force of venture in our history that has brought our nation to where it is. It is up to us to keep it there.

In this age, when so much of scientific man's efforts are to become master of the universe in his own right, the vastness and unseen power of Antarctica, its beauty and its utter peace, put man in his right place. Shackleton and Wild, as they walked across South Georgia at the end of their epic boat journey across 600 miles of stormy Antarctic seas, both record that there was an unseen Guide watching over their footsteps.

Inscribed below the statue to Captain Scott which stands outside the Polar Institute in Cambridge, there is an inscription which in translation reads: "In seeking to unveil the Pole he found the hidden things of God."

Often I have looked out of my tent in the peace that follows an Antarctic blizzard, or watched the unseen force behind the movements of polar ice, with the same feeling. Here at least is a chance for man to sort out the true relationship between himself and his God.

Index

Adams, Capt. ("Chuck"), 137, 162, 164, 166
Adelaide Island, 21
Adie, Roy, 176, 179, 180, 186
Aircraft; American, 136; arrival of, 104, 136; hangar, 107, 132, 148–9; loss of, 166; use of, 126, 148, 154, 162, 170, 171
Airfield glacier, 78
Alarm clock, use of, 73, 75
Albert Medal, 5, 145
Alexander Land, 114, 182
American Antarctic Service, 23
American huts, cleaning of, 52, 59, 103; leaking of, 97; looting of, 108, 128; state of, on arrival, 23–4, 34, 59, 95; storage in, 59
Americans, arrival of, 118, 119; departure of, 184–5
Amundsen, Roald, 137
Antarctic Swimming Club, 98, 139, 154, 180
Argentine Islands, 21, 23, 59
Auster, see Aircraft

Base: A—Lockroy Bay; B—Deception Island; C—South Orkney; D—Hope Bay; E—Storrington Island, see under separate headings
Bath, 32, 37, 132
B.B.C., 97, 165
Beechcraft, aircraft, 136, 138, 151, 171, 181
Bertram, Dr. G. C., 7, 59
Bills Gulch, 78, 109, 115, 119, 125, 138, 175
Bingham, Sgn.-Cmd. E. W., 6, 13, 30, 33, 34, 42, 52, 53, 55, 57, 69, 79 et seq., 85, 94, 124, 128, 179; retirement from F.I.D.S., 99–100

Bingham, Mrs. E. W., 32
Boots; American ski, 156; moccasin, 66–7, 81; sealskin, 66
British Graham Land Expedition, 14, 15, 59, 159; disappearance of base hut, 102; reoccupation of base hut, 102
Burd, "Dick", 102
Burden, Capt., 104
Burton Island, U.S.S., icebreaker, 183
Butler, Major K. R. O. ("Ken"), 22, 29, 30, 33, 34, 56, 98, 99, 161, 168, 173, 184; appointed leader, 99
Butson, Dr. A. R. C., 70, 105, 109 et seq., 132, 139, 145, 160, 168, 173, 181
Byrd, Commander, 137

Cape Keeler, 161, 164, 170
Charcot, Dr., 14, 23
Choyce, M. A. ("Mac"), 18, 102, 176–7
Christmas 1946 . . ., 97, 99; 1947 . . ., 175–6
Clothing, 52–3, 65
Coal, 25, 34
Colonial Office, 7, 78
Crampons, 110

D'Aeth, Air Vice-Marshal N. H., 80
Darlington, Harry, 136, 137
Darlington, Mrs. H. ("Jinny"), 136, 137, 147
Debenham Islands, B.G.L.E. hut, 22, 23, 58
Deception Island, 14, 15, 17, 19, 25, 40, 43; destruction of hut at, 101
Dehydrated food, 35
Dodson, Bob, 137, 143, 144, 146, 153 et seq., 159, 160, 181

Dogs, 16, 19, 34–49, 76, 95, 111, 141, 186; American, 136–7, 147, B.G.L.E., of, 59; casualties, 40, 99, 118, 136, 141, 155; feeding of, 36, 54; food for, 28, 35, 69, 103, 157, 172; Greenland, 43; harnessing of, 41–3, 148, 180; kennel for, 32, 147; Labrador, 40, 43; passage through Tropics of, 40; puppies, 39, 40, 48–9, 91, 140; steering by compass, 45, 46; tethering of, 70, 147; training of, 34, 57–8, 147; whip, 35–6, 45, 72–3, 147

Edisto, U.S.S., icebreaker, 183
Elephant Island, 101
Elliott, Frank, 176, 181
Ellsworth, Lincoln, 14
Endurance, S.S., 18, 101
Equipment, development of, 62; preparation of, 57, 109–10, 146–7
Esse Stove, 26, 29; failure of, 51

Falkland Islands Dependencies Survey, 7, 9, 14, 21, 189; crest of, 98
Falkland Islands, Governor of, 118, 128
Fire, 101, 125
Fiske, Larry, 137, 139, 152–3
Fitzroy, S.S., 16, 21, 123, 124, 128
Fleming, Rt. Rev. Launcelot, 5–6, 58
Fram, 137
Francis, John, 176–7
Freeman, Capt. R. L. ("Reg"), 22, 30, 36, 84, 86, 88, 91, 93, 111, 113, 130, 142, 161, 162, 166, 174 *et seq.*
Fuchs, Dr. V. E., 7
Fumigator, 22, 25, 37, 55, 80, 84, 88–91, 168

George Bryan Inlet, 171
Giorgio, Giorg di, 174 *et seq.*
Gloves, 66, 110
Graham Land, 10, 14, 16, 19, 78
Greenhouse, 98
Gutenko, Sig, 156

Hangar, construction of, 107
Hardy, M. ("Mike"), 106
Harvard Mountaineering Club, 137
Hewitt, Canon Gordon, 7
Hipper, 5
Hoar-frost, 74
Hope Bay, 15–17, 101, 102; expedition from, 170, 173, 175–6
Huskies, *see* Dogs
Hut, building of, 25, 26, 29; siting of, 24–5, 55, 59
Hut lighting, 32

Ice spear, 65
Iquique, 107–8

James, David, 102
John Biscoe, 183–7
Jones, David, 106, 111, 126, 133, 163
Journeys, list of, 47–8, 189
Joyce, Capt. J., ("J. J.") 22, 30, 52, 59, 86, 91, 93, 99, 103

King George VI Sound, 138, 151
Kitchen waste, 23, 34

Labrador, 40, 43, 53, 65
L.5., aircraft, 136, 164, 171
Lassiter, Capt. J. ("Jimmy"), 137, 164, 165, 166, 171, 181
Latady, W. R. ("Bill"), 134, 144, 171, 173, 180–1
Laubeuf Fjord, 124
Laurie Island, 18, 101
Library, 30, 50
Liquor, ration of, 37, 133
Llamas, 134
Lutzow, 5

Maclary, Nelson, 139, 154, 161, 168, 169
Maclean, Don, 168, 169, 175
MacLeod, Ken, 106, 111, 130, 134, 135, 141, 162, 168, 174 *et seq.*
Marguerite Bay, 15, 19, 21, 23, 103
Mason, Capt. D. P. ("Duggie"), 22, 30, 33, 34, 51, 70, 82, 86, 93, 99, 109 *et seq.*, 164, 168, 174

Mattress, reindeer skin, covered with, 63, 64, 71
Mid-winter's Day 1946 . . ., 56; 1947 . . ., 139, 140
Mobiloil Inlet, 109, 172
Mount Tricorn, 138, 151, 161, 168, 169

Nautilus, 137
Navigation: on glacier, 79, 84, 86, 112; on plateau, 117, 122, 177-8
Neny Fjord, 21
Neumayer Channel, 20, 21
Newfoundland, 40
Nicolls, Bob, 134, 144, 146, 153 *et seq.*, 159-60
Nordensjöld, Professor, 14, 179

Onslow, H.M.S., 5, 167
"Operation Tabarin", 5, 13, 15
O'Sullivan, Tom, 40
Owen ("Art"), 146 *et seq.*, 161, 164, 168
Oxygen, lack of, 120

Peltien Channel, 21
Pemmican, British, 68, 73; American, 155, 156, 173
Penguin eggs, 98
Penguins, 20, 96; Emperor, 189
Penola, R.Y., 19, 22, 23, 58
Peterman Island, 23
Petersen, 137, 143; accident to, 144
Polar bear, fur of, 64
Polar Medal, 6
Port Lockroy, 16, 102
Port of Beaumont, 128, 134, 135-6, 183, 184
Port Stanley, 16
Pourquoi Pas, 14, 23
Puppies, *see* Dogs

Queen Elizabeth, H.M.S., 5

Randall, Terry, 130, 135, 186
Rations, British, 67-9; American, 155
Red Rock Ridge, 154, 158

Refuge Island, 154
Reindeer skins, 63-4
Relentless, H.M.S., 13, 102
Roberts, Dr. Brian, 7
Robertson, Jimmy, 137
Robin, Gordon, 102
Ronne, Commander Finn, 128, 134-8, 143, 150, 152, 158, 171, 184
Ronne, Mrs. "Jackie", 136, 138
Rope haul for steep slopes, 81, 86
Rymill, John, 14, 15, 21, 22, 23

Sadler, M. ("Mike"), 22, 30, 36, 37, 79 *et seq.*, 93, 103
Salter, W., 22, 30, 33, 34, 35, 54, 103
Schlossbach, Capt. Ike, 137, 144, 184
Scott, Capt. R. F., base hut of, 184
Scott of the Antarctic, film, 102
Scott Polar Research Institute, Cambridge, 7, 61, 190
Seals, killing of, 35, 96; Leopard, 20
Sealskin boots, 53
Sewing machine, 36, 57
Shackleton, Sir Ernest, 18, 101, 184
Shepherd, Capt., 17, 21, 104
Signy Island, 102
Ski, 58, 67; bindings of, 110
Sledges, 34, 57, 59, 64, 145-6, 152; icing runners of, 124, 172; rope brakes of, 110, canvas tanks on, 148
Sleeping bag, "Mummy", 63, 71
Slessor, Dr. R., 22, 25, 29, 40, 54, 56, 69, 86, 93, 103, 105, 109
Slippers, duffle, 65, 73
Smith ("Smithy"), 170
Snow, drums for water supply containing, 29, 30, 95; melting by dark objects, 95
Snowshoes, 67, 68, 113; preparing sledge track, 87
Sodabread slope, 86-91, 112, 113-4, 172, 174
South Georgia, 14, 18
South Orkneys, 14, 16, 17, 18, 102
South Shetlands, 14, 15
Square Bay, 84, 86, 103
Stephenson, A., 81, 151

Stone, Mr., 129
Stonehouse, Bernard, 106, 130, 134, 139, 162, 166, 173, 180, 186
Sun, return of, 1946 . . ., 60; 1947 . . ., 142

Tents; American, 143; behaviour in high wind of, 84; groundsheet for, 63; oxygen problems in, 120; Pyramid, 62–3, 71, 154; repair of, 109; ventilation of, 63, 71
Thermos, 76
The Times, 107
Thompson, A. ("Andy"), 137, 169, 170
Thomson, T. ("Tommy"), 106, 111, 126, 132, 145, 154, 162, 166, 175
Tonkin, Capt. J. E., 10, 22, 25, 28, 30, 32, 33, 37, 56, 69, 70 *et seq*, 95, 106, 109 *et seq.*, 126, 132, 134, 153, 155, 164, 174 *et seq.*; accident to, 82–3
Training, American method of, 143; British method of, 143

Trepassey, M.V., 13, 16, 17, 20, 24, 26, 27, 40, 52, 101, 102, 104, 118, 123, 124, 125, 128
Tufts College, Mass., U.S.A., 134
Two Ton Depot, 93, 106, 111, 125, 169

Watkins, Gino, 15
Weasel, tracked vehicle, 136, 151, 152, 157, 159
Weddell Sea, 16, 116
Wilkins, Sir Hubert, 14
William Scoresby, R.R.S., 16, 17, 102
Wilson, Edward, 189
Windproofs, 65
Wireless, 30, 34, 86, 111; "S.C.R. 694", 171, 172
Wolverine fur, 66
Wood, Walter, 153, 162, 170
Wordie, James, 7, 101
Wordie Ice Shelf, 149